Rethinking Aggression and Violence in Sport

Some people think there is no place for aggression and violence in sport. Such a view is misguided. Those who understand the real nature of contact sports know that for many players, sanctioned aggression and violence are a primary source of excitement, pleasure and satisfaction and thus a major factor in their motivation for participation.

Others claim that soccer hooligans and other sports rioters are 'yobs' involved in a mindless activity, while the truth is that the motivation behind this behaviour is far from straightforward.

Popular wisdom suggests that observing violent sport has a detrimental effect on viewers, but the latest developments in theory and research suggest that this is not necessarily true.

Rethinking Aggression and Violence in Sport uses numerous illustrative examples from a variety of sports to critically examine important issues associated with aggression and violence in sport, and includes:

- A review of current theory in the psychology of aggression and violence.
- Discussion of sanctioned and unsanctioned aggression and violence in sport.
- An explanation of how players become acclimatised to physical violence.
- Examination of the aggression and violence debate in youth sport.
- Consideration of fan violence and sport riots.
- Exploration of why people enjoy watching violent sport and its effect on observers.

The book utilises the innovative character of reversal theory to rethink the topic and put across a different point of view from those that are generally accepted. It is a must for teachers, students and researchers within sport science/studies, psychology and sociology with an interest in human violence and aggressive behaviour.

John H. Kerr is Professor of Sport Psychology in the Faculty of Health and Sport Sciences at Kokushikan University in Japan.

Rethinking Aggression and Violence in Sport

John H. Kerr

Routledge
Taylor & Francis Group

LONDON AND NEW YORK

First published 2005
by Routledge
2 Park Square, Milton Park, Abingdon, Oxon OX14 4RN

Simultaneously published in the USA and Canada
by Taylor & Francis Inc
270 Madison Ave, New York, NY 10016

Routledge is an imprint of the Taylor & Francis Group

© 2005 John Kerr

Typeset in Goudy by Keystroke, Jacaranda Lodge, Wolverhampton
Printed and bound in Great Britain by TJ International Ltd, Padstow, Cornwall

Every effort has been made to ensure that the advice and information in
this book is true and accurate at the time of going to press. However,
neither the publisher nor the authors can accept any legal responsibility or
liability for any errors or omissions that may be made. In the case of drug
administration, any medical procedure or the use of technical equipment
mentioned within this book, you are strongly advised to consult the
manufacturer's guidelines.

British Library Cataloguing in Publication Data
A catalogue record for this book is available from the British Library

Library of Congress Cataloging in Publication Data
A catalog record for this book has been requested

ISBN 0–415–28663–8 (hbk)
ISBN 0–415–28664–6 (pbk)

For Sarah and Paul

"Serious sport has nothing to do with fair play. It is bound up with hatred, jealousy, boastfulness, disregard of all rules, and sadistic pleasure in witnessing violence: in other words, it is war without the shooting."

George Orwell (1948/1968). The sporting spirit. *Collected essays, journalism and letters of George Orwell, vol. 4*. London: Secker and Warburg.

Contents

Figures and tables

Figures

Tables

Preface

In considering aspects of sport, one almost inevitably goes back to one's own experience. My experience of aggression and violence in sport began with my involvement in rugby. I started to play rugby when I was 11 years old, after making the transition from primary to grammar school. Although we participated in a variety of sports and physical activities at my primary school, the main sport was football (soccer) and the school had a team, made up of pupils in their final year, which played against other school teams. Compared with my contemporaries, I was singularly unskilled at soccer and ended up as goal keeper in the 'B' team. Even though the 'A' team keeper eventually became an international player, mine was a truly ignominious position. With my move to the grammar school, however, came the chance to play rugby union. As a beginner, I knew little about rugby, but learned quickly in the practices and games, where I could use my large body size and strength to advantage. Here was a game where I could be successful and enjoy the experience. I stuck at it, became more skilled and continued my involvement in the game for a further 40 years, initially as a player and subsequently as a coach.

Like many young people who become involved in sport, my single most important reason for playing rugby was enjoyment. In my early rugby days, I enjoyed the thrills of running with the ball in my hands and chasing and tackling opposing players. I enjoyed the physical contact and competitiveness at scrums and lineouts and the aggression and determination required to drive, hit and knock over opponents in loose play. Later, at higher levels, in addition to the pleasures mentioned above, I enjoyed both pitting my skills against individual opponents and being part of a successful team, with the camaraderie and banter that goes along with it. I enjoyed the satisfaction of being able to survive in a game of intense physicality and violent contact, where being aggressive was a necessary component for survival. Often, the better the opponents and the tougher and harder the match, the more I enjoyed it. There was an immense satisfaction from knowing that you had played well under challenging conditions.

My experience is by no means unique. There are many athletes who have played or are currently playing rugby and other games like American football, Aussie Rules football, ice hockey and perhaps soccer who have, or have had, similar experiences. The purpose of these reminiscences is to get across the fact that aggression and violence in sport, especially team contact sport, are intrinsic and positive elements which can be a tremendous source of pleasure for those taking part. There are, of course, more unsavoury aspects of aggression and violence in sport; times when the fine line between sanctioned and unsanctioned aggression and violence in sport is crossed. Indeed, on occasion, I have crossed it myself. Players take pride in knowing that they have 'stood their ground' or 'handed out punishment' when opposing players have, for example, engaged in dirty play or tactics. In addition, some athletes, either of their own volition or under their coach's instructions, are unscrupulous in using unsanctioned aggression and violence in an attempt to physically dominate or injure opponents. Some people may find this hard to accept, but it is part of the reality of team contact sport.

Writers and commentators often concentrate on these latter, unsavoury aspects of aggression and violence in sport, rarely focusing on the positive side. Newspaper articles, television news clips and slow motion replays during televised games, at least on some occasions, appear to draw readers' and viewers' attention to acts of foul play. Similarly, soccer hooligan behaviour, another negative aspect of aggression and violence in sport, draws a great deal of media attention and interest. Even in academic writing, a large literature on the topic has been established.

However, it seems to me that many sports writers, commentators and academics fail to really understand the true nature of aggression and violence in sport. An example of this was the position stand on aggression and violence in sport published on behalf of the International Society of Sport Psychology (ISSP). Having worked in sport psychology for quite a few years, I have read hundreds of articles and papers on a variety of topics, with some of which I have disagreed. However, rarely have I felt strongly enough to respond in writing to try to correct the situation, at least as I saw it. With the ISSP position stand, however, I considered that the authors had both misunderstood the true nature of aggression and violence in sport and failed to differentiate between athlete and spectator violence. In addition, as it was a position stand directly representing the views of the ISSP and, indirectly, sport psychologists in general, I was concerned that if players, coaches and administrators (especially from sports like rugby, American or Aussie Rules football and ice hockey) read the position stand they would dismiss it as interference from ill-informed academics. I did respond and entered into a debate with the authors of the position stand, which resulted in a total of four papers discussing the topic being published (Tenenbaum *et al.*, 1997; Kerr, 1999; Tenenbaum *et al.*, 2000; Kerr, 2002).

It was my own experience of rugby and my concern at the unbalanced view of aggression and violence in sport in the current literature that generated the idea for this book. In researching the topic, I discovered that no books had been published on aggression and violence in sport since Smith's book, *Violence and sport*, and Goldstein's edited book, *Sports violence*, in 1983. Both books were sociology-based works. In sport psychology, there have been a few individual chapters on aggression and violence in general texts dealing with wider topics in sports psychology (e.g. Isberg, 2000; LeUnes and Nation, 1989; Russell, 1993; Thirer, 1994). These more recent chapters also concentrate on negative aspects of aggression and violence in sport and say little more than Smith and Goldstein did in their 1983 books. Some twenty years later, it would seem timely for a book, advocating a new approach, which addresses a number of important issues about aggression and violence in sport, based on sound psychological theory. I hope to add a new dimension to the understanding of aggression and violence in sport by using reversal theory (e.g. Apter, 2001) as a means of rethinking the topic and providing a realistic understanding of the motivation behind such behaviour.

In the book, chapter 1 begins by providing a number of examples designed to illustrate the range of aggressive and violent acts in sport. It goes on to discuss the difficulties authors have had in arriving at satisfactory definitions of aggression and violence (especially in sport), and to critically appraise some of the theoretical explanations of the causes and processes of aggressive and violent behaviour. The second and third chapters are concerned with reversal theory. Chapter 2 sets out the basic concepts of the reversal theory approach to understanding human motivation, emotion and personality and chapter 3 examines some applications of the theory to understanding aggressive and violent behaviour in sport. In chapter 4, sanctioned violence in sport is discussed in relation to the psychological rewards and pleasure that emanate from taking part in, for example, team contact sports. Some of the discussion explores female as well as male athletes' responses to aggression and violence in competition. By way of contrast, chapter 5 focuses on the unsanctioned acts of violence in sport. It also debates some of the differences between sanctioned and unsanctioned aggression and violence, and between official rules and athletes' unofficial 'codes of practice'. Reversal theory is used to examine the motivational processes behind unsanctioned violent play in an attempt to understand why these acts occur.

At focus in chapter 6 is the acclimatisation of young athletes to physical contact and sanctioned aggression and how they learn to enjoy it. This chapter also reflects on what happens when adult models of sport are imposed on youth and children's sport and some of the associated moral issues for those involved. Issues concerning injuries among young athletes are also discussed in the light of athletes' perceptions of their invincibility as a result of new safety measures.

Sports riots and soccer hooliganism come to the fore in chapter 7, where a new typology of sports riots based on reversal theory is proposed. In the latter part of the chapter, a large soccer hooligan confrontation and a hooligan 'non-event' are examined in detail. In chapter 8, the reasons why people watch aggressive and violent sports and the possible effects of observing these sports on individuals are explored. The discussion will also cover children, violence and the media, in terms of violence in general as well as in sport. Chapter 9, the final chapter, will focus on the control of aggression and violence in sport. It will critically examine legal aspects of violence in sport and recommendations by the International Society of Sport Psychology for reducing the incidence of aggression and violence in sport. Alternative proposals for reducing unsanctioned violent acts in sport and for dealing with sports riots, including soccer hooliganism, are put forward.

Finally, the value of an integrated reversal theory framework for understanding aggressive and violent behaviour in sport is summarised.

This book says something new and challenging about the psychology behind aggressive and violent behaviour and should be of interest to all those concerned with aggression and violence in general and, in particular, in the context of sport.

References

Apter, M. J. (Ed.) (2001). *Motivational styles in everyday life: A guide to reversal theory*. Washington DC: American Psychological Association.

Goldstein, J. H. (1983). *Sports violence*. New York: Springer-Verlag.

Isberg, L. (2000). Anger, aggressive behavior, and athletic performance. In Y. L. Hanin (Ed.), *Emotions in sport*. Champaign, IL: Human Kinetics.

Kerr, J. H. (1999). The role of aggression and violence in sport: A rejoinder to the ISSP position stand. *The Sport Psychologist, 13*, 83–88.

Kerr, J. H. (2002). Issues in aggression and violence in sport: The ISSP position stand revisited. *The Sport Psychologist, 16*, 68–78.

LeUnes, A. D. and Nation, J. R. (1989). *Sport psychology: An introduction*. Chicago: Nelson-Hall Inc.

Russell, G. W. (1993). *The social psychology of sport*. New York: Springer-Verlag.

Smith, M. D. (1983). *Violence and sport*. Toronto: Butterworths.

Tenenbaum, G., Stewart, E., Singer, R. N. and Duda, J. (1997). Aggression and violence in sport: An ISSP position stand. *The Sport Psychologist, 11*, 1–7.

Tenenbaum, G., Sacks, D. N., Miller, J. W., Golden, A. S. and Doolin, N. (2000). Aggression and violence in sport: A reply to Kerr's rejoinder. *The Sport Psychologist, 14*, 315–326.

Thirer, J. (1994). Aggression. In R. N. Singer, M. Murphy and L. K. Tennant (Eds), *Handbook of research on sport psychology* (pp. 365–378). New York: Macmillan.

Acknowledgements

My thanks to two fellow athletes, Ian Purcell and Paul Tacon, whose best games, like mine, are behind them. Along with Randall Braman, who has an intuitive understanding of motivation in sport, Ian and Paul provided numerous helpful insights in my discussions with them on aggression and violence in sport. I am also grateful to Ian, Mike Apter and Mieke Mitchell for their constructive criticism of early drafts of this book and to Mieke for her invaluable copy-editing. My thanks are also due to Routledge, especially Simon Whitmore, who initially took on the idea for the book, and Samantha Grant and the production team who saw it through to publication.

The author is grateful to Open University Press/McGraw-Hill Publishing Co., John Wiley & Sons Inc., and Routledge for permission to reproduce material (specific details are included in the text).

1 The state of play

Incidents, definitions and explanations

This introductory chapter is divided into three sections. The first section gives details of some selected incidents of aggression and violence that have occurred in the sport context. Most of these received a high profile in the television and print media. These particular examples have been selected because they illustrate the range and variety of situations that can occur in sport, and because they highlight a number of contentious issues about aggressive and violent behaviour in sport which will be discussed later in this chapter and the rest of the book. The second section is concerned with attempts in mainstream psychology to define aggression and violence in general, and in sport psychology to find satisfactory definitions for aggression and violence in the context of sport. The third section examines the various theoretical explanations that have developed over the years as to why aggression takes place.

Aggression and violence in sport: Some selected examples

Included in these examples are incidents involving athletes (individually or in groups) being aggressive and violent towards opponents, coaches and spectators, and spectators (individually or in groups) being aggressive and violent towards coaches, parents and the police. These incidents have occurred at training as well as during or after competition and serve to emphasise the different forms and contexts for sport violence.

Incident 1: 21 November 1992
Wales versus Australia rugby union test match at Cardiff Arms Park

Just before half-time, Wales attacked down the blind side. Phil Kearns, Wallaby hooker, lined himself up to tackle the first Welsh attacker as the Welsh fullback came into the line in support. The fullback received the ball and was hit by a superb tackle by Willie Ofahengaue. He went down injured and then left the pitch with damaged ribs. Even though it was a violent hit and the Welsh fullback was injured, Willie Ofahengaue's tackle was entirely within the laws of rugby union and was not penalised by the referee (Sims, 1995).

Incident 2: 3 May 2001
Toronto Maple Leafs versus New Jersey Devils in game 4 of the
National Hockey League (NHL) Stanley Cup Eastern Conference
playoffs in Toronto

Devils' Scott Niedermayer was skating along the boards well away from the puck when Maple Leafs' Tie Domi knocked him unconscious with a vicious elbow to the face. Niedermayer was carried from the ice on a stretcher and, although he was able to get up and walk to his dressing room, he was eventually hospitalised overnight. Domi's team were winning 3–1 at the time and there were less than 20 seconds left in the game. NHL officials suspended Domi for the rest of the playoffs ('NHL bans Domi', 2001). Later, Niedermayer claimed that Domi's hit was in retaliation for a previous hit by him on Domi in game 2. Niedermayer's stick had cut Domi over the bridge of the nose, but the action went unpenalised ('Leafs Domi', 2001). Domi, who at the time had played in the NHL for 12 years, was well known in hockey as an enforcer. Although physically relatively small, 5' 5" and 180 pounds, he had a reputation for fighting, often to protect his teammates from abuse. In 1998 he said, 'Fifty per cent of the time I fight just for the sake of fighting, to get things going, it's situational' (Ulmer, 1998). In March 2001, Domi had also received a fine from the NHL for arguing aggressively with a rival spectator after squirting spectators with water while sitting in the penalty box.

Incident 3: 6 January 2002
2nd day of the International Rugby (Union) Board World Sevens
Tournament in Santiago, Chile

In the semi final, New Zealand played Fiji in a close, hard- but fairly-fought game, and came out winners at 19–17. However, after the final whistle at the end of the match, as players began walking from the pitch, a mass brawl developed, involving most of the players from the two teams. The brawl started when Fijian player Marika Vunibaka ran 50 metres and landed a heavy punch on New Zealand player Amasio Valence. This resulted in 'all in' retaliation from the New Zealand players against Vunibaka and the other Fijian players. The fighting continued on the ground after Vunibaka had been 'taken out' by a couple of New Zealand players and turned ugly when Chris Masoe, coming late to the scene and still on his feet, began vigorously stamping on Vunibaka. Coaches and others from the team benches could not stop the fighting and, eventually, Chilean police went on to the pitch and broke up the fracas, but no one was prosecuted.

Both teams were cited for the brawl and the Sevens' judiciary examined videotapes in the days after the match. The outcome was that Vunibaka was banned from rugby for 12 weeks and the Fijian team was warned that they risked losing the 18 points from the Chile tournament if they were involved in any more fighting during the rest of the World Series. In contrast, New Zealand was merely given a severe reprimand for bringing the game into disrepute. This latter decision caused uproar, reported widely in the New Zealand media, because of officials' failure to deal with the prolonged extent of the New Zealand players' retaliation and, especially, the stamping from Masoe (e.g. Coomer, 2002; Perrott, 2002). Both Vunibaka, who plays in New Zealand, and Masoe had previously been involved in violent incidents.

Incident 4: 25 January 1995
Crystal Palace versus Manchester United in a Premier League
soccer match at Selhurst Park, London (Palace's home ground)

Manchester United striker Eric Cantona retaliated after he was tackled from behind by Palace player Richard Shaw. He was seen by the referee kicking Shaw, shown the red card and ordered off the pitch in the 48th minute of the match. As he left the pitch and was walking along the touchline, Palace supporters severely taunted him. Suddenly, he leapt over the barrier and launched a karate-style two-footed kick at one supporter who had been particularly abusive. Punches were exchanged by Cantona and the supporter as teammate Paul Ince and others came to his aid and stewards and police tried to intervene ('Cantona goes', 1995).

The incident was thought to be unprecedented in English soccer and Cantona was charged with 'misconduct which has brought the game into disrepute' by the English Football Association ('Cantona formally charged', 1995). In addition to being fined and suspended from Manchester United and the English Football Association, he was convicted in March 1995 of common assault and sentenced to two weeks in prison. On appeal, this was later reduced to 120 hours' community service, which consisted of teaching soccer to underprivileged children.

Cantona's previous record for aggressive and violent behaviour was not good. This occasion was the fifth time Cantona had been sent off since his transfer from Leeds in 1992. In 1987, while playing for Auxerre, he received a heavy fine for punching his own team's goalkeeper. In 1988, he was banned from the French team for one year after swearing at national coach Henri Michel. In 1989, after being substituted in a match, he kicked the ball into the crowd and threw his shirt at the referee. His club, Marseille, suspended him indefinitely. In 1990, playing for Montpellier, he was suspended for 10 days after smashing his boots into teammate Jean Claude Lemoult's face. In 1991, he was banned by his new club, Nimes, after throwing the ball at a referee. The ban was increased to two months when, at the disciplinary meeting, he approached each committee member and called each of them 'idiot'. This increased suspension provoked Cantona into announcing his retirement from soccer. Soon after, he returned to play soccer in England.

Incident 5: 1 December 1998
US National Basketball Association (NBA) team, Golden State
Warriors, at a team practice

About halfway through a team practice, an altercation took place between head coach P. J. Carlesimo and NBA All-Star player Latrell Sprewell. Apparently, trouble had been brewing for some time before the incident. Carlesimo had the reputation of being a tough coach, but Sprewell had been involved in fighting with teammates on at least two previous occasions. Taylor (1998) described what happened after the two exchanged words:

> Sprewell threatened to kill him and grabbed the coach by the throat, dragging him to the ground and choking him for 10 or 15 seconds before other players tore Sprewell away. About 20 minutes later Sprewell returned while the team was scrimmaging. According to several Warriors players, he went after Carlesimo again and threw punches at the coach, connecting with one glancing blow before he could again be hauled away.
>
> (Taylor, 1998, p. 62)

Initially, Sprewell was suspended from playing for ten games by Golden State Warriors. Then his contract, which had almost three years to run and close to $25 million dollars of income still to come, was terminated. On top of this, he was banned for one year and precluded from receiving payment from any NBA team by NBA commissioner David Stern. Following arbitration, his contract with Golden State Warriors was reinstated and the one-year ban was reduced by five months ('Sprewell wins', 1998).

Incident 6: 5 July 2000
Youth ice hockey practice at Burbank Ice Arena in Reading near Boston

It is perhaps ironic that, when Thomas Junta first approached coach Michael Costin, it was to object to the level of aggression and physical contact in his 10-year-old son's ice hockey practice. Shortly after, the two became embroiled in a physical confrontation that ended tragically. Costin was taken to hospital and died there the next day.

It later transpired that coach Costin, who was on skates and wearing a helmet, had thrown the first punch. It tore a gold chain from around Junta's neck. At this stage, the two were pulled apart by other parents, but they resumed fighting. This time Junta pushed Costin down, banged his head on the ground and punched him repeatedly. One punch from Junta ruptured one of Costin's arteries and this led to his death. Junta was later found guilty of involuntary manslaughter. Both men had previous convictions; Costin for assaulting a police officer and burglary and Junta for assault and battery and destruction of property (Franklin, 2002).

Junta apparently objected to his son's rough treatment at the hands of the other players and had approached coach Costin about allowing too much physical contact. In an interview with police, Junta told them that the practice had turned rough and the boys were hitting, checking and throwing elbows and that coach Costin brushed off his pleas to keep tighter control of the children ('Son supports', 2002; Franklin, 2002).

Incident 7: 20 April 2001
Rugby league match Parramatta versus Canterbury Bulldogs in
Parramatta stadium, Sydney, Australia

After this floodlit National Rugby League game, police were pelted with beer cans and tools thrown out of the darkness. One police officer required stitches after being struck by a full can of beer. Disturbances, rowdy behaviour and assaults continued as violent spectators left Parramatta stadium in the western suburbs of Sydney. The police put the blame on violent visiting Canterbury supporters, who had been involved in fighting and damage to commuter trains at games at their home stadium of Sydney Showground earlier in the year ('Spectators turn', 2001).

At face value, these examples might be considered relatively straightforward, but closer inspection suggests that there are a number of important questions raised by these and other incidents. Why, for example, were criminal charges brought against the perpetrators in only one of the seven incidents described above, the Junta–Costin parent–coach fight? In the ice hockey incident involving Niedermayer and Domi, Niedermayer did not die as a result of Domi's violent action, but, apart from that, the NHL incident is rather similar to the Junta–Costin fight. Why, therefore, did police not arrest Domi and charge him with assault? Why did Chilean police not arrest the brawling Fijian and New Zealand rugby union players in Santiago? Why are some aggressive and violent acts that take place in sport treated differently from similar acts that take place in other contexts? Is there something about the nature of aggressive and violent acts in sport that makes them special? How is it that some aggressive and violent acts in sport are permissible but others are not? What is it that makes spectators turn aggressive and violent and become involved in fighting with other spectators and the police? It is the purpose of this book to answer these and other questions that arise about aggression and violence in sport and to discuss any relevant issues that are encountered.

In the next section, the difficult task of trying to define what constitutes aggression and violence in sport, as opposed to other contexts, is attempted. In so doing, it will be necessary to examine definitions from mainstream psychology as well as those from sport psychology. As part of this task, it will also be important to differentiate between the different forms of aggression and violence which exist in sport.

Definitions of aggression

Almost every author of books on aggression has highlighted the difficulty involved in arriving at a satisfactory definition of aggression. As Renfrew (1997, p. 5) pointed out, at one level, university students may regard aggression as positive or negative, directed or undirected, intentional or uncontrolled, having intent or feeling, as an overt behaviour, or equivalent to anger or frustration. At another level, among professionals from a variety of academic fields, definitions of aggression have frequently focused on the causes of the behaviour, assumptions about the instigators, emotional aspects, and the intent to injure (Edmunds and Kendrick, 1980, p.15). Bandura (1973, p. 2) talked about entering a 'semantic jungle' when attempting to define aggression and Renfrew (1997, p. 5) concluded that 'no clear definition of aggression exists that is commonly accepted by professionals in this area'.

Some psychologists have adopted Buss's (1961, p. 1) definition that aggression is 'a response that delivers a noxious stimuli to another organism' as acceptable. This definition covers a range of aggressive behaviour, including physical and verbal attacks, but does not include the notion of intent to harm or injure and this makes it unacceptable to some other psychologists. Geen (1990), for example, is one of those who argues for a definition of aggression which goes beyond the basic behavioural level. He states:

> The term 'aggression' is applied to a wide array of behaviors that often appear to be highly related, but that on closer analysis prove to be quite different from each other. . . . The problems of definition do not arise until we turn to definitions more elaborate than a basic behavioral one. Aggressive behavior is not as simple or unambiguous as a purely behavioral definition would indicate. Other elements must be added, and these elements create certain complexities.
>
> (Geen, 1990, p. 2)

For Geen (1990) and others (e.g. Kaufman, 1970), these added elements were the intent to harm, and/or the expectation that aggressive behaviour will result in harm to the victim. For example, intent to harm can only be inferred from a person's behaviour and not directly observed, and therefore defies rigorous analysis. Geen (1990) accepted that inferences about intent to harm are difficult, but argued that 'nevertheless some such inference must be drawn in labelling an observed act as one of aggression' (Geen, 1990, p. 3). As a result, he defined aggression as 'the delivery of a noxious stimulus to another person with the intent of harming that person, and in the expectation that the aversive stimulus will reach its destination' (Geen, 1990, p. 28).

Later Geen (2001) modified his definition slightly and included a statement about the motivation of the victim, an additional characteristic of aggression identified by Baron and Richardson (1994). Geen (2001, p. 3) stated that 'aggression is the delivery of an aversive stimulus from one person to another, with intent to harm and with an expectation of causing such harm, when the other person is motivated to escape or avoid the stimulus.' Geen (1990, 2001) also distinguished between affective aggression and instrumental aggression. Affective aggression is accompanied by strong negative emotional states and anger caused by provocation. Instrumental aggression does not have a strong emotional basis, lacks the element of malice towards the victim, and is purely a means to some other end. Geen (2001, p. 5) also pointed out that, recently, the terms 'reactive' and 'proactive' aggression have been used as alternatives to affective and instrumental aggression, and that they are considered to be equivalent, reactive aggression being a self-defensive and angry action in response to provocation (i.e. physical or verbal) and proactive aggression being aggression initiated without provocation and relating to power or mastery over individuals. The terms affective (hostile) and instrumental aggression also appear in association with descriptions and definitions of aggression in the sport psychology literature. This will be further discussed in the following section.

Definitions of aggression in sport

If reaching a consensus about a general definition of aggression in mainstream psychology is a thorny issue, then attempting to find a meaningful definition in the sport context is even more challenging. First, a distinction needs to be made between athlete aggression and violence, and aggression and violence perpetrated by spectators. Definitions here are concerned with the former. The latter will be dealt with in chapter 7. Current definitions of aggression in sport tend to reflect the definitions from mainstream psychology. For example, aggression has been defined as: 'an overt verbal or physical act that can psychologically or physically injure another person or oneself' (Husman and Silva, 1984, p. 247), and 'the infliction of an aversive stimulus upon one person by another, an act committed with intent to harm, one perpetrated against an unwilling victim, and done with the expectancy that the behavior will be successful' (LeUnes and Nation, 1989, p. 193). Also, Terry and Jackson (1985) defined violence as: 'harm-inducing behavior bearing no direct relationship to the competitive goals of sport, and relates, therefore, to incidents of uncontrolled aggression outside the rules of sport, rather than highly competitive behavior within the rule boundaries.'

These definitions, typical of those existing in the sport psychology literature, are rather similar to those emanating from mainstream psychology. At face value they would, therefore, perhaps appear to be valid. Closer examination, however, reveals that they have major shortcomings. A serious criticism concerns the fact that definitions from mainstream psychology are not always applicable to sport because, by its very nature, sport takes place in a unique context and definitions like those above demonstrate a lack of knowledge and understanding of the real nature of aggression in sport. Smith (1983, p. 10) and Russell (1993, p. 181) have understood the special status that sport enjoys with regard to aggression and violence:

> Outside of wartime, sports is perhaps the only setting in which acts of interpersonal aggression are not only tolerated but enthusiastically applauded by large segments in society. It is interesting to consider that if the mayhem of the ring or gridiron were to erupt in a shopping mall, criminal charges would inevitably follow. However, under the umbrella of 'sport', social norms and the laws specifying what constitutes acceptable conduct in society are temporarily suspended. In their stead is a new order of authority, namely the

official rules of the sport. These dictate the forms of aggression that are illegal (e.g., a low blow) and the conditions under which aggression is unacceptable (e.g., a late hit).

(Russell, 1993, p. 181)

Aggressive and violent actions which might be illegal outside sport, or in supposedly non-contact sports like basketball, are legal and sanctioned in the context of combat sports like judo, karate and wrestling, or team contact sports like rugby, American football, Australian Rules football and ice hockey. All these sports are characterised by high levels of aggression and often violent physical contact which is both within the rules of the games and not intended to injure. Re-examining the definitions of Husman and Silva (1984), LeUnes and Nation (1989) and Terry and Jackson (1985), it is clear that they do not take into account forms of physical aggression and violence which are intrinsic and sanctioned in these types of sports (e.g. Russell, 1993, pp. 184–185). The definitions are not flexible enough to, for example, clearly differentiate between an aggressive body check in ice hockey (sanctioned) and one in basketball (unsanctioned). The fine line that distinguishes violent but legitimate actions from vindictive acts of violence is of crucial importance in this context (e.g. Smith, 1983; Russell, 1993; Kerr, 1999, 2002).

Kerr (1997) attempted to formulate a definition of aggression and violence in sport, which does incorporate this distinction:

In general, aggression can be seen as unprovoked hostility or attacks on another person which are not sanctioned by society. However, in the sports context, the aggression is provoked in the sense that two opposing teams have willingly agreed to compete against each other. Aggression in team contact sports is intrinsic and sanctioned, provided the plays remain permissible within the boundaries of certain rules, which act as a kind of contract in the pursuit of aggression (and violence) between consenting adults.

(Kerr, 1997, pp. 115–116)

Publications on aggression and violence in sport have used a number of qualifying adjectives (e.g. legal and illegal, legitimate and illegitimate, acceptable and unacceptable, permissible and impermissible, admissible and inadmissible, sanctioned and unsanctioned) to distinguish between different forms of aggression and violence in sport. In this book, the preferred terms are 'sanctioned' and 'unsanctioned' aggression and violence. The term 'sanctioned' has the advantage of including both the written rules or laws of sports and any unwritten rules or informal player norms (Bakker *et al.*, 1990) concerning aggression and violence in sport. 'Unsanctioned' aggression and violence is any act outside the written and unwritten rules or laws and player norms.

Two similar incidents from the 1994 and 1992 Bledisloe Cup second tests neatly illustrate the difference between sanctioned and unsanctioned aggression and violence. In the 1994 game, following two tries by Jason Little and Phil Kearns, the Australians went into a 17–3 lead. After half-time, the New Zealanders increased the intensity of their play and brought the score back to 17–16. David Knox kicked a penalty for Australia, 20–16. After almost continuous New Zealand attacks and just four minutes from the end of a thrilling game, New Zealand wing Jeff Wilson stepped past four defenders and dived for the try line. In mid-air he was hit by a shuddering cover tackle from George Gregan, the Australian scrum half. The physical contact at the tackle was so hard that the ball was knocked from Wilson's hands and he lost possession over the try line. It was a decisive moment in the game because Australia held on to win. Two years previously, in the 1992 second test, Australia also won the match with wing Paul Carozza scoring two tries. In the first try, in a situation similar to that of Jeff Wilson in the 1994 match, Carozza dived over the try line in the corner. However, after Carozza dived and scored, Richard Loe, the New Zealand prop, was seen to drop down on him and make firm contact with his forearm and possibly his elbow on Carozza's face. Carozza's nose was broken. Although the two incidents are very similar, they neatly illustrate what is meant by sanctioned and unsanctioned aggression and violent action in sport. Gregan's tackle in the 1994 test was a sanctioned violent act, but Loe's forearm smash in the 1992 test was a clear case of unsanctioned violence. Even so, in this case, the New Zealand rugby union authorities found no cause for taking action against Loe (Cameron, 1992).

Before moving on to examine definitions of aggression in sport in depth, it might be useful to examine how aggression relates to violence. The two terms tend to be used interchangeably, but Smith (1983, p. 3) stated that 'physical violence represents the end point on a continuum of aggressive behaviour, it is the most extreme form of aggression'. Although the word violence is often used in the negative sense to mean physical force employed (especially in an unlawful way) so as to damage or injure, it can also be used to mean violent action, as in a severe or violent collision or tackle. This book follows Atyeo's (1979) approach, where the term violence is used in both senses of the word:

> Violence is a threadbare catch-all of a word and I am no doubt guilty of stretching it even thinner. I have used it primarily in the sense of successful aggression towards an object, an animal or another person. Unlike most press reports which see sporting violence only as an infringement of the rules, I have applied the word to both 'legal' and 'illegal' incidents. For the purposes of this book, Mean Joe Greene is guilty of using violence whether he hits his opponent with his fists or blocks him with his shoulder.
>
> (Atyeo, 1979, p. 12)

Intent to harm or injure in sport

As with definitions of aggression from mainstream psychology, the element of intent to harm or injure is somewhat controversial. Several authors have argued that intent to injure is the most crucial element in defining aggressive and violent acts in sport (e.g. Husman and Silva, 1984; Tenenbaum *et al.*, 1997). Others have commented on the difficulties associated with the notion of intent to harm or injure in definitions (e.g. Isberg, 2000, p. 115; Russell, 1993, p. 185; and Smith, 1983, pp. 3–4). A major sticking point is, how does one identify intent to harm or injure during sport competition? Even though, for example in ice hockey, match penalties for intent to injure can be awarded against players who commit acts of unsanctioned violence, the only person who really knows whether or not there was any intent to injure is the athlete who carried out the action. In rugby league, extremely hard and legally violent tackles are part of the sanctioned aggression and violence that is intrinsic to the game. As a player, it is possible to tackle an opposing player as hard as possible, yet have no intent to injure the tackled player. Conversely, it is possible to undertake the same tackle, but have the clear intention of trying to injure the opposing player while doing so. Here, the action is the same, but the motivation behind it is totally different. Therefore, as mentioned earlier in relation to general definitions of aggression, making judgements about a person's motivation in general, and more specifically about intent to harm or injure by indirect means, is problematic (e.g. Apter, 1982, 1989; Frey, 1999; Schachter and Singer, 1962). It is the subjective meaning of the aggressive behaviour to the athlete concerned that is crucial.

A recent legal case from ice hockey shows how problematic the intent to injure element in definitions is, even in connection with an unsanctioned violent act (Kerr, 2002). Boston Bruin Marty McSorley was prosecuted in a British Columbia court and found guilty of 'assaulting Donald Brashear with a weapon, a hockey stick'. The guilty verdict was based on the judge's decision that 'Brashear was struck as intended.' In addition, the National Hockey League banned McSorley from playing for a year. In the incident, Vancouver Canuck Donald Brashear fell to the ice after receiving a heavy blow from McSorley's stick to the side of the face. The back of Brashear's head struck the ice, causing a grade three concussion and a grand mal seizure. The unsanctioned act occurred close to the end of the game when Brashear was well away from the puck. Later, in an interview, McSorley said 'Yes I meant to slash him'. 'Did I mean to hurt him with my stick? No' (Kennedy, 2000, p. 60). Kennedy claimed that McSorley aimed his slash at Brashear's shoulder to provoke a fight and that he did not intend to make contact with Brashear's head. According to Kennedy, video evidence confirmed that McSorley first struck Brashear on the shoulder before making contact with his face. If what McSorley said is true, his act of unsanctioned aggression was not undertaken with the intent to injure.

Perhaps the final point in this discussion on intent to injure is that people who agree to take part in sports involving aggressive and violent physical contact are actually well aware that there is a reasonable chance that they will be injured. Smith (1983), in particular, pointed out:

> It is taken for granted that when one participates in these activities one automatically accepts the inevitability of contact, also the probability of minor bodily injury, and the possibility of serious injury. In legal terms,

volenti non fit injuria – to one who consents no injury is done. On the other hand, no player consents to being injured intentionally.

(Smith, 1983, p. 10)

Further considerations concerning definitions of aggression in sport

Still widely cited in sport psychology publications is the difference between so-called 'instrumental' and 'hostile' (or 'reactive') aggression (Husman and Silva, 1984; Martens, 1975; Smith, 1983; Tenenbaum *et al.*, 1997). Both hostile and instrumental forms of aggression include intent to injure. The relatively common incidents of angry retaliation which occur as the result of provocation in team contact sports can be seen as examples of hostile aggression in sport. The so-called 'professional foul', especially in soccer, where a player is tackled, and usually illegally brought down to prevent the player scoring, can be seen as an example of instrumental aggression. It is interesting that, in sport, acts of instrumental aggression by a player often lead to acts of affective hostile aggression in self-defence or retaliation by the victim. It is often the act of retaliatory hostile affective aggression, rather than the provocative act of instrumental aggression, which is seen and punished by game officials.

It has been argued, however, that all aggressive acts in sport are instrumental and carried out with some end in mind (Smith, 1983). Smith concludes, therefore, that the distinction between instrumental and hostile aggression is not a useful one and is difficult to separate empirically where a particular aggressive act may have a variety of outcomes for the perpetrator. The distinction between hostile and instrumental aggression in sport is similar to the distinction between affective and instrumental aggression from mainstream psychology discussed earlier (Geen, 1990, 2001). Parry (1998) recognised this but, like Smith (1983), found the distinction of only limited value in the sport context:

> Sports psychologists seem to have taken one of the canons of the literature from the parent discipline related to aggression in humans generally, and simply applied it directly to sport, assuming that it will 'fit', and yield productive insights. I think that it has been of some value, but that it obscures more than it reveals.
>
> (Parry, 1998)

It has also been argued that some sanctioned acts of aggression in sport have been mislabelled as 'aggressive' and should actually be called 'assertive' (Husman and Silva, 1984; Tenenbaum *et al.*, 1997; Tenenbaum *et al.*, 2000; Thirer, 1994). Husman and Silva (1984) did concede that attempting to decide whether or not a legal act in sport is aggressive requires subjective assessment of the mood of the athlete concerned. They pointed out that cues from the social environment (e.g. gestures, hostile interactions, game developments) allow a decision to be made about whether behaviour is aggressive or assertive. However, this type of argument suffers from the same limitations as the 'intent to injure' element in definitions of aggression and violence in sport. In addition, calling aggressive behaviour 'assertive' is symptomatic of the general lack of realism about the true nature of sport, especially team contact sports. Tackles, body checks and blocks in team contact sports all require some degree of aggression. Referring to American football, LeUnes and Nation (1989, p. 197) said that 'In view of the generally violent nature of the game of football, it may be argued that all tackles are acts of aggression. Equally plausible, however, is the hypothesis that all of them are merely examples of assertiveness.' For some writers, however, the latter hypothesis lacks plausibility. These are sanctioned aggressive plays and to argue that they are merely assertive is an exercise in splitting hairs. As the present author put it,

> Would anyone who watched the American football Super Bowl, played last year in Florida, really have considered that the players were being assertive rather than aggressive? On the contrary, those watching the game would have seen a game that was replete with aggressiveness, violent physical contact and action, most of it sanctioned and an intrinsic part of the game. To argue that this type of behavior in team contact sports is assertive rather than aggressive lacks credibility and remains unconvincing.
>
> (Kerr, 2002, pp. 71–72)

Causes and processes of aggression and violence

Theoretical explanations of aggression and violence in sport have largely been based on those from mainstream psychology. Aggression, like intelligence, personality and some other concepts in psychology, is the subject of a nature–nurture debate. Early theories of aggression from mainstream psychology can be divided into three major groupings. These are biological theories (e.g. Lorenz, 1966), drive theories (e.g. Dollard *et al.*,1939; Berkowitz, 1962, 1989) and social learning theories (e.g. Bandura, 1973). Later, Geen (1990, 2001) presented a view of aggression in which cognitive, affective, behavioural and emotional variables interact. However, before examining Geen's (1990, 2001) approach, a brief review of the biological, drive and social learning theory explanations of aggressive behaviour will be undertaken. The basic elements, and the advantages and disadvantages of these approaches, are outlined below.

Biological theories of aggression and violence emphasise the innateness of the aggressive stimulus–response sequence. Studies of animals in the wild (e.g. Ardrey, 1966; Lorenz, 1966) and the results of laboratory experiments involving implanted electrodes in the hypothalamus and other parts of the brains of cats, monkeys, or rats (e.g. Maclean and Delgado, 1953; Renfrew, 1969), lent support to this approach. The hypothalamus, for example, was found to have an important role in controlling aggression in lower animals and, because their brain components are structurally and functionally similar, many of the findings from animal research could be generalised to human beings. However, in higher animals it was hypothesised that experience played a greater role in influencing instinctive patterns of aggression because they are controlled by the cortex (Renfrew, 1997).

Over the years, since scientists like Lorenz (1966) studied aggression in wild animals, opinions have changed as to the extent of innate animal aggression. Earlier studies indicated that many species of animals displayed aggression in forms of ritualised fighting, which involved threatening displays and, after confrontation, submissive acts which minimised the chance of the loser receiving fatal injuries. Forms of ritualised fighting were thought to have evolved as a means of safeguarding the survival of the species and typically took place when young were being protected or when animals competed for food, mates or territory. In more recent years, however, this view of animal aggression has had to be revised as evidence of murder and infanticide in the animal world have been revealed (e.g. Atkinson *et al.*, 1990).

Lorenz (1966) developed a theory of aggression which incorporated the notion of catharsis. Lorenz argued that aggressive energy builds up and, unless it can be released in some safe way, may increase to the point where it is released in a sudden aggressive attack. In the case of humans, an enduring belief is that participating in or watching sport acts as a kind of safety valve, a means of discharging aggressive urges through catharsis. Russell (1993, p. 232), however, in summarising research evidence and the views of other psychologists, is critical of the catharsis, sport-as-therapy idea. He states, 'Despite the general popularity of cathartic beliefs, participants and spectators in sports show little evidence of experiencing anything resembling a cathartic response to aggression. Rather, just the opposite usually occurs.'

A major challenge to those biological theories which are based on instinct, or argue that aggressive innate fighting instincts have developed through evolution, was provided by the Seville Statement on Violence (Seville Statement on Violence, 1986). The Statement was drawn up by a group of 20 scientists from 12 different countries meeting in Seville, Spain, in 1986 and later endorsed by some 15 professional organisations, including the American Psychological Association. The Statement challenged a number of popular beliefs based on allegedly scientific findings which have been used to justify violence and war, including the notion that humans have inherited, or possess an instinct for, or are genetically programmed to be violent or make war.

Drive theories of aggression are rooted in psychoanalytic theory and generally take the view that the frustration of instinctive behaviour (e.g. sexual behaviour) arouses an aggressive drive that is reduced only by an aggressive response. Dollard *et al.* (1939) extended the so-called frustration-aggression hypothesis to include the frustration of an individual's goal-directed behaviour which leads to an aggressive drive against the person, or perhaps object, that is causing the frustration. However, whilst the hypothesis seemed to provide a valuable explanation, it was too simplistic to account for the other non-aggressive types of responses that occur when people encounter frustration (e.g. Russell, 1993). Later revisions attempted to account for a wider range of responses to frustration in addition to aggression (Miller, 1941), and to tie frustration to negative affect so that only unpleasant frustrations were seen to lead to aggression (see page 15; Berkowitz,1989).

Elements of behaviourism and the results of research on animal learning can be found in the social learning theory approach to aggression, in which observational learning and the reinforcement and generalisation of aggression are central features. However, in the social learning theory approach, the importance of cognition and observational learning make it different from traditional behaviourism. Perhaps the most important contribution to this approach was the experimental work of Bandura and his colleagues, which focused on the learning of aggressive behaviour through imitation (e.g. Bandura *et al.*, 1963a, 1963b). In their well-known 'Bobo doll experiments' nursery children watched (both live and on film) a young woman being aggressive and violent towards a large inflatable clown doll. Later, children who observed this behaviour accurately imitated the woman's aggressive and violent actions when presented with the doll. Over the years Bandura and his colleagues carried out a large number of variations of this study by, for example, changing the rewards and punishments. The overall conclusion was that the observation of either live or filmed models of aggression increased the likelihood of aggression in the viewer.

However, Bandura's modelling experiments have been subject to criticism. In addition to ethical and moral concerns about the experimental conditions in the experiments, in which some critics argue that the children were trained to be aggressive (e.g. Worthman and Loftus, 1992), there have been other criticisms. For example, some argue that the children were manipulated into responding to the aggressive movie, and not all psychologists agree with the interpretation of the results offered by Bandura and his colleagues. Also, it has been argued that striking a rubber 'Bobo doll', that was specially designed to be hit, is not really aggressive behaviour at all, but simply vigorous play (e.g. Apter, 1982, p. 134). Criticisms such as these pose serious questions about the usefulness of the results for understanding aggressive behaviour.

Among more contemporary theoretical perspectives, Geen (e.g. 2001) considers that affect, cognition and arousal are the processes which mediate aggression. As is evident from the earlier section on definitions, Geen's ideas on aggression have changed somewhat over the years. These changes in his personal view appear to have been influenced by the general changes in more contemporary research and theorising that have taken place over recent years. He stated:

> Cognition has become the major process on which most mediational models are built, with affect and arousal as important parallel mechanisms. The nature of the cognitive emphasis has changed somewhat from what it once was. In the 1980s, the cognitive analysis of aggression was based mainly on the attribution of meaning to the provoking event. More recently the role of cognition has been couched in terms of such matters as the accuracy of social information processing, with processing deficits serving as the underlying antecedent of aggression in provoking situations, and the mechanisms by

which environmental conditions prime aggressive thoughts, feelings and dispositions to act.

(Geen, 2001, p xii)

Also according to Geen (2001), of importance in current theory and research on aggression are the so-called moderator variables: biological inheritance, social learning history, sex, personality and socio-cultural background. These moderator variables moderate the effects of provocative and anger-inducing situations, producing varying amounts and levels of aggression. Together, moderator variables and variables associated with provocative and anger-inducing situations comprise the two factors in affective or reactive aggression (Geen, 2001, p. 61).

This view links back to Berkowitz's work (1989, 1993), which re-examined the frustration-aggression hypothesis first put forward by Dollard *et al.* (1939) and led to the formulation of his cognitive-neoassociationist model of affective aggression. Berkowitz (1989) argued that aversive and unpleasant frustrations lead to aggressive behaviour, highlighting the importance of negative affect in hostile or affective aggression. He further proposed a series of stages in the formulation of the aggression process. Briefly, stage one involved the aversive event and the production of negative affect. In stage two, an associative reaction through experience and learning developed. The negative affect was thought to induce thoughts, feelings (e.g. fear, anger), and expressive-motor reactions associated with the so-called fight or flight tendency. In other words, depending on which tendency was stronger, the individual concerned would either flee from the situation or respond aggressively. These responses were thought to be automatic and, apart from appraising the event as aversive, cognitive processes were thought to have little influence in the early stages. However, in the later stages, cognition was thought to play an important role and was thought to influence subsequent emotional reactions and experiences through higher order processing. This led to the initial automatic responses being modified through causal attributions, evaluatory thoughts and attempts at self-control as part of higher cognitive functioning, which were then considered to either facilitate (anger-out) or inhibit (anger-in) an aggressive response.

Closing comments

In this introductory chapter, some example incidents were described to illustrate the range of aggressive and violent incidents in sport, definitions were examined and explanatory theories summarised, thus setting the scene for the rest of the book. Although not without their critics, each of the theoretical approaches described has played a role in helping to explain the motivation behind aggressive and violent behaviour. The relatively new and innovative reversal theory (Apter, 2001) forms the theoretical background on which this book on aggression and violence in sport is based. As well as being able to explain aggression and violence in general, it is one of the few theoretical approaches which can provide an adequate explanation of the pleasure and satisfaction that athletes obtain from sanctioned and unsanctioned aggression and violence in certain sports (e.g. team contact sports; Kerr, 1997). In chapter 2, the basic concepts of reversal theory are clearly set out and examples are provided to illustrate how those concepts apply to the context of sport.

References

Apter, M. J. (1982). *The experience of motivation: The theory of psychological reversals.* London: Academic Press.

Apter, M. J. (1989). *Reversal theory: Motivation, emotion and personality.* London: Routledge.

Apter, M. J. (Ed.) (2001). *Motivational styles in everyday life: A guide to reversal theory.* Washington DC: American Psychological Association.

Ardrey, R. (1966). *The territorial imperative.* New York: Dell.

Atkinson, R. L., Atkinson, R. C., Smith, E. E., Bem, D. J. and Hilgard, E. R. (1990). *Introduction to psychology.* San Diego: Harcourt Brace Jovanovich.

Atyeo, D. (1979). *Blood and guts: Violence in sports.* Melbourne: Cassell Australia.

Bakker, F. C., Whiting, H. T. A. and van der Brug, H. (1990). *Sport psychology: Concepts and applications.* Chichester: Wiley.

Bandura, A. (1973). *A social learning analysis.* Englewood Cliffs, NJ: Prentice Hall.

Bandura, A., Ross, D. and Ross, S. A. (1963a). Imitation of film-mediated aggressive models. *Journal of Abnormal and Social Psychology*, 66, 3–11.

Bandura, A., Ross, D. and Ross, S. A. (1963b). Vicarious reinforcement and imitative learning. *Journal of Abnormal Psychology*, 67, 601–603.

Baron, R. A. and Richardson, D. (1994). *Human aggression.* New York: Plenum.

Berkowitz, L. (1962). *Aggression: A social psychological analysis.* New York: McGraw-Hill.

Berkowitz, L. (1989). Frustration-aggression hypothesis: Examination and reformulation. *Psychological Bulletin*, 106, 59–73.

Berkowitz, L. (1993). *Aggression: Its causes, consequences and control.* New York: McGraw-Hill.

Buss, A. (1961). *The psychology of aggression.* New York: Wiley.

Cameron, D. (1992, September). Grievous bodily harm. *Rugby World and Post*, pp. 26–27.

Cantona goes over the top. (1995, 27 January). *The Japan Times*, p. 22.

Cantona formally charged by F.A. for spectator attack. (1995, 28 January). *The Japan Times*, p. 22.

Coomer, J. (2002, 11 January). Rugby Union decision gutless, *The New Zealand Herald*, p. A11.

Dollard, J., Doob, L., Miller, N., Mouwer, O. and Sears, R. (1939). *Frustration and aggression.* New Haven, CT: Yale University Press.

Edmunds, G. E. and Kendrick, D. C. (1980). *The measurement of human aggressiveness.* Chichester: Wiley.

Franklin, R. (2002, 12 January). Umpires strike back at parental violence. *The New Zealand Weekend Herald*, p. B9.

Frey, K. (1999). Reversal theory: Basic concepts. In J. H. Kerr (Ed.), *Experiencing sport: Reversal theory.* Chichester: Wiley.

Geen, R. G. (1990). *Human aggressiveness.* Milton Keynes: Open University Press.

Geen, R. G. (2001) (2nd Edition). *Human aggressiveness.* Milton Keynes: Open University Press.

Husman, B. F. and Silva, J. M. (1984). Aggression in sport: Definitional and theoretical considerations. In J. M. Silva and R. S. Weinberg (Eds), *Psychological foundations of sport* (pp. 246–260). Champaign, IL: Human Kinetics

Isberg, L. (2000). Anger, aggressive behavior, and athletic performance. In Y. L. Hanin (Ed.), *Emotions in sport*. Champaign, IL: Human Kinetics.

Kaufman, H. (1970). *Aggression and altruism*. New York: Holt Reinhart & Winston.

Kennedy, K. (2000, 20 November). Up against it. *Sports Illustrated*, 92, 58–62.

Kerr, J. H. (1997). *Motivation and emotion in sport*. Hove, England: Psychology Press.

Kerr, J. H. (1999). The role of aggression and violence in sport: A rejoinder to the ISSP position stand. *The Sport Psychologist*, 13, 83–88.

Kerr, J. H. (2002). Issues in aggression and violence in sport: The ISSP position stand revisited. *The Sport Psychologist*, 16, 68–78.

Leafs Domi threatened Niedermayer prior to vicious hit. (2001, 9 May). *The Japan Times*, p. 23.

LeUnes, A. D. and Nation, J. R. (1989). *Sport psychology: An introduction*. Chicago: Nelson-Hall Inc.

Lorenz, K. (1966). *On aggression*. New York: Harcourt Brace Jovanovich.

Maclean, P. D. and Delgado, J. M. R. (1953). Electrical and chemical stimulation of the frontotemporal portion of the limbic system in the waking animal. *Electro-encephalography and Clinical Neurophysiology*, 5, 91–100.

Martens, R. (1975). *Social psychology and physical activity*. New York: Harper & Row.

Miller, N. E. (1941). The frustration-aggression hypothesis. *Psychological Review*, 48, 337–342.

NHL bans Domi for rest of the playoffs. (2001, 6 May). *The Japan Times*, p. 24.

Parry, J. (1998). Violence and aggression in contemporary sport. In M. J. McNamee and S. J. Parry (Eds), *Ethics in sport* (pp. 205–224). London: E. & F. N. Spon.

Perrott, A. (2002, 10 January). Sevens stomper gets off the hook. *The New Zealand Herald*, p. A3.

Renfrew, J. W. (1969). The intensity function and reinforcing properties of brain stimulation that elicits attack. *Physiology and Behavior*, 4, 509–515.

Renfrew, J. W. (1997). *Aggression and its causes: A biopsychosocial approach*. Oxford: Oxford University Press.

Russell, G. W. (1993). *The social psychology of sport*. New York: Springer-Verlag.

Schachter, S. and Singer, J. (1962). Cognitive, social and physiological determinants of emotional state. *Psychological Review*, 69, 283–290.

Seville Statement on Violence (1986). In J. Grobel and R. A. Hinde (Eds) (1989). *Aggression and war: Their biological and social bases* (pp. xii–xvi). Cambridge, UK: Cambridge University Press.

Sims, G. (1995, June). Willie O. *Inside Sport*, pp. 59–69.

Smith, M. D. (1983). *Violence and sport*. Toronto: Butterworths.

Son supports father over fatal beating. (2002, 10 January). *The New Zealand Herald*, p. B2.

Spectators turn violent after game. (2001, 22 April). *The Japan Times*, p. 21.

Sprewell wins twice. (1998, 6 March). *The Japan Times*, p. 24.

Taylor, P. (1998, 15 December). Latrell Sprewell's attack on Golden State Warriors coach P. J. Carlesimo brought many questions to the fore, none more baffling than, Who is Latrell Sprewell and why did he resort to violence? *Sports Illustrated*, p. 62.

Tenenbaum, G., Stewart, E., Singer, R. N. and Duda, J. (1997). Aggression and violence in sport: An ISSP position stand. *The Sport Psychologist*, 11, 1–7.

Tenenbaum, G., Sacks, D. N., Miller, J. W., Golden, A. S. and Doolin, N. (2000). Aggression and violence in sport: A reply to Kerr's rejoinder. *The Sport Psychologist*, 14, 315–326.

Terry, P. C. and Jackson, J. J. (1985). The determinants and control of violence in sport. *Quest*. 37, 27–37.

Thirer, J. (1994). Aggression. In R. N. Singer, M. Murphy and L. K. Tennant (Eds), *Handbook of research on sport psychology* (pp. 365–378). New York: Macmillan.

Ulmer, M. (1998, 11 March). On-ice thug is really a sensitive guy. *The Ottawa Citizen*, p. C5.

Worthman, C. and Loftus, E. (1992). *Psychology*. New York: McGraw-Hill.

2 Getting started with reversal theory[1]

Step 1 in getting started with reversal theory is to note that reversal theory is a *general theory* of psychology which utilises a *structural phenomenological* approach. In addition, the theory considers human behaviour to be inherently inconsistent and argues that *reversals* between paired *metamotivational states* form the basis of human personality, emotion and motivation (see Figure 2.1). Step 2 involves examining the basic features of reversal theory, and the technical terms they have been assigned, in more detail. Where examples have been provided to illustrate concepts from reversal theory, they have been taken from athletes' experience in sport.

Structural phenomenology

Phenomenology is one of the major approaches in the study of psychology. It concentrates on the individual's subjective experience of life events. Structural phenomenology is the special form of phenomenology which is utilised by reversal theory. In structural phenomenology, the subjective experience of cognition and emotion, as well as one's own motivation, is thought to be influenced by certain structures and patterns. Thus, structural phenomenology provides a perspective on how human motivation is organised. Tied in with the individual focus of reversal theory is the notion that there is an inherent inconsistency in the way that people behave. In other words, an athlete who finds him or herself in the same situation on different occasions may behave in totally different ways.

Metamotivational states and reversals

Metamotivational states are mental states which are concerned with how athletes experience their motives. There are eight different metamotivational states bonded together in four pairs which co-exist separately within *bistable systems*. The concept of bistability has been adopted by reversal theory from cybernetics to explain the rapid changes or psychological reversals that take place backwards and forwards over time between any pair of metamotivational states. In cybernetics, a bistable system is one which tends to maintain a specified variable, despite external disturbance, within one or another of two ranges of values of the

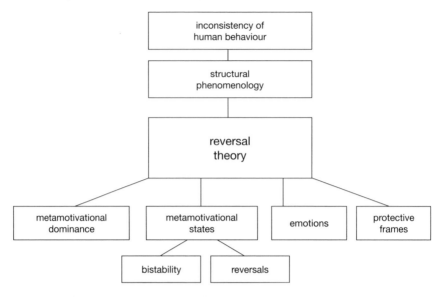

Figure 2.1 The main concepts in reversal theory

Source J. H. Kerr (1994) *Understanding soccer hooliganism* (© 1994 Open University Press). Reproduced with the kind permission of the Open University Press/McGraw-Hill Publishing.

variable concerned. The four sets of partner metamotivational states are known as the *telic and paratelic, negativistic and conformist, autic and alloic* and *mastery and sympathy* states. The first four are primarily concerned with the way an athlete experiences his or her own bodily arousal and are therefore known as the *somatic states*. The latter four states are primarily concerned with interactions with other people or, in some situations, objects (e.g. motorcycles, boats, horses, skis and other sports equipment), and have therefore been labelled the *transactional states*. In reversal theory, the relative importance of one state over the others at any particular time is known as *salience*. Figure 2.2 summarises the major character-istics of the somatic and transactional metamotivational states.

An analogy might be useful in illustrating the relationship which exists between partner metamotivational states. For example, consider a viewer who is particularly interested in sport sitting down to watch television. Two sports events (e.g. track-and-field athletics and tennis) are being transmitted on different channels, say channels 1 and 2, at the same time. Although interested in both events, the person concerned can only watch athletics on channel 1 or tennis on channel 2 at any one time, but by using the remote control to switch back and forth between channels, the viewer can see the best action from both events. Here, channel 1 can be thought of as representing one metamotivational state (e.g. the telic state) and channel 2 its paired partner (e.g. the paratelic state), and the switches between channels can be thought of as the reversals which occur between metamotivational states in everyday life (see Figure 2.3, page 23).

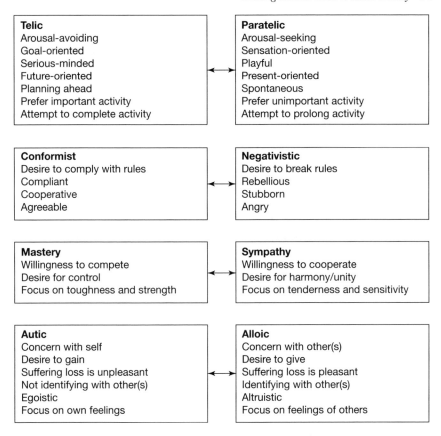

Figure 2.2 Characteristics of the four pairs of metamotivational states.

Characteristics of the somatic states

Telic state

With the telic state operative, an athlete's behaviour is likely to be serious, goal oriented and future related in the sense that it involves considerable planning ahead. This form of behaviour is typical of many training situations where a high workrate and the completion of training goals are to the fore. Also, when in this state, athletes will generally have a preference for experiencing low levels of *felt arousal.*

Paratelic state

With the paratelic state operative, an athlete's behaviour is likely to be spontaneous, impulsive and sensation oriented, and geared to prolonging the immediate enjoyment of ongoing activities. In this state, the athlete prefers high levels of felt arousal and, where goals exist, their purpose is to add to the pleasure in a situation. Scandinavian fartlek distance running training is a good example, where fun is the main objective and distance and time are of lesser importance.

Conformist state

Athletes in the conformist state are usually agreeable and cooperative and have a desire to comply with rules. The written and unwritten rules and conventions of many sports require compliance by the athletes concerned and, as a result, athletes will often be in the conformist state when competing.

Negativistic state

Athletes in the negativistic state tend to be rebellious, stubborn and defiant, feeling the need to act against something or someone. With this state operative, an athlete might react to the aggressive barracking of rival fans and respond by directing a provocative gesture at them.

Characteristics of the transactional states

Mastery state

Athletes may often find themselves in the mastery state when competing against another athlete or team. In the usual competitive situation, they will feel the need to be tough and masterful in order to defeat opponents.

Sympathy state

When the sympathy state is operative, athletes will feel the need to empathise with others, perhaps teammates or supporting spectators. Here feelings of harmony and unity may be important.

Autic state

The focus for individuals in the autic state is themselves and what happens to them personally in any sporting or other interaction. If an athlete perceives him or herself as successful in an interaction, it is a pleasant experience; if unsuccessful, it is experienced as unpleasant. A try-saving tackle in rugby or a diving catch in the cricket outfield executed successfully would engender pleasant feelings for an athlete with the autic state operative.

Alloic state

When the alloic state is operative, the focus for an athlete is what happens to other athletes, coaching staff, or even officials in any sporting interaction. Perceiving these other participants as having been successful will induce feelings of pleasure and satisfaction in that particular athlete. For example, for a player in the alloic state, a winning goal scored by a field hockey teammate in injury time at the end of a close, hard-fought game would be experienced in this way.

How reversals take place

Reversals are thought to be involuntary and sometimes unexpected. In other words, a person cannot suddenly decide that he or she would prefer to be in, say, the telic state and consciously prompt a reversal to that state from the paratelic state. Reversal theory hypothesises that there are three ways in which reversals take place. These have been termed *contingency, frustration and satiation* (see Figure 2.3).

Contingency

A club cricketer plays recreational cricket at the weekend. He is the team's best fast bowler and takes his bowling very seriously, thinking about and planning the series of balls in each over very carefully. When he is bowling, he is typically in the telic state. However, he has never shown much talent or skill with the bat and he regularly bats near the bottom of the team batting order. As a result, his attitude when batting has been to treat it as a bit of a laugh, getting to the crease and swinging his bat with reckless abandon, hoping to notch up a few lucky runs before he gets bowled out. When he is batting he is typically in the paratelic state.

During one particular match in the latter stages of a cup competition, his more talented teammates at the top and middle of the batting order fail to come to terms with a very skilful spin bowler and they are skittled out for a very low score. He finds himself going out to bat with nine wickets down. He and his partner are the last batsmen. Usually when he bats he is in the paratelic state, but now, owing

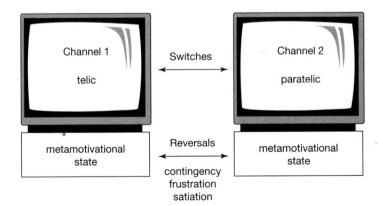

Figure 2.3 Television channel switching illustrating how reversals are induced by the three types of inducing agents.

to the sudden collapse of his team's normally dependable batting and the fact that he has to bat slowly and cautiously to try and achieve a good score and get his team out of trouble, he undergoes a reversal and finds himself in the telic state. In this example, the batting collapse is an environmental event which has induced a reversal from the paratelic to the telic state (e.g. Svebak *et al.*, 1982).

Frustration

A rugby league match involves two teams from a premier division, but with players of very different abilities and playing styles. One team has extremely skilful players who are intent on playing the game to the best of their ability and using team strategy and tactics which involve a flowing, entertaining game. The other team's players are not as skilful and have developed a style of play which is dependent on 'mixing it' with the opposing players and trying to upset their playing style. This often means using physically violent, unlawful tactics which they have employed with some success in previous matches.

Towards the end of the first half of the game, a forward from the skilful team receives the ball and runs at speed, trying to break through the opposition defence. He is tackled by two defenders. One of the defenders has tackled low and taken the attacking forward around the legs. The second defender has tackled around the upper body and, just as the players hit the ground, he elbows the attacker hard in the face. The foul play was unseen by referee and touch judges. In addition, the opposition have been using very dubious tactics since the start of the game, preventing the attacking team from playing their usual open style of play. This is the third or fourth time that the attacking forward has been subjected to foul play. Following the instructions of the team coach, he has not reacted to the previous incidents, remaining in the conformist state and adhering to the coach's instructions and the rules of the game. With the latest incident, however, a reversal from the conformist to the negativistic state takes place, prompted by the repeated acts of foul play. The attacking forward angrily retaliates and a punch-up between the two players develops. This time, however, the touch judge has observed the retaliation and, after consulting with the referee, the attacking forward (feeling even more aggrieved and negativistic) is sent off the pitch to the 'sin bin'. This example illustrates the second type of reversal induction, where a reversal has occurred due to conditions of *frustration*, where an athlete has been unable to obtain satisfaction in an operative state or state combination (see, for example, Barr *et al.*, 1990).

Satiation

A professional volleyball player is a member of a team based in Japan. Prior to the start of the playing season, she participates in pre-season training and attends a special summer training camp. Once the season begins, she becomes a permanent member of the team and plays in all the team's matches. She has a very serious and dedicated approach to volleyball and when she is training and playing she usually has the telic state operative. At the end of a long season, she joins her national team at a four-day international tournament. During her last game, at a stage when the two opposing teams are evenly matched, she suddenly reverses from the telic to the paratelic state. She finds herself in a rather playful mood, making unplanned, spontaneous plays. Even so, her team manages to win and returns to the dressing room. After showering and changing, the player, still with the paratelic state operative, leaves the volleyball facility and goes out on the town for an all-night binge of drinking and partying with some of her teammates. This example illustrates the third type of reversal-inducing agent, *satiation*, which is increasingly likely to induce a reversal if an athlete has been in one meta-motivational state for some time (e.g. Lafreniere *et al.*, 1988).

Although reversals are thought to be involuntary, some research evidence does suggest that people may be able to place themselves in particular situations and contexts, or create environmental conditions which are likely to induce reversals to particular metamotivational states (e.g. Kerr and Tacon, 1999). Some examples of research which examined reversals in sport are: Cox and Kerr (1989, 1990), research on competitive squash; Kerr and Vlaswinkel (1993), a study on long distance running; and Males and Kerr (1996), research on slalom canoeing. Details of these studies and all the latest reversal theory sport research can be found in Kerr (1997, 1999).

Metamotivational dominance

To return to the television analogy used earlier, if the action is especially thrilling, a viewer may spend more time watching one channel than the other. In a similar way, though psychological reversals between metamotivational states are thought to take place frequently, each athlete will vary in the amount of time spent in either one of two partner states. Athletes, therefore, who have a tendency or innate bias to spend more time in one metamotivational state over its partner are said to be, for example, *telic dominant* or *mastery dominant*. Even though athletes may exhibit particular state dominances, they will reverse and spend time in their non-dominant states.

Research examining metamotivational dominance in sport has shown, for example, that telic dominance is associated with participation in and preference for endurance sports, such as long distance running and hiking (Svebak and Kerr, 1989), and paratelic dominance with explosive sports such as baseball and cricket (Svebak and Kerr, 1989), along with risk sports like parachuting, motorcycle racing and snow-boarding (Cogan and Brown, 1998; Kerr, 1991).

Protective frames and parapathic emotions

A *protective frame* is a kind of psychological bubble, or more specifically a phenomenological frame, which provides a sense of safety in dangerous situations or circumstances. This produces a paradox of danger-which-is-not-danger and allows people to enjoy pleasant high arousal associated with arousal seeking in the paratelic state (Apter, 1993, p. 31). There are three main types of protective frames, known as the *confidence, safety-zone,* and *detachment frames*: The confidence frame provides feelings of safety in the face of risk through confidence in one's skills and those of others and the dependability of equipment; the safety-zone frame provides feelings of safety through the perception that in fact there is no source of threat; and the detachment frame provides feelings of safety through the fact that one is merely an observer (Apter, 2001, p. 47). Confidence and safety-zone frames are most important for athletes when performing, and safety-zone and detachment frames are most important for spectators and fans when watching sporting contests.

In special circumstances, where a paratelic protective frame exists, high arousal emotions that are usually experienced as unpleasant in the telic state (e.g. anxiety, anger) can be experienced as pleasant. In this form they are known as *parapathic emotions*. Parapathic emotions can be experienced in any of the safety-zone, confidence or detachment frames, and they then take on a special nature. Apter, describing the special quality of parapathic emotions, stated:

> Nevertheless the reversal theory thesis is that *all* high arousal emotions, however unpleasant in the telic state, can be experienced in some form in the paratelic state, and that they will always be pleasant in this state. However, to be experienced in the paratelic state without a reversal to the telic state occurring, these normally telic emotions have to undergo a type of transformation, the result of which is that they come to have in the paratelic state a special phenomenological quality which differentiates them quite clearly from the corresponding emotions in the telic state.
>
> (Apter, 1982, p. 109)

According to reversal theory, it is by means of paratelic protective frames that recreational or competitive athletes involved in risk sports, such as skydiving, are able to enjoy activities which others perceive as highly dangerous. The skydiver, for example, can experience the unpleasant telic anxiety typically associated with skydiving in a pleasant form, through paratelic protective frames and parapathic emotions. Of course, if for any reason the frame should break (for example, as a result of a sudden equipment failure), the pleasant parapathic emotion (anxiety) will once again be experienced in its unpleasant form. Experiencing protective frames is synonymous with being in the paratelic state. Kerr (1997) has explored the reversal theory concept of protective frames and participation in dangerous sports, and Apter (1992) has explored the concept across the whole gamut of sport, recreational and other activities.

Metamotivational state combinations

Step 3 in getting started with reversal theory is to examine a more complex development, that of *metamotivational state combinations* and the emotions which occur as a result.

Two-way somatic state combinations

Perhaps the best way of illustrating the concept of metamotivational state combinations is to return to the television analogy. The original setup can be extended to include two more channels. There are now four channels available to the viewer: channels 1, 2, 3 and 4. With the split-screen function that is available on some contemporary televisions, a viewer can watch two channels at the same time. However, suppose the split-screen function works in such a way that either channel 1 or 2 can be viewed on one panel and either 3 or 4 can be viewed on the other. This would mean that there are four possible split-screen combinations between which a viewer could channel-switch; channels 1 and 3, channels 1 and 4, channels 2 and 3, channels 2 and 4. Here, as well as channel 1 representing the telic state and channel 2 representing the paratelic state, channels 3 and 4 can be thought of as representing the negativistic and conformist metamotivational states, respectively (see Figure 2.4). Like the switches between channels, reversals between telic and paratelic states and between negativistic and conformist states are possible, and the different split-screen combinations represent possible metamotivational combinations of the four somatic states (telic-negativistic, telic-conformist, paratelic-negativistic, paratelic-conformist).

Some examples from sport may help to illustrate how these two-way somatic state combinations work. The paratelic-conformist state combination is likely to be operative when a person is playing a leisurely game of pool or snooker with a friend. The game finishes and they decide to play another one. However, the friend suggests that in the next game they should have a sizeable wager on the outcome. This changes the players' perception of the seriousness of the play and might well induce a reversal from the paratelic to the telic state. Thus, if a reversal

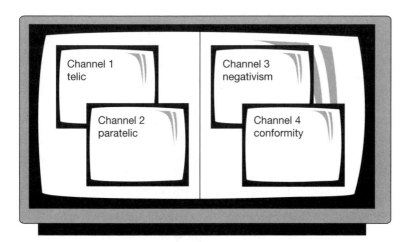

Figure 2.4 The television split screen analogy representing two-way somatic state combinations.

does occur, the person's state combination changes from paratelic-conformity to telic-conformity (conformity because the player has to adhere to the rules and conventions of the game). For professional pool or snooker players involved in top-level competitions, the telic-conformist state combination would be likely to be operative because of the seriousness of the competition and the large amounts of prize money to be won by successful play.

Angry athletes who verbally abuse, push or, very occasionally, strike umpires or referees are likely to be in the telic-negativistic state combination. This usually occurs when the umpire or referee has made what the athlete considers to be an unfair decision against the athlete or the team. The abusive behaviour is a response to perceived injustice.

When athletes' behaviour involves doing something 'just for the hell of it', then it is probable that they are in a paratelic-negativistic state combination. A good example of this is the ethos of the style of play of the Barbarians rugby team (a specially selected team mostly comprised of players from England, Ireland, Scotland and Wales which plays a one-off match against visiting touring teams from other countries), which is representative of paratelic-negativism. The Barbarians' tradition is that they play in an unconventional, entertaining way, throwing caution aside and trying personal skills and team moves and tactics which they would rarely try in their regular telic-conformist-oriented matches. In this way, players can, to some extent at least, enjoy defying the usual expectations and break with the established way of doing things.

Two-way transactional state combinations

What is true for the somatic states is also true for the transactional states. Imagine a second set of four channels, again arranged in two pairs (5–6 and 7–8). Channels 5 and 6 represent the autic and alloic states and channels 7 and 8 the mastery and sympathy states, respectively. In the same way as for the four previous channels, four more channel combinations are possible; channels 5 and 7, channels 5 and 8, channels 6 and 7 and channels 6 and 8 (remember, only 5 or 6 and 7 or 8 can be viewed at any one time). These channel combinations represent combinations of partner transactional states which produce the autic-mastery, autic-sympathy, alloic-mastery and alloic-sympathy metamotivational state combinations (see Figure 2.5).

To take some more sport examples, many athletes involved in elite-level individual sports (e.g. track-and-field athletic events) will have the autic-mastery state combination operative when they perform. They have dedicated themselves to maximising their strength and fitness and have mastered their technique, with a view to defeating their opponents. Their focus is on themselves and being successful, preferably winning. However, a reversal from mastery to sympathy state might occur if the athlete had been unluckily disqualified (e.g. for false-starting, no-throwing or no-jumping). This would result in an autic-sympathy state combination. That is, the athlete would want to be sympathised with and reassured.

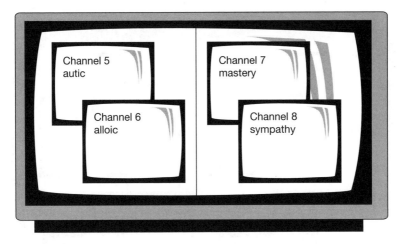

Figure 2.5 The television split screen analogy representing two-way transactional state combinations.

Conversely, a male coach guiding his athlete or team through a tournament will likely be in the alloic-mastery state as he instructs, guides and urges his athlete or team towards victory. The alloic-sympathy state combination might be operative in an athlete who, after competing well, stops at the edge of the playing arena to sign autographs for admiring teenage fans.

Four-way metamotivational combinations

Imagine that the two sets of four channels in the television analogy have been added together and it is now possible for the viewer to watch four channels (one from each pair) at any one time through a four-way split-screen. As shown in Figure 2.6, there are four television channels possible in any combination. This means that, for example, channels 1, 3, 5 and 8 could be viewed together, as could channels 2, 3, 6 and 8. These television channel combinations represent the metamotivational state combinations of telic-negativistic-autic-mastery, and paratelic-negativistic-alloic-sympathy, respectively. Of course, these are examples; several other four-way metamotivational combinations are possible.

Reversals between partner states will occur, and so the component states within any state combination will change relatively frequently. An analogy is real-life cable television which has one channel consisting of an overview of all the other channels, often showing twelve or more channels in miniature on one regular-sized screen. As the viewer watches, the mini-channels change periodically in an apparently random organisation to show brief glimpses of the many cable channels on offer.

This arrangement of metamotivational state combinations is possible through the introduction of the concept of *multistable systems* which, like the bistable system, also originates from cybernetics. In reversal theory, a multistable system

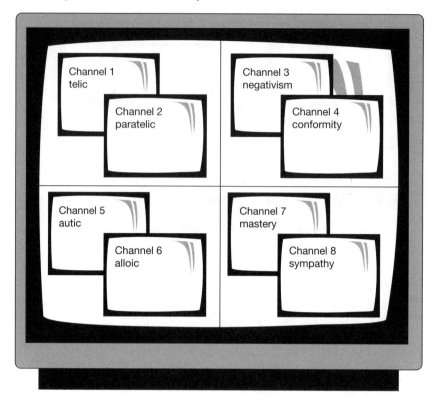

Figure 2.6 The television split screen analogy representing four-way somatic and transactional state combinations.

is really a more complex version of the bistable arrangement that exists between any two partner states. The two sets of somatic states and the two sets of transactional states interact within a multistable system. Thus, reversal theory is a multistable theory of motivation.

Four-way state combinations in sport

The Eco Challenge is a long-distance endurance team race over extremely difficult terrain which involves activities such as hiking, running, swimming, mountain biking, canoeing, rock climbing, abseiling and horse riding. The Eco Challenge is designed to be exactly that: a challenge which pushes the competing teams of three men and one woman to their absolute maximum and beyond. Team members voluntarily suffer excruciating pain from blisters, pulled muscles, cramp, injuries from falls, intense heat and cold, dehydration, lack of sleep and other more serious medical conditions. Teams have to plan their own routes over each stage and all the teams in the race are carefully checked at regular rest and food stops. When a team or individual athlete's long-term health or, in some instances, life is threatened, organisers and medical support staff can prevent them from continuing. Back-up helicopters often have to search for competitors in trouble and airlift them back to base hospitals. All four team members have to finish the race; if one is forced to drop out, then the others have to stop as well.

The Eco Challenge provides a useful example of how metamotivational state combinations and reversals might work in the sport context. In an event like this, lasting several days, where athletes repeatedly encounter new and diffi-cult, challenging situations, it is likely that an athlete will experience numerous different metamotivational states and state combinations. For example, when a team are planning their route for the first stage of the race, team members are likely to be in the telic and conformist states. They are also likely to have the alloic and mastery states operative as team cohesion and the desire for their colleagues to be successful is strong. At a later stage, when faced with a long and tricky abseil down a wet and slippery rock face, the athletes may find themselves firmly in a telic-conformist-autic-mastery state combination as they concentrate hard and use all their skill to personally master the task at hand.

At another stage in the race, a tired team member suffering from severe foot problems may reverse from the operative telic and mastery states to the paratelic and sympathy states, as he jokes with medical staff while they treat his cuts and blisters at a rest stop. His overall operative state combination in this situation is likely to be paratelic-conformist-autic-sympathy, with the autic-sympathy combination being most prominent. Once treatment is complete, and as the time to restart the race approaches, the athlete might reverse from paratelic to telic and from sympathy to mastery states in anticipation of what lies ahead.

In a competitive race such as this, the experience of some states may be less common than others. There would, for example, seem to be few occasions for these athletes to have the negativistic state operative. It must also be kept in mind that, in a race of this kind, although certain metamotivational combinations may be operative for fairly long periods, reversals are always likely to occur as a result of sudden unexpected environmental events, frustration or satiation. For example, a fall off a mountain bike, resulting in severe scrapes and bruises, a slip from a rope while crossing a river, resulting in a complete soaking in freezing cold water, or a canoe capsize in a choppy sea are all unexpected environmental events which might induce reversals. Also, at any one time in a metamotivational state combi-nation, one or two states may predominate over the others. In most of the Eco Challenge race situations, the mastery state may well be salient for many of the competitors.

Metamotivational variables and the sixteen primary emotions

The preference for different levels of felt arousal in the telic and paratelic states has already been mentioned in the subsection 'Characteristics of the somatic states' (page 21). Felt arousal is one of reversal theory's *metamotivational variables*, which are associated with the different sets of partner metamotivational states.

Felt arousal is the degree to which an athlete feels him or herself to be worked up. Other metamotivational variables include *felt transactional outcome* (transactional states; the degree to which a person feels him or herself to have gained or lost in an interaction); *felt significance* (telic and paratelic states; how much a person perceives a goal he or she is pursuing as significant and serving purposes beyond itself); *felt negativism* (negativistic and conformist states; how much a person feels him or herself to be acting against an external rule or requirement); *felt toughness* (mastery and sympathy states; how much a person feels him or herself to be tough, strong or in control); and felt identification (autic and alloic states; how much a person feels him or herself to be egoistic or altruistic).

How different levels of these metamotivational variables are experienced has important implications for an athlete's experience of emotions. In this regard, felt arousal and felt transactional outcome are the two most important metamotivational variables. Felt arousal is a metamotivational variable concerned with the somatic states and its importance in sport has been repeatedly demonstrated by reversal theory sport research (e.g. Cox and Kerr, 1989, 1990; Kerr and Cox, 1989, 1990; Kerr and Vlaswinkel, 1993; Males and Kerr, 1996).

The experience of felt arousal is dependent on whether the conformist or negativistic state is allied with the telic or paratelic state in a two-way combination. An athlete with the telic-conformist state combination operative generally prefers low levels of felt arousal. With the paratelic-conformist state combination operative, high levels of felt arousal are generally preferred. As shown in Figure 2.7, the experience of preferred levels of felt arousal is, in both cases, associated with positive hedonic tone and is experienced as pleasant *relaxation* and *excitement*, respectively. Non-preferred high levels of felt arousal in the telic state and low levels of felt arousal in the paratelic state result in negative hedonic tone and are experienced as unpleasant *anxiety* and *boredom*, respectively. Thus, there are four possible somatic emotions which may result from the experience of felt arousal conditions in the telic- or paratelic-conformist state combination.

Four additional somatic emotions are experienced when athletes are in the telic- and paratelic-negativistic state combinations. Referring again to Figure 2.7, *placidity* and *provocativeness* are the two pleasant and *sullenness* and *anger* the two unpleasant emotions resulting from the various state combinations. In each case, they are also related to the experience of preferred and non-preferred levels of felt arousal, and a reversal between partner states would change the experience of arousal. For example, an athlete might be experiencing unpleasant boredom (paratelic low arousal), but a reversal to the telic state (within a two-way combination with the conformist state) would result in the low arousal then being experienced as pleasant relaxation. Equally, for the two high arousal emotions, unpleasant telic anxiety would be experienced pleasantly as paratelic excitement if a telic to paratelic reversal took place.

Felt transactional outcome is a metamotivational variable concerned with the transactional states. As shown in Figure 2.8, a similar series of state combinations between the autic-alloic and mastery-sympathy pairs of states and the experience

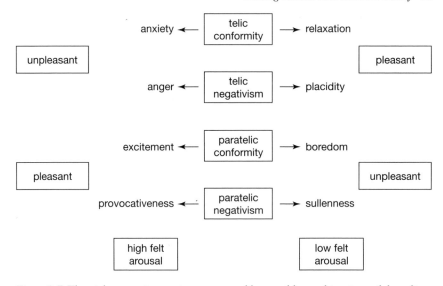

Figure 2.7 The eight somatic emotions generated by possible combinations of the telic-paratelic and negativism-conformity pairs of states.

Source J. H. Kerr (1994) *Understanding soccer hooliganism* (© 1994 Open University Press). Reproduced with the kind permission of the Open University Press/McGraw-Hill Publishing.

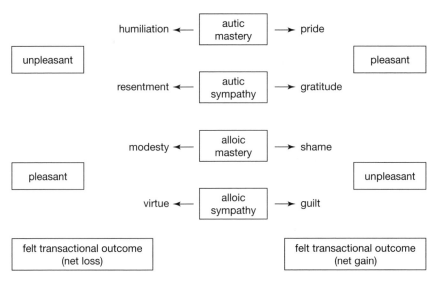

Figure 2.8 The eight transactional emotions generated by possible combinations of the autic-alloic and mastery-sympathy pairs of states.

Source J. H. Kerr (1994) *Understanding soccer hooliganism* (© 1994 Open University Press). Reproduced with the kind permission of the Open University Press/McGraw-Hill Publishing.

of felt transactional outcome in terms of net gain or loss result in the experience of eight transactional emotions. These are *pride, modesty, humiliation, shame, gratitude, virtue, guilt* and *resentment*.

The experience of metamotivational variables in both somatic and trans-actional state combinations contributes to hedonic tone or experienced pleasure. Provided reversals are not ongoing, athletes at any one time will experience one somatic and one transactional emotion, but the strength of two emotions may vary (for example, a judo player who progresses to the quarterfinals of a tournament after injuring his or her opponent in a throw might experience mild excitement and strong guilt). Overall hedonic tone is, therefore, a composite of the two and reflects the strengths of the contributing emotions. Stress may result from mismatches in preferred and felt levels of the metamotivational variables and is reflected in low levels of hedonic tone and the experience of unpleasant emotions (see Figures 2.7 and 2.8). The reversal theory approach to stress is explained in the following, final section of the chapter.

Experiencing stress in sport

Step 4 in getting started with reversal theory focuses on how athletes experience stress and how they can attempt to cope with it. As mentioned in the previous section, any mismatch or discrepancy between felt and preferred levels of metamotivational variables, like felt arousal and felt transactional outcome, will lead to stress. For example, an archer at a competition may typically perform in a specific metamotivational state combination at a preferred level of arousal. If, however, at one particular archery meet, a marked arousal discrepancy occurs between the archer's actual and preferred levels of arousal, the archer is likely to experience stress. In reversal theory, there are two forms or types of stress (Svebak and Apter, 1997). The stress experienced by the archer, caused by a mismatch in preferred and felt arousal levels, is known as *tension stress* and the effort expended by the archer in trying to reduce tension stress is known as *effort stress*. Effort stress is an attempt at coping with discrepancies in levels of metamotivational variables. For example, tension stress and effort stress can be experienced in both telic and paratelic states. In the telic state, tension stress is experienced as unpleasant threat or anxiety, and in the paratelic state it is experienced as unpleasant lack of threat, or boredom. Effort stress in the telic state takes the form of effortful coping, but in the paratelic state it takes the form of responding to challenge(s).

In the case of the archer, let us suppose that the telic state is operative within his or her usual competitive state combination, with accompanying low levels of felt and preferred arousal. The archer will experience telic tension stress if, for example, felt arousal increases as a result of adverse weather conditions during competition. Increased felt arousal interferes with the archer's pursuance of his or her desired goals and results in unpleasant feelings of anxiety. These unpleasant feelings may lead to effort stress as the archer initiates compensatory coping behaviour aimed at reducing tension and minimising interference in the archer's attempts at goal achievement.

Conversely, consider the triple jumper whose preferred performance state combination includes the paratelic state with accompanying high felt and preferred arousal. If, for example, at a certain athletics meet, injury forces the withdrawal of the jumper's main rival, the triple jumper's levels of felt arousal may become lower, and the resultant mismatch in arousal levels will be experienced as unpleasant paratelic tension stress. Instead of the competition being challenging and exciting, it is now experienced by the triple jumper as boring. In order to offset the paratelic tension stress, the triple jumper needs to initiate some form of present-oriented coping activity (experienced as paratelic effort stress) in an attempt to increase his or her level of felt arousal. This might take the form of setting up other challenges, such as trying to beat his or her personal best distance, or perhaps making an attempt at a new record.

For an athlete experiencing telic or paratelic tension stress, there are a number of options for manipulating or managing arousal levels, for example through cognitive intervention. Many sport psychology texts (e.g. Morris and Summers, 1995; Murphy, 1995) suggest that an athlete, like the archer above, experiencing anxiety (telic tension stress) could adopt an arousal reduction strategy such as a self-relaxation technique (Jacobson, 1974) to reduce his or her level of felt arousal. However, this type of intervention would be completely counter-productive for an athlete, like the triple jumper, experiencing paratelic tension stress. It is not a lowering of felt arousal which is required in this case, but the opposite, some form of arousal-enhancing strategy aimed at increasing felt arousal levels.

Another effective option for the athlete experiencing telic or paratelic tension stress is not to attempt to modulate felt arousal levels, but to induce a reversal to the partner metamotivational state. This would allow a reinterpretation of arousal levels and a subsequent reduction in tension stress, as any mismatch in felt and preferred arousal levels is corrected. Figure 2.9 summarises the two options for cognitive intervention available to the athlete experiencing either telic or paratelic tension stress.

In the examples used above, felt arousal was the metamotivational variable and telic and paratelic forms of tension stress were discussed. Equally, the other metamotivational variables and other forms of tension stress could have been used. It should be possible to modulate levels of felt transactional outcome and even felt negativism and felt toughness, or induce reversals between the partner states. Prior to the implementation of any of the possible intervention strategies described above, it is essential that the coach and the athlete are able to determine when the performer is experiencing different forms of tension stress.

Incidentally, reversal theory predicts that athletes' stress response may be influenced by their metamotivational dominance. Research by Summers and Stewart (1993), following on from the work of Martin *et al.* (1987), which examined dominance and the stress response in a general non-sport sample, has confirmed this prediction, showing that, while telic dominant athletes prefer low levels of stress, paratelic dominant athletes actually enjoy moderate levels of stress.

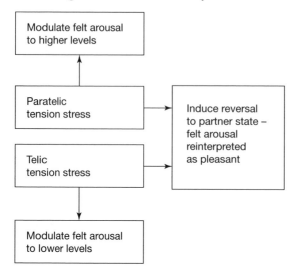

Figure 2.9 The four available options for alleviating tension stress.

Closing comments

If the challenge of summarising reversal theory in a single chapter has been successful, the reader should now have a good grasp of its basic concepts and be ready to proceed to subsequent chapters with confidence. For those who already had some knowledge of the theory, it is hoped that this chapter might have acted as a kind of refresher course. Chapter 2 is also a source to be consulted when the need arises as progress is made through the rest of the book. Chapter 3 will explain the reversal theory approach to aggression and violence and its application to sport.

Note

1   Apart from some minor changes, the contents of chapter 2 appeared as chapter 1 in Kerr, J. H. (2001). *Counselling athletes: Applying reversal theory*. London: Routledge.

References

Apter, M. J. (1982). *The experience of motivation: The theory of psychological reversals*. London: Academic Press.

Apter, M. J. (1989). *Reversal theory: Motivation, emotion and personality*. London: Routledge.

Apter, M. J. (1992). *The dangerous edge*. New York: Free Press.

Apter, M. J. (1993). Phenomenological frames and the paradoxes of experience. In J. H. Kerr, S. Murgatroyd and M. J. Apter (Eds), *Advances in reversal theory* (pp. 27–39). Amsterdam: Swets and Zeitlinger.

Apter, M. J. (Ed.) (2001). *Motivational styles in everyday life: A guide to reversal theory.* Washington DC: American Psychological Association.

Barr, S. A., McDermott, M. R. and Evans, P. (1990). Predicting persistence: A study of telic and paratelic frustration. In J. H. Kerr, S. Murgatroyd and M. J. Apter (Eds), *Advances in reversal theory* (pp. 123–136). Amsterdam: Swets and Zeitlinger.

Cogan, N. A. and Brown, R. I. F. (1998). Metamotivational dominance, states and injuries in risk and safe sport. *Personality and Individual Differences, 27,* 503–518.

Cox, T. and Kerr, J. H. (1989). Arousal effects during tournament play in squash. *Perceptual and Motor Skills, 69,* 1275–1280.

Cox, T. and Kerr, J. H. (1990). Self-reported mood in competitive squash. *Personality and Individual Differences, 11, 2,* 199–203.

Jacobson, P. (1974). *Progressive relaxation.* Chicago: University of Chicago Press.

Kerr, J. H. (1991). Arousal-seeking in risk sport participants. *Personality and Individual Differences, 12, 6,* 613–616.

Kerr, J. H. (1997). *Motivation and emotion in sport: Reversal theory.* Hove, England: Psychology Press.

Kerr, J. H. (Ed.) (1999). *Experiencing sport: Reversal theory.* Chichester, England: J. Wiley & Sons.

Kerr, J. H. and Cox, T. (1989). Effects of metamotivational dominance and metamotivational state on squash task performance. *Perceptual and Motor Skills, 67,* 171–174.

Kerr, J. H. and Cox, T. (1990). Cognition and mood in relation to the performance of a squash task. *Acta Psychologica, 73, 1,* 103–114.

Kerr, J. H. and Tacon, P. (1999). Psychological responses to different types of locations and activities. *Journal of Environmental Psychology, 19,* 287–294.

Kerr, J. H. and Vlaswinkel, E. H. (1993). Self-reported mood and running. *Work & Stress, 7, 3,* 161–177.

Lafreniere, K., Cowles, M. P. and Apter, M. J. (1988). The reversal phenomenon: Reflections on a laboratory study. In M. J. Apter, J. H. Kerr and M. P. Cowles (Eds), *Progress in reversal theory* (pp. 257–266). Amsterdam: North-Holland/Elsevier.

Males, J. R. and Kerr, J. H. (1996). Stress, emotion and performance in elite slalom canoeists. *The Sport Psychologist, 10,* 17–36.

Martin, R. A., Kuiper, N. A., Olinger, L. J. and Dobbin, J. (1987). Is stress always bad? Telic versus paratelic dominance as a stress moderating variable. *Journal of Personality and Social Psychology, 53,* 970–982.

Morris, T. and Summers, J. (1995). *Sport psychology: Theory, applications and issues.* Chichester, England: J. Wiley & Sons.

Murphy, S. M. (1995). *Sport psychology interventions.* Champaign, IL: Human Kinetics.

Summers, J. and Stewart, E. (1993). The arousal performance relationship: Examining different conceptions. In S. Serpa, J. Alves, V. Ferriera and A. Paula-Brito (Eds), *Proceedings of the VIII World Congress of Sport Psychology* (pp. 229–232). Lisbon, Portugal: International Society of Sport Psychology.

Svebak, S. and Apter, M. J. (1997). *Stress and health: A reversal theory perspective.* Washington: Taylor and Francis.

Svebak, S. and Kerr, J. H. (1989). The role of impulsivity in preference for sports. *Personality and Individual Differences, 10, 1,* 51–58.

Svebak, S., Storfjell, O. and Dalen, K. (1982). The effect of a threatening context upon motivation and task-induced physiological changes. *British Journal of Psychology, 73,* 505–512.

3 New beginnings

A reversal theory view of violence

Apter (1982, 1997) has pinpointed a number of major differences between the reversal theory approach to understanding aggressive and violent behaviour and the approach offered by other theories in the social sciences. First, reversal theory does not equate aggression and anger, unlike some other approaches (e.g. Isberg, 2000), but argues that aggression can occur both in the presence and in the absence of anger. Second, reversal theory is concerned with the immediate background of why aggression and violence occur, rather than taking the longer term perspective that other theories, dealing with evolution, genetics, subculture or upbringing, offer (e.g. Lorenz, 1966). Third, reversal theory can provide an understanding of a wide range of different types of aggressive and violent behaviour, where other theories have tended to concentrate on only one form of violent behaviour (e.g. aggression in children as a result of observation and imitation, Bandura, 1973). Fourth, reversal theory seeks multiple causes for aggressive and violent behaviour, where other theories have largely proposed single causes (e.g. drive theory, Dollard et al., 1939).

As with reversal theory explanations of other forms of human behaviour, its explanation of aggressive and violent behaviour is based on metamotivational states, metamotivational state combinations and the reversals that may occur between them. It would, therefore, be erroneous to associate forms of aggression or violence with a single metamotivational state, although some states in particular combinations may play a more influential role than others. Of all the possible metamotivational state combinations, Apter (1997) has argued that, when different forms of violence are examined, four state combinations occur most frequently. These are based on combinations of (1) the telic and paratelic states with the negativistic state, and (2) the telic and paratelic states with the mastery state, but in each case other pairs of states could also be involved. As shown in Figure 3.1, these combinations give rise to four different forms of violence: *anger, thrill, power* and *play violence*, respectively. The following sections will examine each of these forms of violence in detail.

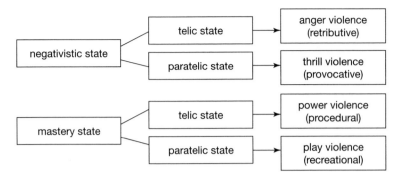

Figure 3.1 Showing the metamotivational state combinations which underlie the different types of violence proposed by Apter (1997).

Anger violence

Anger violence is associated with a metamotivational state combination with the telic and negativistic states salient and therefore it is serious, involves anger and unpleasant high arousal, and tends to be reactive in nature. The influence of the telic state means that the experience of anger violence is serious and characterised by unpleasant high arousal. The reactive negativistic element in anger aggression generally occurs as a result of an individual feeling compelled to act against another individual or group of individuals because of restrictions, requirements or interpersonal actions which are deemed incorrect or unfair. In many cases of anger violence, a person's response is sudden and immediate and those involved often say 'I don't know what happened, something just snapped.' This is indicative of a sudden reversal to the negativistic state. Indeed, the reversal to the negativistic state is part of a basic sequence which is typical of violent episodes involving anger violence.

There are many possible sequences, but, for example, one might begin with the recognition by an individual that something is unfair and the desire to act against that perceived injustice. With this recognition, increases in felt arousal, along with a reversal from a telic-conformist to a telic-negativistic state combination take place, and the individual concerned experiences extreme anger. A violent act then occurs which is likely to be experienced as very pleasant due to the salience of the negativistic state and strong feelings of felt negativism and felt arousal. While the mastery-sympathy and autic-alloic pairs of states will also be involved in metamotivational state combinations associated with anger violence, their role is likely to be relatively minor compared to the negativistic and telic states.

At this point, there are at least three possible outcomes. One, following the violent act felt arousal levels decrease, the telic state again becomes salient and the person involved feels a sense of relief. Two, if the violent act was perpetrated against another person, that person may well also become angry and retaliate and the situation could escalate as levels of anger violence increase on both sides.

Third, once the initial violent act takes place, a reversal from the negativistic to the conformist state in the aggressor means that, if the retaliation is vicious enough, the original aggressor may experience extreme anxiety or fear and flee, as felt arousal levels remain high in the telic state.

Anger violence may take place as a result of an individual being, for example, cheated on by a partner, being accused wrongly of doing something or feeling that someone 'had taken liberties', as in incidents of road rage. Recent protests against large corporations, and against the 'G8' countries at their various meetings around the world, have often led to anger violence responses from protesters and, on some occasions, increased levels of violence have occurred following police restrictions on personal freedom to protest. In some cases, anger violence may even be directed at animals or inanimate objects, as is possible, for example, when a pet dog defecates inside a house or a lawn mower refuses to start. Sport examples from chapter 1 which fall into this category of anger violence would include Junta's attack on ice hockey coach Costin, the retaliation by New Zealand's Sevens players after the match against Fiji, Cantona's fight with a rival soccer team's fan, and possibly basketball player Sprewell's attack on his coach. Other examples from sport are described in chapter 5.

Thrill violence

Thrill violence is primarily concerned with the paratelic-negativistic state combination and, because the paratelic state is operative and salient, is therefore immediate, not serious, and often spontaneous, providing pleasant feelings associated with high levels of felt arousal and felt negativism. The negativistic element in the state combination also means that thrill violence involves individuals in acts they perceive as breaking established norms or being provocative, acts that they consider other people would think of as taboo. There is no real purpose to thrill violence apart from the fact that it is carried out for 'kicks', that is to say, seeking pleasant high arousal experiences for immediate gratification. For thrill violence to occur, a paratelic protective frame must be in operation, providing perpetrators with confidence and the sense that they can get away with it (Apter, 1992). In the presence of a protective frame (see below), it is possible for an individual to experience unpleasant emotions as pleasant in the form of parapathic emotions. This means that if anger is involved in thrill violence, it is parapathic anger and is fundamentally different from the real anger associated with a telic-negativistic state combination.

It is possible to identify at least two examples of metamotivational sequences in which thrill violence might occur. In the first case, it may simply involve an individual who is in a paratelic-conformist state combination under high felt arousal conditions and who experiences a reversal from conformist to negativistic state. In the second case, the sequence begins with the experience of low arousal and feelings of boredom in a paratelic-conformity state combination. A reversal to the negativistic state occurs, accompanied by increased levels of felt arousal and felt negativism and is likely to lead to provocative violent behaviour. A paratelic-negativistic state combination is now operative and a protective frame in place which allows a person to perpetrate a violent act, while they themselves do not feel at risk. With the paratelic state salient, following the aggressive or violent act, the person experiences high felt arousal and feels excitement and positive hedonic tone. If reversals do not occur, and the paratelic-negativistic state combination remains operative there are at least two possible outcomes. First, further acts of violence may be necessary to maintain, or perhaps increase further, already high levels of arousal, felt negativism, and feelings of excitement and provocativeness. Otherwise, the person or persons involved may return to feeling bored and the cycle may start again. Second, if, after the violent act, the victim(s) of the thrill violence retaliate or there is a possibility that the perpetrators might be apprehended (e.g. the sound of police sirens approaching) then it is possible that high levels of arousal and positive hedonic tone would be maintained or possibly enhanced through the experience of parapathic fear.

There are many examples of thrill violence in life in general (Kerr, 1994), including acts of vandalism, weekend brawls at pubs and clubs, gang fighting, and soccer hooliganism. Sport examples from chapter 1 would include the disturbances by Canterbury rugby league supporters at Parramatta, and some of the fighting engaged in by ice hockey enforcer Domi ('Fifty per cent of the time I fight just for the sake of fighting, to get things going, it's situational'; Ulmer, 1998, p. C5).

Power violence

As Apter (1997) pointed out, the most important states in power aggression and violence are the telic and mastery states. This form of violence does have a serious purpose and the mastery state brings the desire to be successful, to dominate and subjugate an enemy, rival or opposing team. In very extreme cases, this is the type of cold, calculated violence that has been seen in inter-racial violence in Rwanda and the civilian casualties that are victims (so-called collateral damage) of bombing raids on 'military' targets (e.g. Baumeister, 1997).

One can recognise a possible sequence to power violence. An individual or individuals come to perceive themselves over time as superior to some other group which constitutes some kind of threat, or they find themselves in a situation in which they believe that the end justifies the means and violence against others becomes somehow acceptable. For this type of violence to occur, the telic-mastery state combination must have been operative for some time. Unlike anger violence, there is nothing sudden or immediate about power violence, rather it appears to build up steadily and can endure over quite a time as the violence becomes routine. It may even involve considerable planning. Resistance by victims of power violence is liable to lead to an escalation of violent acts.

Examples of power violence do exist in sport. Aggression and violence in professional boxing and K1 or extreme fighting might be placed in this category. There is little doubt that the proponents would need to be in a state combination of telic-conformist-autic-mastery, with the mastery state salient, to be successful in these sports. As Patmore put it:

> The boxer's job is to injure, maim, and render his opponent unconscious. Indeed, if the opponent dies from his injuries, it simply means that the fighter who hit him was very good at landing punches where they were most likely to do the most damage.
>
> (Patmore, 1979, p. 175)

One can also think of the infamous 'bodyline' bowling on the 1932–33 England cricket tour of Australia. In order to counter the threat of legendary Australian batsman Donald Bradman, the English fast bowler Harold Larwood, under the orders of Douglas Jardine, his captain, bowled aggressive 'bouncers' directly at the Australian batsmen. These particular bouncers are balls often aimed at leg stump, which, after striking the ground, rear up and, depending on the skill of the batsman, just miss or strike his upper body or head, or force him to give away a soft catch to fielders positioned close on the leg side. England's tactics caused tremendous controversy because, although technically within the laws of the game, they went very much against the spirit of the game at the time. Subsequently, the number of fielders that could be placed on the leg side was restricted by rules to prevent the bodyline strategy. Nowadays, all fast bowlers use bouncers, but there are limits on the number that can be bowled in any one over and batsmen now wear helmets to protect them from head injuries. Neither of these safety precautions were present in the 1930s and several Australian batsmen were injured.

An example of power violence from chapter 1 is ice hockey enforcer Domi's fighting, that is, the fifty per cent not concerned with thrill violence, on occasions when he has been sent on to the ice by his coach to deliberately take out or rough up an opposing player. Most acts of an unsanctioned aggressive and violent nature in sport fall into this category and these will be explored in more detail in chapter 5.

Play violence

The fourth main type of violence identified by Apter (1997) is associated with a state combination where the paratelic and mastery states are to the fore and is therefore about being playful, having fun, experiencing power and enjoying high levels of felt arousal and felt mastery. Many of the best examples of this form of violence are found in sport. In addition, Apter's (1997) concept of play violence is of crucial importance to understanding sanctioned aggression and violence in sport.

In this regard, if sport and these other activities are to work satisfactorily, then the participants involved must stick to the rules. Thus, the paratelic and mastery states associated with play aggression will usually be combined with the conformist state. Indeed, most sports have referees, umpires and officials to make sure that the rules are adhered to and, in the case of some sports, ensure that levels of aggression and violence remain within those rules. In, for example, team contact sports like ice hockey, rugby and American football, and combat sports or martial arts, aggression and violence are legal and sanctioned elements of the sports. However, outside the context of these types of sports (and therefore beyond the boundaries of play violence), acts like hard tackling, tough body checking, tenacious blocking and vigorous throwing of an opponent to the ground are not sanctioned, but prohibited by society and are considered illegal forms of physical assault.

In thinking about a sequence or pattern for play violence, it becomes apparent that opportunities to engage in this type of activity may be either relatively spontaneous or rather more regular and organised. On the spur of the moment, a group of friends may, for example, decide to play a game of soccer, but other individuals may take part in soccer on a more regular basis. In the former case, the sudden decision is likely to have been induced by reversals in one or more of the group. In the latter case, by engaging in activities on a regular basis, people are actually placing themselves in sport or other situations where the necessary metamotivational state combination for enjoying play violence can come into effect. In both cases, the state combination is paratelic-conformist-mastery and will also include the autic or alloic state, depending on the sport or the ongoing situation during play. The paratelic state is likely to be salient and, as in the case of thrill violence, paratelic protective frames (see below) are likely to be involved.

Combinations of different types of violence

The four types of violence may be interlinked, depending on the operative metamotivational state combination and which states are salient. For example, a state combination involving paratelic, negativistic and mastery states could allow either thrill or play violence to occur, depending on which states predominate. Similarly, a combination of telic, negativistic and mastery states could give rise to anger or power violence, with the autic or alloic states again also playing a role. Given conducive conditions, what starts out as one form of violence may change into another form. For example, consider the angry, aggressive and violent flare-ups that sometimes occur between players during matches. These represent a change from play violence to anger (and/or power) violence and occur when an incident (e.g. shirt-pulling in soccer, obstruction in rugby and 'off the ball' incidents in Australian rules football) sparks reversals from a combination of, for example, paratelic-conformist-mastery to telic-negativistic-mastery. The outcome often involves serious unsanctioned aggression and violence.

Paratelic protective frames

Thrill and play violence both involve the paratelic state and therefore paratelic protective frames play an important role in these two types of aggression and violence. It is thought that the vast majority of sports are experienced within paratelic protective frames. It is on these paratelic protective frames that the special nature of sport is built (e.g. Apter, 1992; Kerr 1997). Sport settings can be thought of as being outside the real world and the rules and laws which regulate play allow activities to occur in a special kind of psychological space:

> Usually in sport there is some specially demarcated area – the cricket pitch, the tennis court, the golf course, the gridiron – and these provide clear-cut enclaves within which the problems of the rest of the world are not allowed to enter. Each sport also has its own system of rules which help to construct a psychological space within which only certain kinds of things can happen; and these are known in advance and controlled by referees and umpires. The effect of all this is to produce a kind of safety zone.
>
> (Apter, 1989, p. 44)

Protective frames are 'constructed' by athletes to suit their own idiosyncratic needs within their individual sports. In many sports, the risk to the participant is not only physical; losing or playing badly and injuring one's self-esteem and pride is also a threat. In addition, in team contact sports, athletes need to develop confidence and safety-zone frames which allow them to deal not only with playing badly or losing, but also with the aggression, hard play and physical violence characteristic of their sports and the fact that they face the danger of possible serious injury. In team contact sports, for example, athletes can obtain the maximum enjoyment from their sports activities as long as the protective frame remains intact. The element of physical confrontation adds to the excitement while it remains within what is sanctioned behaviour in the game. Should the paratelic protective frame become ruptured or broken in some way, then the player concerned is likely to reverse to a metamotivational combination where the telic state is salient and the emotions experienced will no longer be pleasant (Kerr, 1997).

Closing comments

When two opposing teams have willingly agreed to compete against each other they have initiated a kind of contract in the pursuit of aggression and violence between consenting adults. In this struggle to frustrate opponents and gain mastery over each other, the aggression and violence is deliberately provoked.

Those involved in team contact sports know that much of the pleasure, satisfaction and enjoyment to be gained from these sports is associated with the intense physicality and with carrying out the skills involved in physically aggressive and violent plays successfully (Kerr, 1997; Russell, 1993). In addition, aspects of danger, concerned with the risk of injury (or infrequent death), associated with the hard physical play add to the attractiveness and pleasure experienced by the athletes. Although the pleasures of being physical are a central feature of some sports, they have rarely received attention in the sport psychology literature. This may have been due to a difficulty in finding an adequate theoretical explanation of why and how athletes can enjoy aggressive and violent behaviour in sport. Where other theoretical explanations have largely proved inadequate in this respect, reversal theory, in its unique manner, can provide comprehensive psychological explanations for the thrills and enjoyment associated with being physical and, indeed, go further to explain how these processes can sometimes develop into other forms of highly aggressive, violent and often physically injurious behaviour on the field. The dynamic nature of reversals between metamotivational states means that, for example, the thrill or play forms can become the anger or even the power varieties of violence. This is the advantage of reversal theory explanations of aggression and violence in sport.

The motivation and emotions of the athletes involved in play violence through sanctioned aggressive and violent acts in sport are central topics in the discussion in the following chapter.

References

Apter, M. J. (1982). *The experience of motivation: The theory of psychological reversals.* London: Academic Press.

Apter, M. J. (1989). *Reversal theory: Motivation, emotion and personality.* London: Routledge.

Apter, M. J. (1992). *The dangerous edge.* New York: Free Press.

Apter, M. J. (1997, July). *The experience of being violent.* Paper presented at the Eighth International Conference on Reversal Theory, University of East London.

Bandura, A. (1973). *A social learning analysis.* Englewood Cliffs, NJ: Prentice Hall.

Baumeister, R. F. (1997). *Evil: Inside human cruelty and violence.* New York: W. H. Freeman.

Dollard, J., Doob, L., Miller, N., Mouwer, O. and Sears, R. (1939). *Frustration and aggression.* New Haven, CT: Yale University Press.

Isberg, L. (2000). Anger, aggressive behavior, and athletic performance. In Y. L. Hanin (Ed.), *Emotions in sport.* Champaign, IL: Human Kinetics.

Kerr, J. H. (1994). *Understanding soccer hooliganism.* Buckingham: Open University Press.

Kerr, J. H. (1997). *Motivation and emotion in sport: Reversal theory.* Hove, England: Psychology Press.

Lorenz, K. (1966). *On aggression.* New York: Harcourt Brace Jovanovich.

Patmore, A. (1979). *Playing on their nerves: The sport experiment.* London: Stanley Paul.

Russell, G. W. (1993). *The social psychology of sport.* New York: Springer-Verlag.

Ulmer, M. (1998, 11 March). On-ice thug is really a sensitive guy. *The Ottawa Citizen,* p. C5.

4 The joy of physical contact

Sanctioned aggression and violence in sport

This chapter will concentrate on sanctioned aggressive and violent play as an accepted part of the action in some contemporary sports. Much of the discussion will focus on the motivation and emotions of the athletes involved, the rewards associated with participating in team contact sport and the development of physical aggression and violence as a particular source of pleasure. Most of the published material on aggression and violence in team contact sport has concentrated on male athletes, but recently there is a small but growing interest in female athletes. Some exploration of female athlete responses to aggression and violence is also undertaken in this chapter. In addition to reversal theory, which is used to provide a theoretical explanation for understanding sanctioned aggression and violence in sport, the Hedonic Tone Management Model of Addictions (Brown, 1997) will be used to explain how an athlete's positive reward from physical aggression and violence develops over time and may eventually become addictive.

Some of the few books available that deal with the topic of aggression and violence in sport begin by pointing out the historical context of 'games' and the violence involved in those games, as the forerunner of contemporary sports. Some authors have gone as far back as the Greek and Roman empires (e.g. Auguet, 1994; Guttmann, 1986) and underline the fact that Greek and Roman games were often quite violent affairs. Here, the historical background to aggression and violence in modern sport is mentioned only in passing, but Guttmann's work (1986, 1998) will be returned to in chapter 8.

It should also be mentioned at this early point in the chapter that the discussion in this and the successive two chapters will focus largely on team contact sports, like ice hockey, soccer, and the other varieties of football. In team contact sports the codes of conduct are somewhat less stringent than, for example, in combat sports and therefore offer a better contrast between sanctioned and unsanctioned aggressive and violent acts. Individual combat sports, such as judo, sumo, some forms of karate and other combat sports also involve sanctioned aggression and violence (indeed, in some of these sports, lack of aggression on the part of the contestants is penalised), but the codes of conduct for competitors in these sports are so strict that acts of unsanctioned aggression and violence rarely occur.

Boxing is a particularly interesting case among combat sports because, along with K-1 or 'ultimate' fighting, it is one of the very few sports where the use of physical violence to injure opponents is sanctioned and acceptable:

> . . . two men enter a small ring, each with the sole intention of inflicting pain directly on the body of the other and, if possible, knocking the other senseless (with all the attendant risks of injury and worse entailed) in the shortest possible time.
>
> (Jefferson, 1998, p. 83)

Some aficionados might make a distinction between amateur and professional boxing, and/or between skilful 'boxers' (e.g. Muhammad Ali early in his career) who are geared to out-pointing opponents, and bruising 'fighters or scrappers' (e.g. George Foreman) who aim to knock out their opponents. However, this distinction may be largely irrelevant in terms of what actually takes place in the boxing ring, where even the most skilful boxers can end up with damage to their retinas, concussion and other, sometimes fatal, brain damage. Although, for some, boxing can undoubtedly be exciting to watch (e.g. Schlesinger *et al.*, 1998) because of the 'raw' violence epitomised in the ferocity of fighters like Mike Tyson, others feel uncomfortable watching it.

Boxing might be considered an exception amongst combat sports in terms of codes of conduct. Although boxing does have certain rules and violence is sanctioned within those rules, the use of the head in clinches and low blows to the pubic area are not uncommon. Indeed, the infamous incident in which Mike Tyson bit off part of Evander Holyfield's ear during the 1997 heavyweight championship bout provides a rather unusual, but classic example of unsanctioned aggression and violence in boxing. In that case, the boxing authorities were very quick to hand down a very severe punishment and, at the time, there was some doubt if Tyson would ever box again.

Facilitating positive experience

Boxing and K-1 fighting are examples of power violence, with protagonists in a telic-conformist-autic-mastery state combination, with telic and mastery states salient. However, most instances of sanctioned aggressive and violent acts in sport take place in a paratelic-mastery-conformist metamotivational state combination in what has been termed by Apter (1997) as the play form of violence. With this form of aggression and violence, it is important to remember the role that paratelic protective frames play in providing a secure environment where the enjoyment of sanctioned aggression and violence in team contact sports can take place. If this secure environment and the special nature of sport are to be maintained, then the participants involved must, in general, stick to the rules. Also, particular aspects or features of team contact sports facilitate an athlete's chance of obtaining positive experience. These features include the exciting nature of the sports themselves, mastering personal skills, as well as mastering opponents and exploiting weaknesses, the hard physicality of the play, winning, belonging to a team of athletes with similar aims and objectives and a common love of the sport, and playing in front of fans. Although they are linked in terms of an athlete's overall experience, for convenience each of these features will be explored separately.

The exciting nature of the sports themselves

For athletes and spectators alike, it is the intrinsic excitement of team contact sports which draws them to play or watch. For those who have played team contact sports, there will be very few, if any, who can forget the thrill and excitement of the moment when they ran or skated clear of the opposing defence just long enough to race through for a try or touchdown or to attempt a shot on goal, or the desperate chase after an escaping attacker to bring off a score-saving tackle. Jennings, in describing rugby union, captures this feeling well:

> I have always thought that the supreme joy of rugby is running – running after a man who has got away and is threatening one's side with danger; running through the defence, or, best of all, running for your very life for the try line.
> (Jennings, 1966, p. 129, cited in Morell, 1966, p. 105)

Jennings' comments on rugby could also be applied to some other team sports that do not involve physical contact, but Brink (1995) introduces the attractiveness of the physical contact element in team contact sports, linking the running or motion aspect of play to other captivating features of the game:

> Much of the attraction of rugby lies in its extreme physicality. But its full fascination is determined by the way in which brute force and athletic speed are married to quick thinking, the ingenuity and anticipation of a chess player, the absorption of the individual within a large, fluid motion, the creation of moving patterns and changing rhythms.
> (Brink, 1995, p. 29)

Take, for example, the classic semi-final ice hockey match which took place between Canada and the Czech Republic at the 1998 Winter Olympics in Nagano, Japan. The Canadians had been favourites to win, and most knowledgeable observers thought that it would be a game dominated by the two goal-tenders, Patrick Roy for Canada and Dominik Hasek for the Czechs. Hasek and Roy both brought off some terrific saves as the Czech Republic took the lead in the third period and Canada equalised with just over a minute left in regulation time. The Czechs eventually won in the shoot-out, after 10 minutes of sudden death overtime. It was ice hockey at its best, played by two superb teams; a game of tremendously exciting end-to-end action, involving superb hockey skills and extremely hard sanctioned physical confrontation. After the game, although disappointed, Marc Crawford, the Canadian coach, alluded to the quality of the play when he said, 'History will say that this was a great hockey game played by two great hockey teams. In the shoot-out we just weren't equal to the task. It was a classic game, I just wish we were on the other end of the score' (Smaal, 1998, p. 24).

Close games, between well-matched teams like this Canadian–Czech Olympic semi-final, are the most exciting and pleasurable for the athletes involved. In this type of game, athletes can become totally engaged in the 'cut and thrust' of the game, with the result that the performance of aggressive and violent plays is most satisfying for all concerned. One-sided games are not as much fun for either the winning or losing team and performing aggressive and violent plays is likely to be much less satisfying for the players where the result has been decided long before the end of the game.

Mastering personal skills

Being able to learn, master and perform the skills (often under pressure) required to play team contact sports with confidence is another source of pleasure and reward for athletes. There are, of course, many individual athletes who stand out in their particular sports for their outstanding skills. Ice hockey's Wayne Gretsky, rugby union's David Campese, rugby league's Laurie Daley, Aussie rules' Dermott Brereton, American football's Dan Marino and soccer's David Beckham are a few who come to mind. Take Daley, for example: Australians certainly are in no doubt that Daley was as superbly skilled as they come in his chosen sport of rugby league. Other observers outside Australia have come to the same conclusion. Irvine (1997), for example, compared him to Wally Lewis, a legend in Australian rugby league, when he wrote:

> When injury forced Wally Lewis from the Australia side in 1990, no one could have imagined that the young Daley would supplant 'King Wally'. At Wembley on Saturday, there were echoes of Lewis' genius, the nonchalant prising open of gaps, the ability to compress time and create space for his trickery and the inch-perfect tactical kicks, short, long or into the out-stretched arms of his wing.
>
> (Irvine, 1997)

In the same article, Irvine quotes Daley as saying:

> I take a lot of pride in my performance, but when you put pressures and expectations on yourself, that's when it's all too much to live up to. . . . When you're confident, you're enjoying it that much more.

Daley, like the other players mentioned above, is noted for his 'creative' skills, not that he was any slouch when it came to aggressive defensive skills. However, there are players who specialise in and are better known for the performance of aggressive and violent skills in, for example, tackling or blocking.

Rugby union player Willie Ofahengaue, mentioned in chapter 1 for his sanctioned aggressive and violent tackle on the Welsh fullback, is one such player and
other team contact sports have them too. Jack Tatum, the legendary American
football linebacker, put it like this:

> As a defensive player I had resigned myself to the fact that I was never going
> to rush for 1,000 yards during a season and I would never score many touch-
> downs. But at the same time I vowed to earn my reputation in professional
> football with aggressive tackling. . . . I never make a tackle just to bring
> someone down. I want to punish the man I'm going after and I want him to
> know that it's going to hurt every time he comes my way.
>
> (Tatum and Kushner, 1979, pp. 10–11)

A player's reputation as a hard and tenacious tackler can have an important
impact on the thinking of opposition players, sometimes sowing seeds of doubt
and anxiety unless the opposition players are equally tough. Reputations like
Ofahengaue's or Tatum's are built on the successful execution of aggressive
and violent plays. Going into a tackle or body check as hard as possible is not the
only requirement. An aggressive and violent play which is mistimed or misjudged
will neither enhance the reputation of, nor provide much satisfaction for, the
player involved. Initiating aggressive plays is not the only source of satisfaction
and pleasure; the ability to 'take the hit' and still lay-off or pass the ball or puck
to a teammate is also an important element.

Mastering opponents and exploiting weaknesses

In today's age of computer-aided video analysis, it is almost impossible for a
weakness in any team to go unnoticed. At the top levels, teams employ analysis
experts to assist the coaches and players in the job of analysing the strengths and
weaknesses of other teams. Taking advantage of any weakness that might be
apparent in the opposing team is one of the keys to success in contemporary team
contact sports. Even without the help of technology, the players become adept at
probing and testing their opponents, ensuring that, unless they put in a high-level
performance, they will be exposed. This applies to non-aggressive skills, strategies
and tactics in general, as well as to the physical domination of opponents through
the development of aggressive strategies and tactics. Any physical weakness, lack
of skill, or lack of enthusiasm for aggressive and violent aspects of play detected
in opposing teams will also be ruthlessly taken advantage of as play continues.
Thus, aggression and violence are often used strategically. As Barnes (1996)
observed, after watching the extremely exciting, close-run 1996 rugby league
English Challenge Cup final where St Helens narrowly defeated the Bradford
Bulls by 40 points to 32:

> Players and coaches think up acts of cruelty in the night and practise them
> during the day. Come the match, they seek to inflict their cruelties before

cruelties are inflicted on them. That is what sport means. Weakness does not excite compassion. Weakness is opportunity: the road to victory leads through another's weakness. Mercy can lead only to defeat.

(Barnes, 1996, p. 26)

Research by Colburn (1985,1989) has shown that many players do give considerable thought to, and exercise a degree of decision-making over, when and how they use aggressive and violent plays. Colburn's (1985, 1989) research work on ice hockey was carried out over a period of eight years in Ontario, Canada and Indianapolis in the US. During this time, he was a participant observer, acting as trainer with a junior ice hockey team, and also conducted extensive open-ended unstructured interviews with over 150 amateur and professional ice hockey players. His two publications demonstrate clearly how different forms of aggression and violence are used in ice hockey. Some of his observations will be presented in this chapter, yet others will be covered in the following chapter on unsanctioned aggression and violence.

Colburn (1989) has noted that players informally acquire a repertoire of hockey skills, including what he calls 'the strategic uses of violence'. This means, for example, that players routinely 'test' opponents and expect to be tested themselves. This testing or physical intimidation is aimed at distracting or interfering with the performance of opposing players:

> I use violence in my work as a defenseman. Not cheap stuff, but good, solid body checks. This makes others keep their heads up. They become intimidated, that makes them throw away the puck that much faster.
>
> (Colburn, 1989, p. 72)

Responses to (sanctioned) physical intimidation can take a number of forms. One often effective response is to 'respond in kind, giving as good as you get' or, in other words, counter physicality with equivalent (or greater) physicality. This often denies the opposition the advantage sought. Ignoring physical intimidation is likely to lead to further and more excessive intimidation. A player may respond to (sanctioned) physical intimidation with unsanctioned acts which, in turn, may change the form of, and escalate the level of, aggression and violence:

> Well it is basically your job as a defenseman to own your own end of the ice, from the blue line back to the goal crease, you own it and you control the play. And if some guy is getting into your corner and you find he is getting around you, you get into the body contact part of it where you take him out of the play and just exactly how you do it depends on other things.
>
> (Colburn, 1989, p. 73)

Colburn (1985, 1989) also drew attention to the discretion and professional judgement that players possess as to what type of aggression (i.e. sanctioned or unsanctioned) and the degree or severity of the physical violence that they implement in any given situation. The type of aggression used and the degree of severity of the physical violence is dependent on a number of factors. These include the player's own fighting skills, the player's estimates of whether team-mates will back him up if other opposition players get involved, or whether a penalty at this point would be detrimental to the team's chances of winning. The athletes see this merely as a 'part of their job' and, in general, players recognise the professional limits placed on the discretionary use of violence.

The hard physicality of the play

In spite of the risk of physical injury, it is not hard to find anecdotal evidence that team contact sports are attractive and enjoyable precisely because of the physical contact involved. Messner (1992) interviewed an American football lineman who made his enjoyment of aggression and violence quite clear:

> This guy we played against in Denver by the name of Walt B . . . we battled. He enjoyed it, and I enjoyed it. But never was it a cheap shot, never did he have me down and just drive my head into the ground, you know the unnecessary stuff. We played a good clean game of football, because we respected each other. Now, if he could knock me on my butt, he'd do it. And I'd do it to him and help him up. Talk to him after the game. Sit and talk with him like I'm sitting here talking to you. But while we're out there, now, we go at it. And I loved it. Yeah, I loved it.
>
> (Messner, 1992, pp. 68–69)

A similar point was made by Novak (1976), again with reference to American football:

> . . . football allows you to use your body in harmony with your mind. You not only have an inward attitude toward your opponent; you must also physically hit him as hard, as cleanly, and as devastatingly as you can. There is intense joy in using one's body as the language of emotion – a kind of serenity and honesty.
>
> (Novak, 1976, p. 79)

These quotes seem to confirm what the present author has previously stated: 'The truth is that much of the pleasure, satisfaction and enjoyment to be gained in team contact sports is associated with the intense physicality.' (Kerr, 1997, p. 84), a point which has also been made by some other writers on aggression and violence in sport (e.g. Russell, 1993).

In team contact sports, the element of physical aggression is one of the essential components of success as a team. Physical domination of the opposition by what is often called 'controlled aggression' is a recognised tactic, as the following quote from former Queensland coach Wayne Bennett illustrates. In the quote he is referring to the first game of the 1996 'State of Origin' rugby league competition which Queensland lost. (State of Origin is a ferociously contested annual series of three matches played between Queensland and New South Wales in Australia.) Bennett said:

> Controlled aggression is what everyone in rugby league seeks but rarely finds and it's true that Origin 1 probably lacked bodies being put on the line, sacrifices in order to inflict as much pain on an opponent as possible in the eternal endeavour to make his [*sic*] lose the plot. Remember these are the finest players in the game and quite used to taking punishment.
>
> (Bennett 1996, p. 28)

To take (and hand out) 'punishment' in contact sports, it should be obvious that the athletes in rugby league and other team contact sports need to have a special attitude to physical contact and be mentally and physically harder and tougher than those playing most other team sports. What is this special quality of hardness or toughness that is required in team contact sports? Jefferson (1998) summed it up neatly when he stated:

> First, an indifference to the body's (often painful) fate, an attitude quite opposed to the displayed body beautiful of the muscular-body builder. Second, courage or bravery, qualities of mental toughness which have nothing necessarily to do with muscle. Many sports, like motor racing, though physically demanding, do not require hard muscles. But indifference to pain and mental toughness are de rigueur. Over and above physical aptitude, talent, ability, judgement, vision and all the other qualities drawn upon to discuss the undisputed male 'giants' of sport, hardness, this willingness to risk the body in performance, is what, for me, is the perennial sub-textual answer to the sports journalists' insistent question: how are these men different?
>
> (Jefferson, 1998, p. 81)

Although it is argued here that the physical side of team contact sports is a source of enjoyment and pleasure to many players, it is also obvious that not everyone may share this experience, as not every player is endowed with the kind of qualities described by Jefferson (1998) and sought by Bennett (1996). In fact, most teams are composed of a variety of players, with a few players, who are perhaps highly skilled but less aggressive and violent, being 'carried' and 'protected' by other players in the team who relish the physical aspects of play. Wayne Gretsky, the former ice hockey player, is a prime example of a player who fell into this category. His personal skills and passing and scoring ability were second to none, and while he did not necessarily shy away from physical contact he was, however, not known for being an aggressively physical player.

Winning

Experienced players are familiar with the feelings associated with both winning and losing. It is interesting in the present context that some reversal theory research has examined the different psychological effects of winning and losing. Kerr and van Schaik (1995) and Wilson and Kerr (1999) examined possible changes in affect, mood and emotions in top-level Dutch rugby union players as a result of winning and losing matches. The results of both studies showed that players responded differently to winning and losing matches. Winning produced a range of pleasant emotional outcomes and reductions in arousal and stress, while losing produced strong increases in negative affect, and a reduction in arousal. In the Wilson and Kerr (1999) study, for example, winning produced significantly higher scores on relaxation and gratitude, and significantly lower scores on anger, sullenness, humiliation, shame and resentment, than did losing. Winning produced a significant decrease in arousal and stress, but losing only produced a significant decrease in arousal and not stress. Arousal levels decreased for both winners and losers; this was likely to be a consequence of the game being over after a period of intense activity involving high demands on energy and physical effort. However, for losers, the continuing high levels of stress reflected the game outcome. Thus, winners' experience was one of pleasant emotion, low stress and relatively high levels of hedonic tone; losers' experience was one of unpleasant emotion, stress and low levels of hedonic tone.

However, more recent research suggests that emotional responses after games may go beyond simple game outcome. In a study of elite female field hockey players playing in an Olympic qualifying tournament, Kerr *et al.* (2004) found a difference in the pattern of emotions at two losing games. In the first game, the team lost after playing poorly; in the second game the team also lost, but played very well. The pattern of emotions at the second defeat was similar to the pattern at other games where the team had won and was characterised by increased levels of pleasant emotions and positive hedonic tone. It seems likely that perceived performance may be an additional factor in the production of emotional experience of players after games.

In general, most teams win often enough for the players to obtain the psychological benefits or rewards that come with winning, at least on an irregular basis, and these benefits outweigh negative feelings when they lose. In addition to perceived performance, pleasant or unpleasant feelings after the game are partly associated with interactions with teammates, opponents and others.

Belonging to a team

Belonging to a team of athletes with similar aims and objectives and a common love of a sport, the 'mateship', and what these days is termed 'bonding', associated with training, practising and playing together is rewarding for any athlete involved in team sports. 'It's very real, says guard Aaron Taylor. You have a sense of belonging, of something special. It means something to say you are with the

Green Bay Packers' (Weber 1997, p. 133). However, it may even be possible to say that, in team contact sports, the feelings of belonging and camaraderie are even stronger than in other team sports. There is something about the physical side of those sports which pulls the players even closer together and, in some cases, produces a special sense of identity. For example, referring to rugby union in New Zealand, Zavos (1988) observed that:

> Most New Zealand males, from erudite scholars to burly shearers, have experienced the dying fall of light after a hard match and the liniment scented mateship of the dressing room. It is one of those tribal experiences that has helped to create that unique and underrated species, the New Zealand man.
>
> (Zavos, 1988, p. 118, cited in Nauright and Black, 1996, p. 206)

The mateship in team contact sports is about taking the physical 'knocks' to attain shared goals. Players take punishment themselves to spare teammates from taking it and, most important of all, they rely on each other for protection and back up when they 'lay their bodies on the line'.

Playing in front of fans

Many athletes would agree that playing in front of large numbers of fans can add to an athlete's positive experience. This was certainly true for England soccer international David Platt when meeting the fans for the first time prior to a training session at Italian club Bari:

> As soon as I heard my name I trotted out onto the pitch. The scene was unbelievable and the crescendo of noise absolutely deafening. Bari's stadium holds 60,000 people and to see it over half full for a simple training session was inspiring to say the least. Three sides of it were a mass of people, singing and waving their red and white banners and scarves. Red flares were lit, and fireworks were set off. The giant screens at each end of the ground displayed my name and picture as I made my way to the centre circle where all my teammates were lined up.
>
> (Platt, 1995, p.124)

David Ginola, the French soccer player who came to England and played for Newcastle, was also in little doubt that playing in front of spectators was beneficial. He stated:

> When you are playing football, being in a passionate environment is such an advantage – it's what you look for – and I found this in Newcastle. The fans are always at the club, always around the players. The fans come to the training ground in far greater numbers than I was used to in France. They want success and that rubs off on you. If you are having a bad game they push

you to find your best form; if you lose, the next game they are here in force full of encouragement. It's inspirational.

(Ginola, 1996)

In general, Ginola and Platt, both very successful players, are correct. Playing in front of fans can be inspiring and uplifting for athletes, adding to their positive experience of play and improving their levels of hedonic tone. This may be especially true in European soccer, where many fans are long-time followers of particular teams. However, a slightly more cynical view is that fans are actually quite fickle in their support of teams and individual players. This means that fans will be generous in support while things are going well, but this support may be withdrawn if a team is struggling to win and/or a player is struggling to find his or her best form. Whether a team is winning or losing may ultimately affect the fans' experience while watching games and how they respond (Kerr *et al.*, 2004). Similarly for athletes, winning and losing games can affect the nature of their experience of play.

Is it the same for women?

In the period from the late 1980s/early 1990s until the present time, there has been an increasing trend for women to take part in sports activities that were formerly considered the preserve of men. This trend has been across the whole range of sports, including team contact sports, where it is now commonplace to find women's teams actively involved in competition, some to a high level (e.g. Women's World Cups in soccer and rugby union and women's ice hockey in the Olympics). Some media reports have promoted female participation in these sports. For example, Bud MacRae, a coach and convenor of a high school rugby union competition in Canada, was quoted in an article by Ferguson:

Traditionally, women's sport has leaned toward non-contact games like field hockey, ringette, volleyball and basketball. . . . But the majority of girls I have coached admit that they play the sport because they can really mix it up. We've had scrimmages with our boys' teams and, believe me, the girls have no qualms about nailing some guy with a lot of zest. They don't pull their punches.

(Ferguson, 1994)

Theberge (1999) reports a research study undertaken during fieldwork with a Canadian women's ice hockey team (the Blades) during the 1992–93 and 1993–94 seasons. The players involved in the study ranged from 16 to 30 years of age and included some members of the national team. The research sought to pinpoint sources of pleasure and satisfaction in women's ice hockey and interviews with the players revealed important insights into physicality in these female athletes. Many of the players talked about the attraction of physical contact and Theberge herself noticed that, after particularly intense games, the athletes were especially animated and excited in the changing room. As one player in an interview said:

> I like a physical game. You get more fired up. I think when you get hit – not a cheap shot – but something like when you are fighting for a puck in the corner, when you are both fighting so you're both working hard and maybe the elbows are flying, that just makes you put more effort into it. You are using your body that much more which means you're exerting that much more energy. It creates more of a game.
>
> (Theberge, 1999, p. 147)

The rules in men's and women's hockey are essentially the same, with the exception that, in the women's game, intentional body checking is prohibited. Only one fight was witnessed over two seasons. Although there are no violent collisions or the cross-checking that characterises the men's game, intentional and unintentional body contact is still part of the women's game. According to the players in Theberge's (1999) study, the game is probably faster as a result of the ban on body checking. It was not always the case, as some of the players had played full-contact hockey before the rules were changed and standardised across Canada in the late 1980s. Many of these players, in comparing the two versions of the game, regretted that body checking had been prohibited and expressed a sense of pleasure and accomplishment in being able to give and take a body check well.

The player quotes from Theberge's (1999) research are very similar to those found in Colburn's (1985, 1989) work with male ice hockey athletes. An enduring theme from these studies is the pleasure and satisfaction that both men and women ice hockey players get from being physical. Theberge (1999) felt strongly enough about the importance of this aspect of the game for women that she stated:

> my research has provided clear and strong evidence of the enjoyment and sense of accomplishment that women hockey players (and all athletes) derive from the physicality of sport. I am suspicious of efforts to promote women's sports by distancing them from images of strength and power. While there has been much to criticize in the model of men's sport, in our efforts to devise alternatives we need to retain features that provide pleasure, satisfaction and a sense of empowerment.
>
> (Theberge, 1999, p. 155)

Reversal theory and the motivation behind sanctioned aggression and violence

In the previous sections, particular aspects of team contact sports were examined from the point of view of how they contribute to an athlete's positive emotional experience when playing team contact sports. However, how can this be interpreted in terms of reversal theory? Examining the aspects of team contact sports highlighted above, it becomes clear that they are associated with individual states or combinations of states and motivational variables. For example, according to reversal theory, excitement is a pleasant emotion, associated with a paratelic-conformist state combination. In the case of team contact sports, excitement is experienced as a consequence of the nature of the sports themselves, specifically features of the play in general, in addition to the added ingredient of the hard physicality of sanctioned physical confrontation. It almost goes without saying that the high levels of arousal generated by play have to be interpreted as pleasant for the athlete to experience excitement. Also, the self-explanatory motivational variable, felt toughness will also likely be involved in any experience related to the physical side of team contact sports. Felt toughness is associated with an autic-mastery state combination. The mastery state comes into prominence when the need to dominate opponents, and exploit any weaknesses that they might have, is considered. Here, the athletes' physicality is a reflection of the meta-motivation associated with this state, where felt toughness and the ability not to reverse to the sympathy state when an opponent is vulnerable, are desirable. Society usually disapproves of behaviour that exploits the weakness of others and, in many countries, laws have been passed to try and protect the welfare of weaker individuals or groups. However, in team contact sports there is every opportunity to dominate and exploit the weakness of opposing teams, allowing the victors to experience pride and the vanquished to feel humiliated. Provided aggressive behaviour remains within the rules of the individual sports, such behaviour is legal, condoned and encouraged.

Another motivational variable associated with the mastery (and sympathy) state is felt transactional outcome, which is concerned with the sense of gain or loss experienced in interactions. It can be important in terms of mastering personal skills, where players have to perform successfully with balls, pucks, sticks and other equipment, but also in interactions with teammates, opposing players, officials and spectators. For example, in reversal theory terms, feelings of belonging to a team are tied up with the personal relationships that an individual has developed with the other members of his or her team. Specific emotional responses will be based on a player's experience in the (self-centred) autic and (other-centred) alloic and mastery-sympathy states. A player, for example, may enjoy intense feelings associated with a (paratelic-conformist-) alloic-mastery state combination if he or she combines with the other players in a 'set play' which leads to the winning score in a hard-fought game.

The reality of team contact sports is that they are much more dynamic than perhaps has been the impression given here. For example, the focus between autic and alloic experience may change back and forth quite often. In any one period of time during a game, interactions might involve reversals between different pairs of metamotivational states and changes of metamotivational state combinations. Unless reversals do occur, the predominant state combination when playing team contact sports is likely to be paratelic-conformist-autic or alloic-mastery. It is this predominant metamotivational state combination which is associated with Apter's (1997) category of *play violence*. It should be reiterated here that the enjoyment of sanctioned aggression and violence is only possible through the mechanism of paratelic protective frames described in chapters 2 and 3.

Developing an excessive appetite for sanctioned aggression and violence

Experienced team contact sports players may develop *excessive appetites* for sanctioned aggression and violence. Excessive appetite is a term proposed by Orford (2001) to describe over-attachments, addictions or dependencies to a drug, object or activity. More specifically, players may become dependent on the high levels of felt arousal, felt transactional outcome and felt toughness which emanate from competitive play and physical confrontation.

It is interesting that among the 40 potentially addictive activities listed by Witman *et al.* (1987), physical violence, as well as playing sports, both feature alongside 22 substance-oriented activities and 16 other non-substance addictive activities. The high levels of positive affect obtainable through sanctioned aggression and violence in team contact sports may work in a similar way to the changes in affect associated with other addictions such as gambling or alcoholism, in the manner outlined by Brown (1991, 1997). Indeed, achieving improved affect is also thought to be one of the major causes leading some athletes, especially long distance runners, cyclists and swimmers, to develop excessive appetites for exercise (e.g. Annet *et al.*, 1995; Blaydon *et al.*, 2002). In extreme cases, the hard physical training and demands of games could potentially result in the exercise component of team contact sports working as an added ingredient to aggression and violence in the situational highs of the athletes and give rise to the formation of a kind of dual dependency.

If dependence on aggressive confrontation and violent plays and/or exercise is a possibility, then, like other addictive behaviours, it is likely to follow a series of similar developmental stages (Brown, 1997). The present author has applied Brown's (1997) Hedonic Tone Management Model of Addictions to understanding addiction in soccer hooligan behaviour (Kerr, 1994) and to aggressive confrontation and violent plays in team contact sports (Kerr, 1997). With respect to team contact sports, Kerr has outlined how the process of dependency can develop through school and youth sport, through adolescence to early adulthood and full maturity as an experienced team contact sport player. The various stages of dependency development as set out by Brown (1997), applied to team contact sports by Kerr (1997) and linked to reversal theory, are shown in Figure 4.1

Stage 1 for athletes is when they first become acquainted with a team contact sport and find that they enjoy the activity. At this early stage, the exciting nature of the play and the pleasure of being (playfully) aggressive, both of which are linked to the experience of pleasant high arousal, are likely to be sources of enjoyment. The paratelic metamotivational state is likely to be salient at this stage.

In Stage 2, as players continue practising and playing their sport, levels of physicality are gradually increased and other features of the game, like mastering

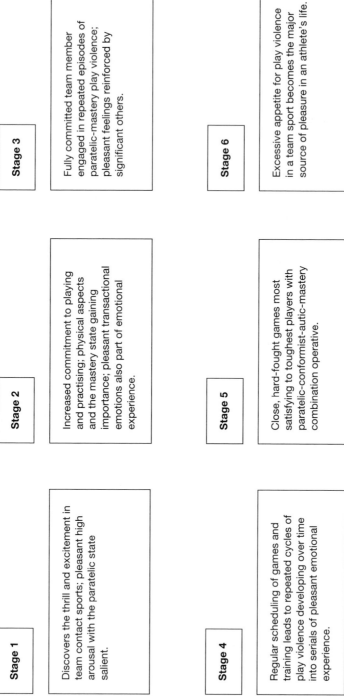

Stage 1

Discovers the thrill and excitement in team contact sports; pleasant high arousal with the paratelic state salient.

Stage 2

Increased commitment to playing and practising; physical aspects and the mastery state gaining importance; pleasant transactional emotions also part of emotional experience.

Stage 3

Fully committed team member engaged in repeated episodes of paratelic-mastery play violence; pleasant feelings reinforced by significant others.

Stage 4

Regular scheduling of games and training leads to repeated cycles of play violence developing over time into serials of pleasant emotional experience.

Stage 5

Close, hard-fought games most satisfying to toughest players with paratelic-conformist-autic-mastery combination operative.

Stage 6

Excessive appetite for play violence in a team sport becomes the major source of pleasure in an athlete's life.

Figure 4.1 Brown's (1997) Hedonic Tone Management Model of Addictions linked with reversal theory (Apter, 2001) and applied to team contact sports.

personal skills and opponents, winning, and belonging to a team will become increasingly important. In this second stage, transactional emotions (e.g. pride), associated with the autic and mastery states, start to play a greater role in the individual player's pleasant subjective experience. At the same time, important others, coaches and teammates and possibly parents, provide positive reinforcement which acts as a powerful motivator for keeping athletes involved in the sport.

By the time Stage 3 is reached, the athletes have become established members of a team with all the commitment that is required in terms of maintaining and improving levels of health, fitness and successful skills performance in practice sessions and games. This includes the development of aggressive and violent skills (e.g. body checking or tackling hard) as the domination of opposing athletes becomes crucial to success. Being aggressive and violent is now firmly entrenched in players and has become a major source of pleasure, which, in turn, again serves to strongly reinforce behaviour through potent positive feedback loops. In Brown's (1997) Hedonic Tone Management Model of Addictions, the development of what he termed repeated episodes (e.g. for the addicted gambler, a visit to a casino), which eventually build into serials, are important aspects of this stage.

In Stage 4, the regular scheduling of training, practice sessions and games during the playing season provides players with 'officially approved' opportunities to maintain and develop their dependency experience. In simple terms, players can achieve emotional highs on a regular basis through their regular weekend games (cycles or episodes). Practice and coaching sessions may help to add to or maintain these positive emotional states in the periods between games over the season (serials). The injection of extra games, perhaps through extra cup matches, may also mean that even more emotional highs are available to players. If, towards the end of a playing season, a team manages to qualify for the final playoffs against the other top teams, the emotional rewards for players are likely to become higher as they come closer to and eventually win a trophy (Kerr 1997, p. 126).

By Stage 5, intense experience within a paratelic-conformist-autic-mastery state combination is what is desired from team contact sports. The physical and violent side of the game has become inextricably linked to the pleasures that players obtain from playing, and close, hard-fought battles will be the most satisfying. As a result, only the toughest, hardest and most durable players can survive in the sport and, for many of these athletes, playing team contact sports may well now be a major source of emotional reward. Stage 6 is the final stage in the dependency process. When players reach this stage, participation in team contact sports has become the major source of reward and pleasure in life and has taken over their life in the same way as any other excessive appetite or dependency.

There is reversal theory-based research evidence to suggest that athletes are generally proficient at achieving the mental states and arousal levels that they desire for performance (Kerr and van Schaik, 1995; Males and Kerr, 1996). Further evidence suggests that particular locations, including sports locations, may induce certain metamotivational states or state combinations (Kerr and Tacon, 1999). Based on these results, it is likely that, for regular players, going to a team contact sport venue, undertaking their usual pre-performance routines in and around the pitch, field or rink and the changing rooms, will induce the paratelic-conformist-autic-mastery state combination. This combination facilitates the enjoyment of sanctioned aggression and violence in sport, and thus this particular metamotivational state combination becomes associated with the episodes and serials that form part of the process of dependency development. It is in this state combination that the heightened levels of felt arousal, felt transactional outcome and felt toughness, and overall increased hedonic tone that are frequently obtained when playing team contact sports, become a major source of pleasure in the athlete's life.

It is important to emphasise that the Hedonic Tone Management Model, like reversal theory, is also an ongoing and dynamic model with feedback links hypothesised between the different stages of the addiction or dependency process. The process may start slowly, but builds up steadily over the period of an athlete's involvement until it may become a fully fledged dependency by the middle and latter years of an athlete's playing career. In addition, although it has been stated that a paratelic-conformist-autic-mastery state combination is likely to be induced during competition, this may not always occur as reversals to or from each of these individual states could possibly take place before or during competition. If this should occur, the experience of the athlete or athletes concerned would be very different.

Some support for the notion of athletes developing excessive appetites or becoming addicted to or dependent on team contact sports comes from Messner (1992):

> You know if you do drugs, you'll get a good feeling; you try to duplicate the highs you get on the field off the field. Because after you get off the field, you go back to normality and become normal again. And after you've just left being on one of the most extreme highs that you'll ever get in life – then you have to come back to life.
>
> (Messner, 1992, p. 125)

The fact that retirement or withdrawal from American football may result in athletes searching for other means of boosting their levels of positive affect (e.g. through alcohol or drug use) indicates that players have indeed developed excessive appetites for the 'highs' of playing American football or possibly other team contact sports. By doing so, they may well simply be swapping one dependency for another. Partly as a result of problems like alcohol and drug abuse, in recent years there has been a focus on retirement planning for athletes. Along with a growing literature in sport psychology, national sport organizations are beginning to carry out research and develop programmes to help athletes cope when their sporting careers are over (e.g. Lavallee and Wylleman, 2002).

Closing comments

In this chapter, the discussion has concentrated on sources of pleasure provided by various aspects of sport in general and team contact sport in particular. Specific aspects of sanctioned aggressive and violent acts in team contact sports, acts which generally fall within the category of play violence (Apter, 1997), have been at focus. Also, how players develop an affinity for sanctioned aggression and violence and how it develops into a major source of reward has been outlined. In addition, it has also been shown how these positive rewards can become so strong that they become potentially addictive. However, this is also true for other forms of aggression and violence. In the next chapter, unsanctioned aggression and violence in sport is the theme and this will mean that some of the other categories of aggression and violence described in chapter 3 (Apter, 1997) become relevant to the discussion.

References

Annet, J., Cripps, B. and Steinberg, H. (1995). *Exercise addiction*. Leicester: The British Psychological Society.

Apter, M. J. (1997, July). *The experience of being violent*. Paper presented at the Eighth International Conference on Reversal Theory, University of East London.

Apter, M. J. (Ed.) (2001). *Motivational styles in everyday life: A guide to reversal theory*. Washington DC: American Psychological Association.

Auguet, R. (1994). *Cruelty and civilization: The Roman games*. London: Routledge.

Barnes, S. (1996, 29 April) Gripping spectacle of Graham's torment. *The Times*, p. 26.

Bennett, W. (1996, 3 June). 'Controlled aggression' talk a Gee-up. *The Australian*, p. 28.

Blaydon, M. J., Lindner, K. J. and Kerr, J. H. (2002). Metamotivational characteristics of eating-disordered and exercise dependent triathletes: An application of reversal theory. *Psychology of Sport and Exercise*, 3, 223–236.

Brink, A. (1995, 24 June). Dirty old habits die hard. *Guardian*, p. 29.

Brown, R. I. F. (1991). Gambling, gaming and other addictive play. In J. H. Kerr and M. J. Apter (Eds), *Adult Play* (pp.101–118). Amsterdam: Swets and Zeitlinger.

Brown, R. I. F. (1997). A theoretical model of the behavioural addictions – applied to criminal offending. In J. Hodge, M. McMurran and C. Hollins (Eds), *Addicted to crime* (pp. 13–65). Chichester: Wiley.

Colburn, K. (1985). Honor, ritual and violence in ice hockey. *Canadian Journal of Sociology*, 10, 153–170.

Colburn, K. (1989). Deviance and legitimacy in ice hockey: A microstructural theory of violence. In D. H. Kelly (Ed.), *Deviant behaviour*. New York: St. Martins Press.

Ferguson, B. (1994, 30 April). Girls tackling rugby with a vengeance. *The Ottawa Citizen*, p. G6.

Ginola, D. (1996). *From St Tropez to St James*. London: Headline.

Guttmann, A. (1986). *Sports spectators*. New York: Columbia University Press.

Guttmann, A. (1998). The appeal of violent sports. In J. Goldstein (Ed.), *Why we watch* (pp. 7–26). New York: Oxford University Press.

Irvine, C. (1997, 6 November). Daley stands out as rare vintage. *The Times*, p. 45.

Jefferson, T. (1998). Muscle, 'hard men' and 'iron' Mike Tyson: Reflections on desire, anxiety and the embodiment of masculinity. *Body and Society*, 4, 77–98.

Jennings, H. D. (1966). *The DHS story 1866–1966*. Durban: [publisher unknown]; cited in J. Nauright and T. J. L. Chandler (Eds) (1996) *Making men: Rugby and masculine identity*. London: Frank Cass.

Kerr, J. H. (1994). *Understanding soccer hooliganism*. Buckingham: Open University Press.

Kerr, J. H. (1997). *Motivation and emotion in sport: Reversal theory*. Hove, England: Psychology Press.

Kerr, J. H. and Tacon, P. (1999). Psychological responses to different types of locations and activities. *Journal of Environmental Psychology*, *19*, 287–294.

Kerr, J. H. and van Schaik, P. (1995). Effects of game venue and outcome on psychological mood states in rugby. *Personality and Individual Differences*, *19 (3)*, 407–409.

Kerr, J. H., Wilson, G. V., Nakamura, I. and Sudo, Y. (2004). Emotional dynamics of soccer fans at winning and losing games (submitted for publication).

Kerr, J. H., Wilson, G. V., Bowling, A. and Sheahan, J. P. (2004). Game outcome and elite Japanese women's field hockey players' experience of emotions and stress. *Psychology of Sport and Exercise* (accepted for publication).

Lavallee, D. and Wylleman, P. (2002). *Career transitions in sport: International perspectives*. Morgantown, WV: Fitness Information Technology.

Males, J. R. and Kerr, J. H. (1996). Stress, emotion and performance in elite slalom canoeists. *The Sport Psychologist*, *10*, 17–36.

Messner, M. A. (1992). *Power at play: Sports and the problem of masculinity*. Boston: Beacon Press.

Morell, R. (1966). Forging a ruling race: Rugby and white masculinity in colonial Natal, c. 1870–1910. In J. Nauright and T. J. L. Chandler (Eds), *Making men: Rugby and masculine identity* (pp. 91–120). London: Frank Cass.

Nauright, J. and Black, D. (1996). 'Hitting them where it hurts': Springbok–All Black rugby, masculine national identity and counter-hegemonic struggle, 1959–1992. In J. Nauright and T. J. L. Chandler (Eds), *Making men: Rugby and masculine identity* (pp. 205–226). London: Frank Cass.

Nauright, J. and Chandler, T. J. L. (Eds) (1996). *Making men: Rugby and masculine identity*. London: Frank Cass.

Novak, M. (1976). *The joy of sports*. New York: Basic Books.

Orford, J. (2001). *Excessive appetites: A psychological view of addictions*. Chichester, England: John Wiley.

Platt, D. (1995). *Achieving the goal*. London: Richard Cohen Books.

Russell, G. W. (1993). *The social psychology of sport*. New York: Springer-Verlag.

Schlesinger, P., Haynes, R., Boyle, R., McNair, B., Dobash, R. E. and Dobash, R. P. (1998). *Men viewing violence*. London: Broadcasting Standards Council.

Smaal, R. (1998, 21 February). Czech this: Canada booted in semis. *The Japan Times*, p. 24.

Tatum, J. and Kushner, B. (1979). *They call me assassin*. New York: Everest House.

Theberge, N. (1999). Being physical: Sources of pleasure and satisfaction in women's ice hockey. In J. Cloakley and P. Donnelly (Eds), *Inside sports* (pp. 146–155). London: Routledge.

Weber, R. (1997, December). The Green Bay effect. *Inside Sport*, p. 133.

Wilson, G. V. and Kerr, J. H. (1999). Affective responses to success and failure: A study of winning and losing in rugby. *Personality and Individual Differences*, *27*, 85–99.

Witman, G. W., Fuller, N. P. and Taber, J. I. (1987). Patterns of polyaddictions in alcoholism patients and high school students. In W. R. Eadington (Ed.), *Research in gambling: Proceedings of the Seventh International Conference.*

Zavos, S. (1988). In praise of rugby. In M King (Ed.), *One of the boys? Changing views of masculinity in New Zealand.* Auckland: [publisher unknown]; cited in Nauright and Black, 1996, p. 206.

5 When things turn ugly

Unsanctioned aggression and violence

This chapter is concerned with unsanctioned, malicious violence in the form of foul or dirty play and the psychological processes which lie behind such acts. It begins with a brief return visit to the problems of differentiating between sanctioned and unsanctioned aggression and violence and the grey areas that exist and which can sometimes cause difficulty in distinguishing between the two. The focus here moves to the importance of players' rules or norms as well as the rules of the particular sport. Following this, further discussion of intimidation and retaliation, beyond the points raised in chapter 4, are explored in relation to unsanctioned aggression and violence. The discussion also examines those athletes, sometimes known as 'athletic psychopaths', whose acts of unsanctioned violence are deliberately calculated to attempt to start trouble or injure players by unprovoked violent attacks on opponents. Finally, the motivation behind the behaviour of athletic psychopaths as well as other forms of unsanctioned violence will be explored using reversal theory and Apter's (1997) categories of violence.

Revisiting the difference between sanctioned and unsanctioned aggression and violence

The distinction between sanctioned and unsanctioned aggression and violence in sport has been neatly summarised by Brink (1995):

> Because the game is so relentless by its very nature, the borders between the permissible and the inadmissible are not always very clear-cut. Both are inherently violent. But surely the distinction between hard play and foul play lies in the resort of the latter to violence of an underhand, malicious, treacherous kind. It is a condition of foul play that it is not supposed to come to light, to be exposed, because it is not directed to the unfolding of the game but to the private goals of rage or revenge, to 'get at' a specific opponent, to 'prove' oneself. It foregrounds the individual, not the team.
>
> (Brink, 1995, p. 29)

This quote relates to rugby union, but it could equally well describe any of the other team contact sports. The terms 'permissible' and 'hard play' refer to acts of violence within the laws or rules of the sport (i.e. sanctioned) and, conversely, 'inadmissible' and 'foul play' refer to acts of violence outside the rules of the game (i.e. unsanctioned). The importance of carrying out aggressive and violent plays within the laws or rules of individual team contact sports, as sanctioned acts, has been emphasised earlier in this book. However, closer examination indicates that there are actually two sets of rules in operation. First, there are the formal rules of the game and, second, the informal unwritten rules or norms of the players playing the game. In different ways, they both serve to censure unacceptable actions. Even within the formal rules of the games, the existence of, for example, yellow and red cards in soccer and 'sin bins' in rugby league and rugby union, indicate that there is an assumption that players will break those rules and will need to be penalised. The match officials' task is difficult, because they must not only enforce technical rule infractions and try to keep the game flowing, but also prevent severe violations of the rules with respect to aggression and violence. It is not surprising, then, that officials sometimes fail to spot player misdemeanours or decide to 'let things go'. In spite of their efforts to be consistent, players know that officials' calls are often situational or contextual (Colburn, 1989, p. 77). Players' unwritten rules usually come into effect when opposing players overstep the mark by repeated rule infractions or unacceptably violent play or unsanctioned acts which remain unpenalised by the officials. Patmore (1979), also talking about rugby union, stated:

> Much has been said about the 'unwritten laws' of the game. One unwritten law not usually mentioned is that, as a player, you do not allow yourself or your team-mates to be publicly brutalized by an opposing team in the course of play. You are duty bound to level the score; if you don't your reputation for toughness and pride is immediately compromised.
>
> (Patmore, 1979, p. 172)

If players' rules are broken, they often take the law into their own hands and usually retaliate with acts of unsanctioned violence. As a consequence, when discussing sanctioned and unsanctioned acts of aggression and violence, players' rules as well as the rules of the game must be taken into account. This is discussed in the next section, where a unique example of players' rules in action actually proves to be an exception to the previously established distinction between the two types of aggression and violence in sport.

Sanctioned fighting: The unique case of ice hockey

Some readers, especially those interested in ice hockey, may have realised that in North American ice hockey at least, and unlike the other team contact sports, fighting between players on the ice is currently sanctioned by both players and coaches, and, to a large extent, condoned by the authorities. Fighting in hockey is, therefore, a sanctioned form of an activity which is technically unsanctioned aggression and violence. According to Colburn (1985, 1989), players in hockey distinguish between the fist-fight and other violent acts. He sees it as a social ritual which acts as a means of establishing or re-establishing respect and honour among opposing players, a form of social control which has a moderating effect on more serious violent acts between players. As such, fist-fights are viewed as legitimate (sanctioned) according to the players' rules, just as stick assaults are illegitimate, unsanctioned violence. 'Fist-fights may be proscribed and their occurrence penalized by the official rules, but players view the matter differently. As I have heard many players, fans and officials say on numerous occasions, fist-fights are "part of the game".' (Colburn, 1985, pp. 156–157). Not only are they considered a part of the game, but there is a set of expectations as to how players behave during the course of a fist-fight. First, the players square up to each other, then the antagonist drops his gloves and stick so that the opponent can see them come off. Then the opponent either skates away (not recommended or sanctioned by most players) or, in turn, drops his gloves and stick and the two engage in the fist-fight (Colburn, 1985). Rarely, it seems, is any real damage done:

> Nobody gets hurt in a fist-fight. . . . In a fight where punches are thrown, like what the hell, you've got maybe eight, six inches of your head that is showing, the rest of you is covered in equipment. So in a fight maybe you'll get hit, or maybe you'll get a fat lip, but I have never seen any teeth knocked out in a fist-fight. All the teeth I have seen knocked out are by sticks.
>
> (Colburn 1985, p. 156)

The reason for revisiting the distinction between sanctioned and unsanctioned aggression and violence was to underline the fact that there are 'grey areas' which exist between these two types of aggression and violence. These grey areas are often specific to particular team contact sports and focusing on the case of sanctioned fist-fighting in North American ice hockey provides a neat example of what would be considered unsanctioned violence in other team sports. This all serves to show how difficult it is to provide blanket definitions of what is, and what is not, sanctioned and unsanctioned violence in sport. Indeed, this situation is even more complicated in ice hockey because there are some types of fist-fight that are not considered legitimate or sanctioned (Colburn, 1985). These are calculated or pre-meditated unsanctioned acts of aggression and violence and are fundamentally different in character from the spontaneous fist-fights that occur between willing opponents. Virtually all acts of unsanctioned aggression and violence can be classified as intimidation or retaliation. The next part of this chapter is concerned with examining intimidation and retaliation in detail. When these acts occur during team contact sports, they are often linked, with acts of intimidation producing retaliation. For convenience here, however, they will be dealt with separately.

Intimidation

As pointed out in chapter 4, players are constantly seeking to exploit any weakness in opposing players or teams. Testing for weaknesses can involve the strategic use of (sanctioned) physical intimidation. However, it may also take the form of unsanctioned acts which, to use Brink's (1995) words, are of 'an underhand, malicious, treacherous kind'. The Larwood and England bodyline bowling controversy described in chapter 3 provides a good example of the strategic use of physical intimidation within the rules, if not the spirit of the game. Also, a recent television programme, *Hardball: Baseball from the inside out* (Deadline Company, 2002) showed that pitchers in baseball can and do adopt similar intimidatory tactics. If intimidation is used in cricket and baseball, two sports with only minimum physical contact, then it can certainly be used in team contact sports.

As Conrad Dobler, who played guard for the American football teams Cardinals, Saints and Bills from 1972 to 1981, and who was regarded as the dirtiest player in the 1970s, stated in an interview with Silver:

> I hear coaches say intimidation is not part of the game – that's bull——. The NFL is trying to make people think this is not a violent sport. It's almost as if they are trying to turn it into a gentlemen's sport instead of the blood sport it used to be. . . . For decades no one said anything about late hits or dirty play. . . . It's only in the last 10 years that it has become an issue. The league wants to protect its star players, the quarterbacks and receivers, because when a star goes down it hurts ticket sales, and the club has to pay big money for a replacement.
>
> (Silver, 1998, p. 52)

The purpose of unsanctioned aggressive and violent intimidation is to distract an opposing player or team from the main objective of playing well and winning the game. It can take the form of testing a player's 'bottle' or mental toughness by roughing him or her up. In other words, if a player is anticipating, watching for and trying to avoid further acts of unsanctioned aggression and violence, then he or she is not fully attending to the play. Decision-making, carrying out pre-planned moves and the performance of individual skills may break down as a result of intimidation. In American football, for example, pass rushing and nailing the quarterback has always been the goal of defensive players. If the defensive players can tackle the quarterback before he throws, then they may affect his confidence and thus his ability to make effective passes, and possibly prevent touchdowns. This of course is a sanctioned act, but the same action performed after the ball has left the quarterback's hand (a late hit) is an unsanctioned violent act. What Dobler, in the quote above (Silver, 1998), is alluding to is that, in recent years, the rules have been changed to provide the quarterback with more protection from opponents' unsanctioned violent acts.

Although not concerned directly with the quarterback, Dan Turk, the deceased former Redskins player, explained how intimidation was used by him and his teammates:

We'd have competitions to see how many defensive backs we could pick off or how many linebackers we could knock off their feet. We had two great moves: the knife where the guard acts like he's pass-blocking his man and I'd shoot in from the side and cut him; and the fork, where I'd pull back and one of the guards would take out the nose tackle. Then we'd make a lot of false fork and knife calls to freak out the defensive linemen. It would take them out of their game.

(Silver, 1998, p. 57)

Similarly, in ice hockey, butt-ending, spearing, slashing, elbowing and high sticking are all unsanctioned violent acts which players use to intimidate opponents in an attempt to get them to lose concentration on the game. An ice hockey player described how it works:

When you are trying to think about hockey, that's enough for one person to do at one time. But when you also got to think or worry about the guy behind you, if he's going to hit you or just exactly what he's going to do to you, it just throws you off your hockey game 'cuz you can't think about two things at once – it's either hockey or fighting.

(Colburn, 1989, p. 74)

Alternatively, intimidation may involve deliberately 'taking out' (often a euphemism for deliberately injuring) a player so that he or she cannot score or can no longer take part in the game. This type of intimidation may be as a result of an individual decision by an individual athlete during play, or even be a planned decision on the part of coach and players as an integral part of team strategy to win particular games. The so-called 'professional foul' in soccer (except where it involves 'handball') is an example of an individual athlete making a decision to take out a player to prevent him or her from scoring. One of the best examples of this form of unsanctioned act took place in the 1982 World Cup between France and Germany. At a crucial time in the game, Harald Schumacher, the German keeper, rushed out of goal and viciously took out an unsighted Patrick Battiston who was in a good scoring position. As a result of the collision, Battiston's jaw was broken and he immediately fell into a coma. He was stretchered off the pitch and taken to hospital, taking no further part in a game which Germany won 3–2.

Coaches and players may deliberately decide to take out a key player as part of their strategy to win a particular game. An infamous example of this form of intimidation involved Hawthorn player Dermot Brereton and Geelong player Mark Yeates. Now retired, Brereton is a legend in Australian Rules football after an outstanding career with Hawthorn, where he won five premierships, and later with the Sydney and Collingwood clubs. The incident occurred in the 1989 Australian Football League (AFL) Grand Final, thought to be one of the best AFL Grand Finals ever. When the game began, right at the first bounce, Brereton went up for the ball, but Yeates cut through the centre square and hit him with a deliberate shoulder charge below the ribs. Brereton went down and, although badly hurt and requiring attention, he continued to play and was a crucial factor in Hawthorn's subsequent win. Later, it was claimed that Yeates' unsanctioned violent act of intimidation had been planned by the Geelong Coach prior to the game (Stocks, 1995). Not only was Brereton a tough competitor, not unknown for handing out punishment himself, but he was also a crucial attacking player for Hawthorn. Had this act of intimidation succeeded, it might have tipped the scales in favour of Geelong in this match. The Australian Football League did not punish offending player Yeates; however, they did make a rule change to prevent this type of incident recurring.

Retaliation

As is the case with intimidation through sanctioned aggression and violence, unsanctioned acts of intimidation in team contact sports often lead to retaliation against the perpetrator by the athlete who has been targeted, or one or more of his or her teammates. When retaliation takes place, levels of violence may escalate and almost certainly will involve more unsanctioned aggression and violence. The question among team contact sport players often arises as to whether a player should retaliate against intimidation immediately or wait until later in the game or even a future game to strike back. Opinion is generally divided. In ice hockey, if the intimidatory act is considered outside players' rules and norms, the gloves come off and, as described earlier in this chapter, an immediate fist-fight occurs. However, ongoing acts of intimidation and retaliation may occur with relative immediacy when two warring players' paths cross during the play. The same is true in other team contact sports. For example, consider an incident involving Kevin Gogan, a 6' 7", 330 pound American football guard for the San Francisco 49ers, which occurred in the Pro Bowl, a post-season exhibition game between selected teams in which not much is usually at stake. The incident resulted in Gogan being ejected from the game, along with his antagonist Neil Smith. In an article which included some interview comments from Gogan, Silver (1998) described what occurred:

> . . . amid the pushing and grabbing he saw a smidgen of daylight between himself and Neil Smith, the Denver Broncos defensive end who seconds earlier, in retaliation for a punch in the chest, had slugged Gogan in the back of the head. Even if he deserves it, Gogan doesn't take a poke from anybody, and Smith was about to experience the swift kick of injustice. 'It was amazing', Gogan recalls. 'All of a sudden, this space opened that was the perfect size for me to get my leg through and kick him in the nuts.' . . . 'The referee told me it was the most vicious kick to the groin he had seen in 23 years'.
>
> (Silver, 1998, p. 48)

Being ejected from the Pro Bowl is an unusual occurrence, but there had been bad blood between Gogan and Smith since their days playing for the Raiders and the Chiefs, respectively. They had merely resumed their battle at the Pro Bowl game.

A different type of retaliation was perpetrated by former Republic of Ireland and Manchester United soccer captain Roy Keane. Keane was already a controversial figure after being sent home from the Irish training camp at the 2002 Korea/Japan World Cup following a conflict with Mick McCarthy, the Irish manager. He found himself in even more trouble with the soccer authorities when admissions that he made in an autobiography caused a great deal of contention. A violent tackle by Keane in a derby match between Manchester United and Manchester City in 2001 seriously injured Norwegian player Alf Inge Haaland. Keane went in very forcefully at knee height with two feet and studs showing and caught Haaland hard on the leg. It was a harsh foul even by the standards of modern European soccer. Keane was sent off and Haaland never really recovered from the injury. Keane admitted in the autobiography that he deliberately set out to injure Haaland in the match in a premeditated act of revenge. He was asked if had any regrets about the Haaland incident in an interview with the *Observer* newspaper (Campbell, 2002). He replied:

> 'No. Even in the dressing room afterward. I had no remorse. My attitude was f*** him. What goes around comes around. He got his just rewards. He f***ed me over and my attitude is an eye for an eye.' Asked if he would do the same thing again, Keane paused before replying: 'Probably, Yeah.'

There was nothing immediate about Keane's unsanctioned violent tackle. It was cold and calculated and, by his own admission, he intended to hurt Haaland. Keane had not forgotten what Haaland had done in a game three years earlier and when an opportunity presented itself he took his revenge:

> 'I'd waited almost 180 minutes for Alfie, three years if you looked at it another way,' he says in the book. 'I'd waited long enough. I hit him hard. The ball was there (I think). Take that.'
>
> ('FA throws book', 2002)

In order to survive in the competitive jungle that exists in team contact sport, individual athletes and teams have to develop and maintain a reputation that they will not stand by and be intimidated without responding in a way that exceeds the level of the initial intimidatory act. The old cliché, kill or be killed, has a ring of truth about it in this context, and retaliation when player norms have been violated helps to build and maintain a reputation for hardness (Weinstein et al., 1995, p. 836). Players have to stand up for themselves on an individual level:

> 'It is getting back to that intimidation point we were talking about earlier where somebody knows I'll back down from a fight. Then I'll just get my own self into trouble 'cuz next game there's going to be six guys after me to fight. You know then they're going to be trying all the little dirty tricks on me'.
>
> (Colburn, 1989, p. 75)

Colburn (1985, p. 162) has argued that it is a matter of honour to counter opponents' disrespectful acts of intimidation by violent physical retaliation. It is almost as if the use of unsanctioned intimidation breaks the terms of the implicit contract (in the pursuit of aggression and violence) that Kerr (1997, pp. 115–116) has suggested exists in team contact sports and this contract must be renegotiated through retaliation. Keeping the opposition's aggression and violence within both game and players' rules is also important on a team level. An act which transgresses those rules requires retaliation on a group or team basis. Both coaches and players know that an act of unsanctioned violent retaliation committed by several team members can benefit performance, in the sense that it can act as a motivational boost for those players and the whole team (Colburn, 1985, p.167; Smith, 1983, p. 94).

Spracklen (1996), studying professional and amateur rugby league football, found that notions of team loyalty and looking after teammates are extremely powerful, even in unusual circumstances:

> Some of the players thought I must be gay [because of his initial fear and real name Cecil], which is not a reputation anyone would want in professional rugby. Yet though they were a tough bunch. . . . I shall be indebted to them for the rest of my life. They were hard but courageous and generous too. Because they knew I always gave my best on the field, they looked after me. A player can easily be hurt (if) there is a collision between an opponent's fist and your face, but my team mates always protected me from unfair play . . . twelve of my mates would retaliate if I went down. It gave me a hugely comforting feeling.
>
> (Thompson, 1995, p. 25, cited in Spracklen, 1996 with his additions in parentheses)

It takes time for a new player to be accepted by teammates, but as Thompson (1995) underlined, once accepted into the 'community' of his rugby league team, he became an insider, worth standing up for against opposing players guilty of foul play. Not all players are willing or able to perform unsanctioned violent acts. Most teams have at least a few 'hardmen' who act as policemen, 'keeping the opposition honest' when the need occurs. These players are respected by other players and only infrequently have to retaliate by fighting, as their menacing reputation for being tough acts as a deterrent to those who might want to use unsanctioned acts of intimidation against them or their teammates (Smith, 1983, p. 94). However, there are some players in team contact sports whose reputation is rather different. These players are constantly looking for trouble. If no incidents occur, they will find ways to start trouble themselves by trying to intimidate opposition players with unsanctioned violent acts in an attempt to spark fights. These players, often called nutters, goons, hitmen, head-hunters or hatchet men, are generally well known in their particular sports by both athletes and fans. Kevin Gogan, of the 'kick in the nuts' incident mentioned earlier in this chapter, might well be placed in this bracket, as one of the dirtiest players in American football:

What sets Gogan apart is the zest with which he seeks a physical con-frontation. 'It seems like guys always want to mess with people who don't want to be messed with,' Gogan says. 'I'm the guy who enjoys going after the instigators. Sometimes I don't even go where the ball is. I just go after the man.'

(Silver,1998, p. 48)

Tony Twist (the Twister), the St Louis Blues left wing and well-known National Hockey League enforcer, might well be another. In 'Fighting for a living', a *Sports Illustrated* article, Murphy, (1998) pointed out that:

Thanks to the Twister's lurking presence, Blues snipers such as wings Brett Hull and Geoff Courtnall enjoy much more elbow room. 'The respect he gets on the ice for our team is huge,' says Courtnall. . . . 'He throws hammers,' says San Jose Sharks right wing Owen Nolan, who also played with Twist on the Nordiques in the 1990s. 'He throws to kill. I've seen him crack a helmet with a punch. If I hadn't seen it, I wouldn't have believed it.'

(Murphy, 1998, p. 43)

Some observers have even suggested the behaviour of these players may well be psychopathic (e.g. McIntosh, 1979) and the term 'athletic psychopaths' has been applied to them (e.g. Kerr, 1997). Further discussion on the possible psy-chopathic behaviour of some players will be discussed in the next section of this chapter, which examines unsanctioned aggression and violence in sport from the point of view of reversal theory. The reversal theory view of psychopathic behaviour is important in the context of aggression and violence in sport.

Reversal theory and the motivation behind unsanctioned aggression and violence

Intimidation and retaliation can be used as umbrella terms to classify almost all forms of unsanctioned aggressive and violent acts committed in team contact sports. In similar fashion to sanctioned aggression and violence, the unsanctioned variety is also concerned with motivational variables and those specific combi-nations of metamotivational states associated with different types of violence (Apter, 1997; see chapter 3 of this volume). However, one type, *play violence*, should be excluded, as it is mostly associated with intimidation and retaliation as forms of sanctioned aggression and violence.

Acts of unsanctioned violence are primarily associated with *power, anger* and *thrill violence* (see Figure 3.1, page 39). The examples of acts of intimidation given in this chapter are all instances of power violence. These unsanctioned acts were initiated in order to subjugate and eventually defeat a rival athlete or team. The mastery state is therefore of prime importance, along with the telic state, because acts of power violence have a serious purpose. When soccer player Keane, Australian Rules player Yeates, American footballer Gogan, ice hockey player

Twist, and the teammates of rugby league player Thompson were 'at their work', there is every likelihood that they were in a metamotivational state combination of telic-mastery. If acts of intimidation are successful, then the player(s) will feel tough and masterful and experience the satisfaction of achieving their goal (of taking out, punching, kicking, or committing some other unsanctioned act against an opposing athlete). The negativistic-conformist and autic-alloic pairs of states will also be involved, but in a lesser role. For example, it is likely that Keane's metamotivational state combination during his foul tackle on Haaland would have been telic-negativistic-autic-mastery. However, in general, it is difficult to infer which states of the negativistic-conformist and autic-alloic pairs would be operative. For example, the negativistic state may have been operative when goalkeeper Schumacher took out Battiston, as he knew he was breaking the rules. However, when an ice hockey enforcer like Twist or Domi goes into action, they may be conforming to the coach's instructions or expectations and have the conformist state operative. The same is true for the autic and alloic pairs and depends what was in the mind of the perpetrator at the time (e.g. defending a teammate or asserting personal mastery over an opponent).

Turning now to retaliation, many of the unsanctioned acts which can be called retaliation are examples of anger violence. This comes about when an athlete is provoked by an unfair, unsanctioned act of intimidation and feels the need to respond in kind. Anger violence involves a metamotivational state combination where the telic and negativistic states are foremost, with accompanying high levels of felt arousal and felt negativism. Again, the mastery-sympathy and autic-alloic pairs of states will also be involved. A retaliatory act may put an end to an opponent's intimidation, but it could also lead to an escalation of violence as the intimidator, now the target of retaliation, has to respond with greater levels of power violence to defend himself and his honour, thus provoking even more retaliation. This appears to be what occurred in the American football Pro Bowl when Gogan and Smith were ejected from the game after a series of incidents of intimidation and retaliation.

It should also be stated that not all acts of retaliation are examples of anger violence. Experienced players, used to the tough competition and physicality of team contact sports, are wily enough to know that there is a good chance that opposing players and teams will try acts of intimidation sooner or later. In a sense, they expect it. This means that, when an aggressor attacks a player, the player may retaliate while keeping a clear head and not becoming angry, merely to re-establish the balance of power. In this case, the retaliatory act would be an example of power violence, and one form of power violence (retaliation) being used to counteract another (intimidation).

Experience is also a vital ingredient in the formation of a paratelic protective frame which is strong enough to handle unsanctioned violent acts. In chapter 4 it was stated that, for paratelic protective frames to work and for a secure environment to be maintained, play had to remain within the rules of the game. This is true at one level, but, at another level, battle-hardened, experienced athletes continue to play and enjoy the aggression and violence of games even when those games involve unsanctioned aggressive and violent acts. It would appear that these athletes have developed extra-resilient confidence frames, in the sense that they are confident that they can deal with any level of aggression and violence which occurs in games; that is, they are tough enough as fighters, or are skilful and speedy enough to generally avoid the worst incidents, or both. Safety-zone frames allow the athletes to take part in team contact sports in spite of the risk of injury from both sanctioned and unsanctioned aggression and violence. For some athletes, both types of violence are essential ingredients in team contact sports, adding to the positive psychological experience associated with playing these sports.

For experienced players, placing themselves in situations where they may take risks, encountering and having to deal with physical violence may become especially emotionally rewarding. Players who are successful at defending themselves and find themselves winning confrontations may begin to enjoy the high felt arousal and feelings of excitement and provocativeness, just for the sake of it. These feelings are associated with a metamotivational state combination of paratelic-negativistic-autic-mastery, with the paratelic state salient, and what Apter (1997) would classify as thrill violence. Team contact sport players engaging in thrill violence might be thought of as arousal seekers in the same way as might people who take part in dangerous sports like downhill skiing, snowboarding or motorcycle racing (Cogan and Brown, 1998; Kerr, 1991). These players commit acts of violence, not in anger or as part of trying to master their opponents, but rather for the immediate gratification or 'kicks' that come from fighting. If trouble starts, even if they are not involved, they will immediately join the fray in order to take advantage of the situation. If their games stay free of unsanctioned violence for too long they may also find themselves deliberately provoking trouble and fighting through acts of intimidation. It is likely that this form of violence can only be enjoyed after experience and confidence have been built up and established over a few years of a player's career, allowing them to develop a protective frame for this type of violence. In the early stages of a career, players are more likely to engage in anger or power violence. If the emotional rewards from thrill violence (also likely to include high felt toughness, high felt transactional outcome and feelings of personal pride) become strong enough, it is possible that players may develop excessive appetites for unsanctioned aggressive and violent acts.

The reversal theory-linked explanation of the development of what have been variously termed excessive appetites, dependencies or addictions, which was applied to sanctioned aggressive and violent acts in chapter 4, can equally well be applied to the type of unsanctioned aggression and violence described in this chapter (Brown, 1997; Gresswell and Hollin; 1997: Kerr, 1997).

Kerr (1997) discussed the possibility that some athletes, sometimes described as athletic psychopaths, might actually be real psychopaths, as recognised in psychology. The truth is that insufficient research has been carried out for definite conclusions to be drawn, but, in team contact sports, there is the opportunity for athletes to engage in 'abnormally aggressive or seriously irresponsible conduct'

(Gregory, 1987). It is interesting that mainstream thinking in psychology considers that this abnormally aggressive or seriously irresponsible conduct is the result of a 'persistent disorder of the mind' (e.g. Gregory, 1987) However, reversal theory argues that it is possible for an individual only to exhibit psychopathic behaviour on specific occasions. In other words, rather than being a persistent disorder or particular arrangement of personality traits, psychopathic behaviour can arise as a consequence of a certain constellation of metamotivational states being operative at particular times; just which combination of metamotivational states, and which state might be salient, is still under discussion. Apter (1982) originally argued that the paratelic and negativistic states and paratelic dominance were crucial. Later, research on psychopathic individuals (Thomas-Peter, 1988, 1993; Thomas-Peter and McDonagh, 1988) indicated that psychopaths were telic rather than paratelic dominant, but did also confirm that psychopaths were more negativistic dominant than other offenders and control group members.

If the reversal theory view of the possibility of psychopathic behaviour having a temporary nature is correct, then it may be acceptable to suggest that the term 'athletic psychopath' is also correct. Thus, a few athletes may be able to use team contact sport to further their temporary psychopathic behaviour. It is also possible that athletic psychopaths may be similar to the hardcore soccer hooligans that Kerr (1994) suggested might, on match days, be 'psychopaths for the day'. In the absence of direct evidence, this must remain as speculation, but McIntosh (1979) lends some support to the notion:

> One of the most disturbing features of modern sport, especially contact sports at the top level is the permission and even encouragement of behaviour verging on the psychopathic. This is particularly the case in failing to control or reverse the increase in violence in various codes of football.
>
> (McIntosh, 1979, pp. 102–103)

Closing comments

This chapter set out to explain the motivation behind unsanctioned aggression and violence by examining different types of intimidation and retaliation in detail. Reversal theory and Apter's (1997) conceptualisation of anger, power and thrill categories of violence provided a framework on which meaningful explanations of many different examples of unsanctioned aggression and violence in sport could be built. The three different types of violence were dealt with separately, but it is important to remember that, with reversals between states, one form of violence can easily change into another.

Much of the material in this chapter (e.g. the acceptance by coaches and players that, in certain circumstances, acts of unsanctioned violence are necessary) dealt with violent aspects of team contact sports that are not often openly discussed outside the locker rooms and team meetings. Some might see this as an unwanted, unsavoury side of team contact sports; others might think of it as just part of the reality of team contact sports. Until perhaps fairly recently, there has been a tendency in some team contact sports not to air dirty washing in public. Unsavoury matters were dealt with 'in house' and, if possible, what happened on the playing field or the ice was left there. High media profile incidents (e.g. Keane's tackle on Haarland), and sometimes subsequent legal action, are bringing these incidents out into the open. Thus, in recent years, sport administrators are being forced into greater transparency as they not only have to do something about these incidents, but also have to be seen, by interested bodies and the general public, to deal with them appropriately. This topic will be returned to in chapter 9, when more consideration will be given to legal aspects of unsanctioned aggression and violence, and attempts by particular team contact sports to eliminate them.

Part of a player's skill involves the ability to show courage in the face of possible violence and to avoid potential injury (Purcell, 2001). Like any other aspect of skill development, this must be learned in the early years of an athlete's career. The next chapter describes the development of contact skills in youth players and also explores some of the issues and problems associated with children and youth in team contact sport as they relate to aggression and violence.

References

Apter, M. J. (1982). *The experience of motivation: The theory of psychological reversals.* London: Academic Press.

Apter, M. J. (1997, July). *The experience of being violent.* Paper presented at the Eighth International Conference on Reversal Theory, University of East London.

Brink, A. (1995, 24 June). Dirty old habits die hard. *Guardian,* p. 29.

Brown, R. I. F. (1997). A theoretical model of the behavioural addictions – Applied to offending. In J. E. Hodge, M. McMurran and C. R. Hollin (Eds), *Addicted to crime,* (pp. 13–65). Chichester: John Wiley.

Campbell, D. (2002, 7 September). No remorse Keane sent off once again. *The Japan Times.*

Cogan, N. A. and Brown, R. I. F. (1998). Metamotivational dominance, states and injuries in risk and safe sports. *Personality and Individual Differences, 27,* 503–518.

Colburn, K. (1985). Honor, ritual and violence in ice hockey. *Canadian Journal of Sociology, 10,* 153–170.

Colburn, K. (1989). Deviance and legitimacy in ice hockey: A microstructural theory of violence. In D. H. Kelly (Ed.), *Deviant behaviour.* New York: St. Martins Press.

Deadline Company (Producer, in association with ESPN) (2002). *Hardball: Baseball from the inside out.* (based in part on R. Scheinin (1994). *Field of screams.*) New York: W. W. Norton.

FA throws book at Keane (2002, 17 October). *The Japan Times,* p. 24.

Gregory, R. L. (1987). *The Oxford companion to the mind.* Oxford: Oxford University Press.

Gresswell, D. M. and Hollin, C. R. (1997). Addictions and multiple murder: A behavioural perspective. In J. E. Hodge, M. McMurran and C. R. Hollin (Eds), *Addicted to crime* (pp. 139–164). Chichester: John Wiley.

Kerr, J. H. (1991). Arousal seeking in risk sport participants. *Personality and Individual Differences, 12,* 613–616.

Kerr, J. H. (1994). *Understanding soccer hooliganism.* Buckingham: Open University Press.

Kerr, J. H. (1997). *Motivation and emotion in sport: Reversal theory.* Hove: Psychology Press.

McIntosh, P. (1979). *Fair play: Ethics in sport and education.* London: Heinemann.

Murphy, A. (1998, 16 March). Fighting for a living. *Sports Illustrated,* pp. 43–45.

Patmore, A. (1979). *Playing on their nerves: The sport experiment.* London: Stanley Paul & Co. Ltd.

Purcell, I. (2001, 25 May). Personal communication.

Silver, M. (1998, 26 October). Dirty dogs. The NFL's dirtiest players: Who they are, what they do. *Sports Illustrated,* pp. 45–57.

Smith, M. D. (1983). *Violence and sport.* Toronto: Butterworths.

Spracklen, K. (1996, July). *Playing the ball: Constructing community and masculine identity in rugby.* Unpublished doctoral dissertation, Leeds Metropolitan University, Leeds.

Stocks, G. (1995, 21 November). Class act left his stamp on Hawks. *The West Australian,* p. 83.

Thomas-Peter, B. A. (1988). Psychopathy and telic dominance. In M. J. Apter, J. H. Kerr and M. P. Cowles (Eds), *Progress in reversal theory* (pp. 235–244). Amsterdam: Elsevier.

Thomas-Peter, B. A. (1993). Negativism and the classification of psychopathy. In J. H. Kerr, S. Murgatroyd and M. J. Apter (Eds), *Advances in reversal theory* (pp. 313–324). Amsterdam: Swets and Zeitlinger.

Thomas-Peter, B. A. and McDonagh, J. D. (1988). Motivational dominance in psychopaths. *British Journal of Clinical Psychology, 27,* 153–158.

Thompson, C. (1995). *Born on the wrong side.* Edinburgh: Pentland Press. Cited in K. Spracklen (1996, July). *Playing the ball: Constructing community and masculine identity in rugby.* Unpublished doctoral dissertation, Leeds Metropolitan University, Leeds.

Weinstein, M. D., Smith, M. D. and Wiesenthal, D. L. (1995). Masculinity and hockey violence. *Sex Roles, 33,* 831–847.

6 Taking the hard knocks
Children's and youth sport

This chapter examines aspects of the involvement of young athletes in team contact sports. It begins with a discussion of some of the difficulties that arise when adult models of sport are imposed on children's and youth sports. These include, for example, problems associated with a coach's emphasis on winning, young athletes' attitudes to the use of unsanctioned aggression and violence, and the moral responsibility of the coach. The chapter goes on to explain how reversal theory's metamotivational concepts can be used as a basis for developing optimal learning experiences for young athletes. In addition, it describes how young athletes learn to enjoy physical contact and charts the stages involved in this process, as well as providing an explanation of the psychological changes that accompany them. Finally, the problem of injuries involving young athletes in team contact sport is discussed, using the introduction of additional safety measures in Canadian ice hockey to illustrate how unexpected outcomes may occur.

The state of play in children's and youth sport

There is a difference between adult-organised sports for children, and youth- and child-organised activities that take place on the street or in the local park. In the latter, the emphasis is on playing and having fun, rules are minimal, scoring unimportant, the players are self-regulating and supervisory parents or officials unnecessary. In the former, the opposite is true; the emphasis is on taking the game seriously, rules are rigorously enforced by officials, winning is very important and coaches and parents dictate who plays, which position they play and for how long they play in any game. The elements of fun, playfulness and spontaneity that should be a part of children's and youth sport have diminished to such an extent that they have almost been totally obliterated (e.g. Gilroy, 1993; Smoll, 1986). For example, Michael McClenaghen (2003), involved in ice hockey coaching in Canada, drew attention to this problem in a letter to *The Vancouver Sun* newspaper, in which he stated:

> It's time for us to stop talking about whether to allow body-checking in hockey programs where young participants are clearly not at the physical

or psychological developmental stage to be able to handle this part of the game. We need to wake up and make changes in children's sport that respect the needs and the rights of the young people who play them. Some of these needs are to have fun and play, make friends, learn new skills and develop existing skills, and to be challenged through fair competition. Children are telling us what they want in their sports but adults are too obsessed with imposing adult models of sport on young people who just want to play.

(McClenaghen, 2003, p. C13)

Parents and coaches are generally far too serious about children's sport participation and they are imposing adult models of sport on the children, when research has shown that all children want to do is take part with friends and have fun (e.g. Roberts and Treasure, 1992; Weiss and Chaumerton, 1992). Incidents recently reported in the media have illustrated the increasingly serious attitude to children's sport: a parent in the US (whose son was not actually playing) who ran onto a soccer pitch and punched an opposing high school player; a father of a 13-year-old rugby player in New Zealand who, standing on the sidelines, tripped an opposing player who was about to score a try; and a Canadian mother who decided to sue her son's ice hockey coach because he chose another goalie to play in an important match. The pendulum in children's and youth sport has swung too far to the serious side and some redress is necessary (e.g. Gilroy, 1993; Roberts and Treasure, 1992; Smoll, 1986; Weiss and Chaumerton, 1992).

This serious approach to youth sport is reflected in current attitudes to aggression and violence. Many coaches, administrators and players involved in professional sport would argue that young players need to have a taste of the reality of team contact sports early in their careers in order to see if they are made of the right stuff for progressing to higher levels. Tough coaching regimes are seen as a necessary part of the hardening and filtering process which allows the most talented, physically strong and mentally tough to rise to the top. This 'taste' would include having regular experience of intense competitiveness and sanctioned (or even unsanctioned) acts of aggression and violence. In their view, athletes need to learn how to deal with the reality of their particular team contact sport early in their careers, so that it will not be a problem later on. This approach raises a number of fundamental and crucial questions. For example, what is the best age for this filtering process to begin? Do all players have to go through it? Are some coaches working with younger athletes pushing them too hard too soon with regard to the physicality of their sports? What effect does a coach's emphasis on winning have on young athletes' attitudes to the use of unsanctioned aggression and violence?

Young athletes and the use of unsanctioned violence

Based on their investigations of over a thousand children and adolescents aged from 8 to 19 years, Conroy *et al.* (2001) found that violence and aggressive behaviour is encouraged and rewarded as part of the normal socialisation in collision sports, especially where the violent and aggressive behaviour is seen as a functional act which is designed to increase the probability of winning. The researchers compared the responses of those from their sample who had engaged in so-called collision (e.g. ice hockey, American football), contact (basketball, women's field hockey, soccer), or non-contact (baseball, golf, tennis) sports and some respondents who were non-participants. In this study, participants were found to be more tolerant of aggression when the probability of punishment was low or the instrumental value of the aggression was high, and aggression was found to be perceived as being more acceptable when an athlete was competing at higher levels of sport.

Smith (1979), some twenty years earlier, undertook a similar kind of study on the legitimacy of violence in ice hockey. He asked three groups of young ice hockey players (minor midget through juvenile, Pee Wee through Bantam, and Junior B and Junior A) to respond to the following statements:

> 'If you want to get personal recognition in hockey it helps to play rough. People in hockey look for this'; 'Roughing up the other team might mean getting a few penalties, but in the long run it often helps you win'; 'Most people in hockey don't respect a player who will not fight when he is picked on'; 'To be successful most hockey teams need at least one or two tough guys who are always ready to fight.'

Young athletes from all three groups indicated widespread agreement with these statements, and their level of agreement increased with age.

If the results obtained by Conroy et al. (2001) and Smith (1979) can be generalised to other groups in other team contact sports, it would appear that young athletes are very much aware of the nature of acts of aggression and violence in sport and perceive them as expected and legitimate under certain circumstances. However, there is no evidence that young athletes carry these perceptions about the legitimacy of violence over into everyday life. Rather the opposite is true, as, Conroy et al. pointed out:

> From a moral reasoning perspective, however, this relationship between competitive level and perceptions of legitimacy may be interpreted as an extension of Bredemeier and Shields' (1986) concept of bracketed morality. Not only is there a difference in perceptions of legitimacy between sport and life contexts, but also there may be differences in perceived legitimacy as a function of the level of competition.
>
> (Conroy et al., 2001, p. 415)

Evidence from a recent study of violence and high school sports participation (Levin et al., 1995) adds some support to the notion of athletes being able to differentiate between sport and everyday life with regard to the legitimacy of using unsanctioned violence. In this study, contact sport athletes and non-athletes were found to be similar in terms of their participation in non-sports-related violent (assaulting other people in an offensive and antagonistic manner) or delinquent behaviour (damaging property, stealing, carrying a weapon). In other words, the aggression and violence that athletes encounter in contact sports does not appear to make them more aggressive and violent in everyday life than non-athletes. The authors concluded that:

> The data presented here . . . do not support the contention that contact sports breed violence and delinquency.
>
> (Levin *et al.*, 1995, p. 386)

Coaches and moral responsibility

One of the arguments put forward to explain the discrepancy between moral reasoning in sport and in everyday life is that coaches and officials have the power of decision and moral responsibility in sport. Therefore, athletes temporarily abdicate their own moral responsibility to the coach (Shields and Bredemeier, 1989). As the authority figure, the coach then tends to transfer his values in terms of moral climate and attitude towards winning to the young athletes. If the team environment is one which encourages inappropriate action in pursuit of winning, then young athletes will tend to conform to the view that inappropriate behaviours are acceptable (Dunn and Dunn, 1999). They also report their intention to engage in inappropriate acts, and engage in them with greater frequency, when they perceive a team environment which permits or encourages unsanctioned acts of aggression and violence (Kavussanu *et al.*, 2002). In a nutshell, the results of these studies point to coaches as a (or even the) major influence on their young athletes in the use (or not) of unsanctioned aggression and violence in sport.

Teachers and coaches working with children are generally considered to have a duty of care to protect the children from unnecessary and unreasonable risks and, in the UK at least, are understood to be *in loco parentis*. In addition, they are supposed to have high moral standards and operate under a code of ethics. Take, for example, this quote from the American Football Coaches' Association code of ethics adopted, just over 50 years ago, in 1952:

> The welfare of the game depends on how the coaches live up to the spirit and letter of ethical conduct and how coaches remain ever mindful of the high trust and confidence placed in them by their players and by the public. Coaches unwilling or unable to comply with the principles of the Code of Ethics have no place in the profession.
>
> (Bricknell, 1989, p. 138)

When children and youth become involved in and continue to participate in team contact sport, the hope is that they will gain from their experience. The opportunities are there for players to benefit physically, psychologically, socially and perhaps morally. Some young athletes may even benefit financially later in their careers. However, not all who try participating in team contact sports enjoy the possible benefits. For some, the experience may be potentially damaging, rather than adding to their personal development. Keeping these concerns in mind, educator and philosopher Peter McIntosh's thoughts on competitive sport provide some reassurance, if at the same time raising an important related issue:

> The strongest argument for compulsory competitive sport seems to me that in a competitive society defeat, failure, and humiliation are as inevitable as victory, success and self-satisfaction, and that in a well-organised and controlled sporting programme both kinds of experience can be had by children without irreparable psychological or physical damage being done. The weakness of this argument is that such a society is not inevitable or necessarily desirable and that by socialising children into it we may be acquiescing in what we believe to be wrong. The choices in moral education cannot be divorced from moral choices in and for society at large.
>
> (McIntosh, 1979, p. 179)

Given McIntosh's views about the resilience of young people, it might be prudent for coaches to keep in mind that good coaching can increase the performance potential of children, give enjoyment and contribute to their development as people (Lee, 1993). To achieve this, Lee (1993) argued, coaches need to be clear about their motives for coaching; they need to examine their own value systems and the relationship between their motives, values and behaviour. At the same time, coaches need to understand their athletes' motives and values and should be aware of the values they are transmitting to the athletes in their care. The importance of the coach as a role model should not be underestimated. Many of those who have been coached in sports as children or youth know this to be true and will acknowledge the tremendous influence that a coach or coaches had on them.

Using reversal theory concepts to provide balance in coaching and optimal learning experiences for young athletes

There is a tendency for some teachers, coaches and parents to maintain a telic-conformist-autic-mastery metamotivational 'adult sport climate' around children's and youth sports activities. Reversal theory would argue that it is important to strike a balance in metamotivational experience by facilitating at least occasional reversals to partner states. Kerr illustrated this point by stating:

> It is interesting that, unlike adults, young athletes often show a concern for their opponents. However, this sympathy for others, it seems, does not take long to disappear. The same kind of attitude from sport educators that drives young athletes and teams to focus on defeating opponents, also encourages them to think of their participation in sport purely from their own point of

view. Opponents are disparaged and some coaches even try to foster in their athletes an active dislike for other competitors.

(Kerr, 2001, p. 30)

The message from reversal theory for coaches (and parents) is that there are liable to be considerable psychological benefits to young athletes if their activities can be balanced across all four pairs of states. On some occasions, sports activities need to be approached in a serious and composed manner, but on other occasions they should be perceived as interesting, fun activities which offer exciting challenges. Too much of the former and young athletes become over-challenged and anxious, too much of the latter and they become under-challenged and bored. Striking a balance provides young athletes with optimal learning experiences (Rea, 1995). Equally, superimposing adult norms on children's and youth sport also means that the activity takes on a 'win at all costs' orientation. The focus is on mastering opponents rather than mastering skills and techniques, and performance is evaluated in terms of competitive outcomes with others. Young athletes are not slow in picking up cues about teachers' and coaches' real expectations and soon understand what their real goals are. Game outcome is emphasised, even though individual achievement in a mastery-learning climate has been shown in sport psychology research to be important in maintaining the motivation and involvement of young athletes (e.g. Roberts and Treasure, 1992; Weiss and Chaumerton, 1992).

However, it is not desirable to completely eliminate competition from sport, especially team contact sports, where the physical nature of the sport adds an extra dimension to any competitiveness. Sanctioned aggression and violence, albeit at much less intensity than in the adult game, is perfectly acceptable. What is desirable for producing optimal learning experiences at child and youth level is a better balance between competing against opponents and against oneself in terms of learning skills and techniques. When this balance is distorted towards winning, there is a much greater likelihood of acts of unsanctioned aggression and violence taking place at this level. Indeed, research carried out by Leith (1989) on 14- to 17-year-old high school students supports this view. He used a modified version of street hockey in which both stick checking and body checking were allowed in an experiment to examine the effect of direct participation in physical activity on aggressiveness. Among other findings, he found that losing resulted in significantly more elicited aggressiveness than winning. Participants who found themselves losing became more aggressive in their efforts to win.

In the reversal theory approach, there is also a need to strive to keep a state of equilibrium between being egoistic and altruistic in children's and youth sport, between keeping the autic and alloic elements in balance. Some parents, by strongly focusing on their child's progress, rather than on their child's team or the child's particular role within the team, encourage the selfish 'me' mentality in young athletes. For example, the Canadian mother who took legal action against her son's coach showed little consideration and respect for her sons' teammates and coach, encouraging an egoistic attitude in her son.

The final element in the balanced approach to young athletes in team contact sports is for teachers, coaches and parents to take into account both the negativistic and conformist elements of metamotivation. This is difficult in sport because, much of the time, young athletes must conform to game rules and etiquette. There may be some opportunities within teaching or coaching sessions to modify the rules or change the size of the playing area which might allow the players the chance to escape from their usual restrictions and enjoy a sense of freedom for a time (e.g. rugby players might be allowed to pass the ball in all directions, rather than backwards, in small-side basketball-style games, as a variation in training). Creativity and innovation are also associated with the negativistic state and coaches may even obtain benefits from athletes having to devise creative solutions to new challenges. For example, taking advantage of the negativistic state in a productive way, athletes may be able to devise unexpected plays which will surprise opposition teams.

Balanced metamotivational experience in sport, through the provision of optimal learning environments for young athletes to develop, is likely to lead to increased possibilities for keeping more athletes motivated and involved and for reducing drop-out rates. Out of all the many thousands of young players involved in team contact sports, only a relatively small number are destined to make it to the very top of the pyramid and become elite-level athletes. However, broadening the base of the pyramid could produce a larger pool of skillful and versatile athletes and improve playing standards at top levels.

Becoming acclimatised to physical contact: An example from rugby union

One of the crucial factors in getting young athletes acclimatised to physical contact is keeping interest and motivation high by maintaining a teaching or coaching environment which provides the pleasant playful feelings that are linked with play violence and a state combination of paratelic-conformist-autic or alloic-mastery. In practice, this means that physical contact has to be introduced gradually and not become too intense too early in the experience of young beginners. Take rugby union, for example, and 7- or 8-year-olds learning tackling: soft padded tackle bags are used to get across the basic head, shoulder and arm positions and other elements of sound tackling. The young players, who usually regard this as great fun, land or fall on top of the bags, roll about and can generally avoid hurting themselves. Sometimes, starting tackle practice in a gym or sports hall, using tackle bags in combination with padded floor mats, is recommended before moving outside on to a grass pitch. When things have progressed enough and the time comes for players to learn to tackle each other, some coaches recommend that this skill should be introduced on a soft grassy pitch with players removing their boots, as some young beginners are afraid of the metal studs screwed to the sole of the rugby boots. By removing the boots, this element of fear can be eliminated. Of course, the boots have to be replaced fairly quickly as movement to the next stage takes place. Teaching progressions (both without and later with boots) begin with those being tackled first standing, then walking, jogging and finally running. Tacklers start from kneeling and 'sprint start' positions, before also moving on to walking, jogging and eventually running. They tackle opponents from the rear, side, and progress to head-on tackles from the front. By teaching in small progressive steps, young beginners not only learn how to tackle, but also build self-confidence in their ability to master the skill, and begin to conquer their fear of getting injured. All of this is designed to maximise the possibility of success by maintaining the fun element as learning progresses. Once these young athletes begin to play games, using modified rules (e.g. variations of 'touch' and partial contact rather than full contact rugby) and smaller balls and pitch sizes, young players begin to experience excitement arising from the play itself, and from discovering the pleasures of being playfully aggressive. They also begin to achieve satisfaction through their improving mastery of skills and opponents. Coaches, teachers, parents and their teammates often provide positive reinforcement, which adds to their subjective feelings of pleasure. 'During these early stages, aggression and violence may not be a major feature of their experience, but players are gradually being weaned onto a diet of physicality that will later develop into something much stronger' (Kerr, 1997, p. 124).

As these young players progress through the teams to youth and eventually second and first teams, they are well on their way to becoming established players. Levels of physicality increase steadily from early playing days through to the teenage years. Players will improve their strength, speed and overall fitness and will also develop the degree of mental toughness that is necessary to survive in the rivalry and competition for team places. It is at this stage that the ability to be aggressive and, when necessary, violent in order to dominate opponents begins to become an important part of a player's repertoire. Those players who can hit and tackle hard will be strongly encouraged to do so by their peers. Many will have already been subject to at least minor acts of intimidation and may well have engaged in acts of retaliation. Along the way, through psychological processes described in chapter 4, they will have become accustomed to high levels of physical contact during play and, with a paratelic-conformist-autic-mastery state combination frequently operative, like it. Their ability to perform contact skills successfully under pressure will provide them with increases in positive hedonic tone through enjoyment of high felt arousal, felt toughness and felt transactional outcome. Many of these players will have come to relish the sanctioned, and some the unsanctioned, aggression and violence associated with rugby union.

It would appear that similar developments take place in other team contact sports. In relation to the development of young players in ice hockey, Smith pointed out that:

> Canadian boys typically enter organized hockey around age seven. The ablest are quickly funnelled into highly competitive 'select' leagues and begin training at the end of which, around sixteen, those who remained emerge into, as Vaz (p. 212, 1976) puts it, 'a tough fighting unit prepared for violence

whose primary objective is to win hockey games'. Fighting and other illegal forms of assault (though not hard body contact) tend to be discouraged among younger boys, but around thirteen to fourteen years of age the criteria for player evaluation begin to change, for it is then that potential for junior professional and professional hockey is thought to reveal itself. By midget age (i.e. fifteen) coaches are looking for players who can mete out, and withstand, illegal physical coercion; indeed some youngsters this age are upwardly mobile primarily because they are good fighters.

(Smith, 1979, p. 76)

It is clear, however, that not everyone enjoys the physical side of team contact sports. Returning, for a moment, to our rugby union beginners in the very early stages of learning to tackle each other, it goes without saying that, in spite of the best efforts of teachers and coaches, a number will not enjoy the activity. For them, tackling, even in its watered down, 'depowered' form, is liable to be anxiety-filled and distinctly unpleasant. Unless forced by school curricula to continue with rugby union, these beginners will likely try to avoid the physicality of rugby by choosing to participate in other sports. These beginners never really come to enjoy the playful aggression associated with playing rugby. In reversal theory terms, they remain with the telic state salient, when having the paratelic state salient would be more suited to the activity, and do not feel in control enough for the mastery state to play any kind of major role. As a result, the metamotivational state combination (paratelic-conformist-autic or alloic-mastery) which is fundamental to being able to enjoy play violence is rarely, if ever, operative for them. As a result, rather than being able to enjoy high felt arousal in the form of paratelic excitement, their experience is one characterised by telic anxiety. Furthermore, the fact that they are 'scared', and do not develop skill and confidence, may add to their unpleasant feelings as their interactions with other, more competent beginners may result in feelings of shame, guilt, humiliation or resentment as the influence of the transactional states unfold.

This was true for student participants in a reversal theory study which compared physical education classes involving easy running, basketball, and rugby union (Kerr and Svebak, 1994). Although not in the 7- to 8-year-old age bracket, these students were relatively inexperienced as far as rugby union was concerned. In the rugby union class, students participated in a warm-up, intensive tackle practice and a period of full contact competitive play; in basketball, warming up, skills practice and competitive play; while in the third class, students in small groups ran at a comfortable pace in a non-competitive way. The students completed a psychological questionnaire (the Tension and Effort Stress Inventory; e.g. Svebak et al., 1991) just before and immediately after the classes. The results indicated that, in the rugby union group, pleasant emotions decreased significantly, unpleasant emotions increased significantly and the greatest increases in stress and effort were found after playing rugby. Compared with the other two sports, the largest pre- to post-session changes were found in rugby. It seems likely that it is only over the longer term that beneficial changes to positive affect, described in chapter 4, can be acquired through playing rugby union and then, perhaps, only to regular and/or more experienced athletes (Kerr and van Schaik, 1995; Wilson and Kerr, 1999).

Relatively few athletes reach the top levels of their particular team contact sport. Many more withdraw along the way. Although there are other reasons why this occurs, for many young athletes it is for reasons related to some aspect of the hard physical contact that drives them away. Withdrawal from a team contact sport because of an inability to handle the physical nature of the sport is perfectly possible at any stage in an athlete's career. Often this occurs when the player's paratelic safety-zone protective frame has been ruptured or broken, perhaps as a result of being injured, observing another player being seriously injured, or even having been the target of unsanctioned violence. This may lead to the loss of the feelings of confidence that are associated with the confidence frame. The loss of the protective frames may be limited to a specific period within a game, endure over a few games, or, in the worst cases, be impossible to reinstate at all. If this occurs, the athlete involved will likely abandon his or her team contact sport.

Young athletes, physical contact and injuries

Team contact sports do involve physical contact and there is always the risk that young athletes may be injured. Concern with severe injuries has led the authorities in some team contact sports to allow the use of protective headgear, or to modify the rules in an attempt to reduce the chance of injury. For example, in Japan, rugby union players at high school level or below must wear protective headgear and rules concerning the scrum have been changed so that a team may not push the opposition scrum back more than one metre. Sanctioned aggressive and violent acts are acceptable at this level, but these types of changes are aimed at reducing the 'intensity' of these acts with the idea of preventing severe injuries. Possibly adding to the problem, for younger players, are the mismatches in physiological maturation which result in large differences in height, weight, strength and speed among players of the same chronological age. In an attempt to deal with this problem, some countries, like New Zealand, have tried organising games in rugby union on the basis of size and weight, rather like the weight divisions that occur in judo and some other contact sports. A related but more recent problem in New Zealand rugby union, concerning ethnic differences in physiological maturation between young Polynesian athletes and those whose background is European, has caused increasing numbers of 'European' parents to take their children out of rugby because they consider them at too big a risk of injury from their earlier maturing, and therefore physically bigger (sometimes much bigger) Polynesian peers (Nauright and Chandler, 1996, p. 214; 'White flight', 2001).

Where severe injuries have taken place, they have generally occurred as 'accidents' during play as a result of play violence. Unfortunately, however, occasional acts of unsanctioned violence in youth sport which have led to severe injuries do come to light. Fifteen-year-old ice hockey player Neal Goss was paralysed from the chest down after one such incident in suburban Chicago. Apparently, after scoring a hat-trick in New Trier's 7–4 victory over Glenbrook North, Goss was cross-checked from behind after the game had ended and he was about to leave the ice (Swift and Munson, 1999). The illegal hit drove him head-first into the boards. The perpetrator was charged with two counts of aggravated battery. The Goss family lawyer also brought a civil suit against the perpetrator and his coach, Adam Smith, who, it is claimed 'persistently heckled and derided Goss' and encouraged his players to 'target [Goss] during as well as after the game' (Swift and Munson, 1999, p. 34).

Tragic incidents like the one involving Neal Goss have focused attention on the controversial issue of body checking in Canadian children's and youth ice hockey. Unexpected checks from behind in ice hockey are thought to be the leading cause of spinal injuries, especially when the player strikes the boards with his head. As recently as February 2003, there was a huge outcry in Canada about a recommendation by the Canadian Hockey Association (CHA) to lower the age of body checking to players aged 9 in the 'Atom' leagues. This led to calls by provincial ministers, coaches, parents and others to eliminate body checking not only from Atom and Pee Wee leagues, but also in the one-year-older Bantam leagues (Mason, 2003). Following the protests, in May 2003 the annual general meeting of the CHA's board of directors approved a motion that increased the age for body checking back up to 11- and 12-year-olds playing at Pee Wee level.

Just about a year before the controversy over body checking in young Canadian ice hockey players arose, a special video entitled *Smart hockey: More safety, more fun*, geared specifically to Atom, Pee Wee and Bantam league players, was telecast nationally on the TSN channel and digitally on the National Hockey League (NHL) network. A number of groups were involved with the production of the safety video, made with the cooperation of the NHL, including Canadian spinal research organisations, equipment manufacturers, commercial sponsors, the NHL Players' Association and the Canadian Hockey Association. The stimulating video, full of action shots, interviews and tips from current and former NHL star players, aimed at reducing brain and spinal cord injuries in young hockey players, is very effective. A major theme of the video was 'never to hit from behind' (especially in the danger zone 3 to 4 feet from the boards) or have arms or stick up checking high to the head or face. Young players are given advice on how to avoid injury when they find themselves in these situations. On the negative side, however, no real advice is given to young players about how they should try to deal with the emotional side of playing; advice that might, for example, have dealt with how players should handle the pressure in important games where the scores are very close, what they should do in situations where they might get angry with an opponent, and how they might cope with the disappointment of losing, or being dropped from a team's starting line-up.

It is interesting to consider the introduction of safety measures in Canadian ice hockey and subsequent developments. In the early 1960s five players died from head injuries, and helmets were made mandatory in Canadian amateur hockey in

1965. However, a surprising turn of events took place. The newly mandatory helmets prevented deaths, but the medical authorities noted that the number of concussions increased noticeably after they were introduced. Helmets gave players the idea that opponents were protected and could not be hurt and that they themselves were invincible. As a direct consequence, reckless checking and hitting increased dramatically. Similarly, since face shields came in, there have been increases in high sticking and elbows to the head and, over the last 15 to 20 years, referees have not been calling penalties on high hits to the head and face as often as they should (*Smart hockey: More safety, more fun*, 2002).

In terms of reversal theory's paratelic protective frames, each time an additional piece of protective equipment (helmets and later face shields) was introduced, players' safety-zone and confidence frames became enhanced or reinforced. Players' feelings of security and confidence increased and a belief that they and their opponents were better protected from injury led to more and more reckless, risky behaviour, in the form of unsanctioned acts of violence. In this unexpected way, the addition of safety equipment designed to prevent injuries and make the game safer actually had the opposite effect, resulting in both an increase in unsanctioned acts of violence and an increase in a different type of injury.

Closing comments

The first five chapters in this book have generally focused on aggression and violence as it relates to athletes in the playing arena. To recap, chapter 1 explored several examples of different types of aggression and violence in sports, most of which were returned to as the discussion unfolded in subsequent chapters. In addition, definitions of aggression and violence were explored and previous theories on aggression and violence were reviewed. Chapter 3 dealt with reversal theory's different types of violence, along with some illustrative examples from sport, and laid the groundwork for the reversal theory explanations and interpretations of athlete behaviour which follow later in the book. In chapter 4, a detailed look at different aspects of physical contact and sanctioned aggressive and violent acts was undertaken, which specified the special role that play violence plays in team contact sports. In chapter 5, unsanctioned aggression and violence, in the form of intimidation and retaliation, were examined; anger, thrill, and power violence came to the fore. In the current chapter, a number of important issues concerning young athletes in team contact sports were addressed. In the next chapter, however, the discussion moves away from athletes to concentrate on aggression and violence in sports spectators, supporters, or fans and the riots that have taken place at some sporting events.

References

Bredemeier, B. J. and Shields, D. L. (1986). Game reasoning and interactional morality. *Journal of General Psychology, 147*, 257–275.

Bricknell, J. (1989). The coaching responsibility. In R. E. Lapchick and J. B. Slaughter (Eds), *The rules of the game: Ethics in college sport*. New York: Macmillan.

Conroy, D. E., Silva, J. M., Newcomer, R. R., Walker, B. W. and Johnson, M. S. (2001). Personal and participatory socializers of the perceived legitimacy of aggressive behavior in sport. *Aggressive Behavior, 27*, 405–418.

Dunn, J. G. H. and Dunn, J. C. (1999). Goal orientations, perceptions of aggression and sportspersonship in elite male youth ice hockey players. *The Sport Psychologist, 13*, 183–200.

Gilroy, S. (1993). Whose sport is it anyway? Adults and children's sport. In M. Lee (Ed.), *Coaching children in sport: Principles and practice* (pp. 17–26). London: E. & F. Spon.

Kavussanu, M., Roberts, G. C. and Ntoumanis, N. (2002). Contextual influences on moral functioning of college basketball players. *The Sport Psychologist, 16*, 347–367.

Kerr, J. H. (1997). *Motivation and emotion in sport: Reversal theory*. Hove, England: Psychology Press.

Kerr, J. H. (2001). The importance of psychology for the future of sport education. In *Proceedings of the Japanese Society of Sport Education International Conference*, Osaka (pp. 27–34).

Kerr, J. H. and Svebak, S. (1994). The acute effects of participation in sport on mood: The importance of level of 'antagonistic physical interaction'. *Personality and Individual Differences, 16*, 159–166.

Kerr, J. H. and van Schaik, P. (1995). Effects of game venue and outcome on psychological mood states in rugby. *Personality and Individual Differences, 19*, 407–410.

Lee, M. (1993). Why are you coaching children? In M. Lee (Ed.), *Coaching children in sport: Principles and practice* (pp. 27–38). London: E. & F. Spon.

Leith, L. M. (1989). The effect of various physical activities, outcome and emotional arousal on subject aggression scores. *International Journal of Sport Psychology, 20*, 57–66.

Levin, D. S., Smith, E. A., Caldwell, L. L. and Kimbrough, J. (1995). Violence and high school sports participation. *Pediatric Exercise Science, 7*, 379–388.

Mason, G. (2003, 20 February). Hockey head leads charge to check body checks. *The Vancouver Sun*, p. C9.

McClenaghen, M. (2003, 20 February). No body checking for children [Letter to the editor]. *The Vancouver Sun*, p. C13.

McIntosh, P. (1979). *Fair play: Ethics in sport and education*. London: Heinemann.

Nauright, J. and Chandler, T. J. L. (Eds) (1996). *Making men: Rugby and masculine identity*. London: Frank Cass.

Rea, D. (1995). Motivating at-risk students with serious fun. In D. Rea and R. Warkentin (Eds), *Youth at risk: Reaching for success* (pp. 22–36). Dubuque, IA: Brown & Benchmark.

Roberts, G. C. and Treasure, D. C. (1992). Children in sport. *Sport Science Review, 1*, 46–64.

Shields, D. L. and Bredemeier, B. J. (1989). Moral reasoning, judgement, and action. In J. Goldstein (Ed.), *Sports, games and play: Social and psychological viewpoints* (pp. 59–81). Hillsdale, NJ: Erlbaum.

Smart hockey: More safety, more fun (2002, January). Presented by TD Waterhouse, Think First Canada and the TSN television channel.

Smith, M. D. (1979). Social determinants of violence in hockey: A review. *Canadian Journal of Applied Sport Science, 4*, 76–82.

Smoll, F. L. (1986). Coach-parent relationships: Enhancing the quality of the athlete's sport experience. In J. M. Williams (Ed.), *Applied sport psychology: Personal growth to peak performance* (pp. 47–58). Palo Alto, CA: Mayfield Publishing Company.

Svebak, S., Ursin, H., Endresen, I., Hjelmen, A. M. and Apter, M. J. (1991). Back pain and the experience of stress, efforts and moods. *Psychology and Health, 5,* 307–314.

Swift, E. M. and Munson, L. (1999, 20 December). Paralyzing hit. *Sports Illustrated,* 34–35.

Vaz, E. W. (1976). The culture of young hockey players: Some initial observations. In A. Yiannakis, T. D., McIntyre, M. J. Melnick and D. P. Hart (Eds), *Sport sociology: Contemporary themes* (pp. 211–215). Dubuque, IA: Kendall-Hunt.

Weiss, M. R. and Chaumerton, N. (1992). Motivational orientations in sport. In T. S. Horn (Ed.), *Advances in sport psychology* (pp. 61–99). Champaign, IL: Human Kinetics.

'White flight' in New Zealand rugby (2001, January). *New Zealand Rugby.* Cited on Planet-rugby.com website.

Wilson, G. V. and Kerr, J. H. (1999). Affective responses to success and failure: A study of winning and losing in rugby. *Personality and Individual Differences, 27,* 85–99.

7 Beyond the pale

Fan violence and sports riots

Any psychology-based study of aggression and violence in sport must give some attention to aggression and violence among team supporters or fans, and this chapter focuses on that topic. While this form of aggression and violence can sometimes be prompted by violent action involving players, or other events during a game, sport-related disturbances and riots often occur for other reasons. It is necessary, therefore, to examine the aggressive and violent behaviour of supporters or fans as separate phenomenon.

The first part of this chapter discusses fan violence and sports riots in general, applying reversal theory to develop a new typology of sports riots. The second and third sections are concerned with probably the most enduring form of sports violence and rioting, soccer hooliganism. No chapter on sport fan violence would be complete without some reference to soccer hooliganism. It is ten years since *Understanding soccer hooliganism*, the first book to use reversal theory to explain soccer hooligan behaviour, was published in 1994. In those ten years, soccer hooliganism has continued almost unabated in several European countries. Among those countries is the Netherlands, and the second part of this chapter is comprised of a study of a large soccer hooligan confrontation there, where one man was killed and several others seriously injured. Soccer hooliganism has also been a cause for concern at major international soccer tournaments during this period. The World Cups in France in 1998 and Euro 2000 in Belgium–Holland both had major soccer hooligan incidents. The third part of the chapter examines events around World Cup Korea–Japan 2002, where no real soccer hooligan incidents took place in either country during that tournament in spite of the fact that the England team were playing.

In the discussion that follows, 'spectators' are defined as those who go to watch matches for the enjoyment of the play without having a particular allegiance to either team, 'fans and supporters' as those who attend games for enjoyment, but who have followed a team for some time and have an emotionally vested interest in a team's success or failure, and 'hooligans' (most often associated with soccer) as those who attend games primarily to engage in aggressive and violent behaviour. Although hooligans may claim to be passionate followers of a team, they utilise this affiliation as a kind of flag of convenience to accommodate their fighting.

A new typology of sports fan violence and riots

Attempts have been made to categorise different types of sports riots into group-ings with common characteristics. Mann (1979) and Smith (1983) have both proposed typologies of sports riots. As shown in Table 7.1 Mann (1979) had five separate categories of riots: *frustration, outlawry, confrontational, remonstrance,* and *expressive* riots. Smith (1983) had a continuum of six overlapping categories of riots: *defeat, entry, confrontation, demonstration, victory* and *time-out* riots. Examining the characteristics of these sports riots, it would appear that Mann's expressive (anger) riots share common ground with his frustration category, while within Smith's typology of riots, the motivation behind entry and defeat, and victory and time-out riots are similar, apart from the situational aspects of the labels. There would also appear to be considerable overlap between the two typologies. For example, from the descriptions, Smith's category of demonstration riots is similar to Mann's remonstrance riots, Smith's separate categories of victory and time-out riots would fit into Mann's expressive (euphoria) category, and Smith's defeat or entry category might match up with Mann's frustration or expressive (anger) grouping.

While these typologies have been of use, crowd disturbances and riots can also be classified using a new reversal theory typology. One advantage of the reversal theory typology is that, unlike either of the other typologies, it is based on a comprehensive general psychological theory which views riotous behaviour in a systematic way, and, unlike Smith's (1983) typology, the classification is based on the motivation behind crowd disturbances, rather than situational variables concerned with, for example, when the riot happened or game outcome. As shown in Table 7.1, both Mann's (1979) and Smith's (1983) categories of sports riots can easily be incorporated into the reversal theory typology.

In chapter 3, the four different reversal theory forms of violence (Apter, 1997) were explained. These were *anger, thrill, power,* and *play* violence and each was associated with particular combinations of metamotivational states where certain states were salient: anger violence with a telic-negativistic state combination prominent; thrill violence, a paratelic-negativistic combination; power violence, a telic-mastery combination; and play violence, a combination in which paratelic and mastery states were the most important. Earlier in this book, these four types of violence were applied to aggression and violence among athletes, but they can equally well be applied to crowd disturbances and sports fan riots. Some examples, associated with recent sports events, will serve to illustrate the different types of fan riots and violence involved in the proposed new reversal theory typology.

Anger riots

When trouble occurred at a Jacksonville versus Cleveland National Football League American football game, it was a decision by an official during the game that prompted a violent response from fans ('Brownout in Cleveland', 2001). Jacksonville were leading Cleveland 15–10 in the final minute of the game when

Table 7.1 A new reversal theory-based typology of crowd disturbances or sports riots

Reversal theory typology	Salient metamotivational combination	Mann's (1979) typology	Smith's (1983) typology*	Characteristics
Anger riots	Telic-negativistic	Frustration riots Expressive (anger) riots	Defeat riots Entry riots	Angry, violent reaction to some restriction or perceived unfairness
Thrill riots	Paratelic-negativistic	Outlawry riots Confrontation riots	Confrontation riots [Defeat riots Entry riots]	Vandalism or fighting between rival fan groups; arousal or thrill-seeking behaviour
Power riots	Telic-mastery	Remonstrance riots	Demonstration riots	Serious attempts to gain power over sports authorities and police to further a cause (the end justifies the means)
Play riots	Paratelic-mastery	Expressive (euphoria) riots	Victory riots Time-out riots	Aggressive attempts to dominate, engaged in as a kind of game; largely for fun

*Note: Several of Smith's categories of riots (defeat, entry, victory, time-out) could be placed in different categories depending on the presence or absence of negativism and/or anger.

officials, having initially allowed play to continue, decided to review a previous play on the television review monitor and, with just 48 seconds left in the game, overturned a call denying Cleveland a first down at Jacksonville's nine yard line. Beer bottles and cups of ice were thrown at Jacksonville players and game officials, and they had to run for safety. 'We feared for our lives,' wide receiver Jimmy Smith said. 'It was like dodging bullets' ('Brownout in Cleveland', 2001). As a result of the incident, play was suspended for approximately 30 minutes. After this unscheduled break, when many fans had left and things had settled down, only Jacksonville's offence and Cleveland's defence returned to the field to play out the remaining 48 seconds of the game.

This incident is a good example of reversal theory's anger riots category. Anger riots often involve a sudden reaction to something considered to be restrictive, unfair or incorrect, which provokes fans to reverse to the telic-negativistic state combination and leads to an angry reaction. In this regard, it is the reactive element of negativism which is important. Cleveland Fans reacted to an official's decision which denied their team a last-minute chance to win. Anger is a high felt arousal emotion and, in this case, was likely to be accompanied by intense feelings of felt negativism and felt identification, as the alloic state was also possibly operative.

Thrill riots

The example, in chapter 1, of crowd trouble at a Parramatta versus Canterbury Bulldogs rugby league match in Australia, provides a good illustration of a thrill riot. After the game, beer cans, tools and other items were thrown at police, and rowdy behaviour and assaults occurred as violent spectators left the Parramatta stadium. Police blamed Canterbury Bulldogs' supporters, who had a previous history of fighting and vandalism, similar to soccer hooligans, for causing the trouble ('Spectators turn', 2001).

In thrill violence and riots, a paratelic-negativistic state combination is prominent. Negativism here is likely to be of the proactive variety, which means that individuals have a desire to be rebellious and break the rules just for the hell of it. In thrill riots, the paratelic-negativistic combination produces a desire for stimulating and entertaining situations, while in anger riots the telic state gives the negativistic element a much more serious orientation. Another example of reversal theory's thrill riot category will be found later in this chapter, where a Dutch soccer hooligan confrontation is discussed.

Play riots

In Maryland, university fans set bonfires and shot off fireworks to celebrate their team's 64–52 victory over Indiana University in the US College Basketball Championships. Police on horseback pushed thousands of revellers, ecstatic over the school's first National Collegiate Athletic Association (NCAA) basketball championship, off the streets. About ten people were arrested as police tried to regain control ('Indiana fans', 2002). Similarly, after the 2003 NCAA ice hockey championship final, in which Minnesota beat New Hampshire 5–1 in Buffalo, New York, winning Minnesota fans threw bottles and rocks, smashed store windows and set trash bins on fire. Police arrested 11 people after the celebration caused damage to shops near the university ('Fans riot', 2003). These celebrations by fans after a victory that turn violent are good examples of play riots.

In play riots, the crucial metamotivational state combination is paratelic-mastery. Fans experience high felt arousal as pleasant excitement, but also high levels of felt toughness as they vicariously experience the power and mastery of their team over the losing team and opposing fans. The alloic state is also likely to be operative and, as a result, fans will have a sense of high felt identification and allegiance with their team. The conformist state may also be operative as fans congregate and go along with the actions of the crowd.

Power riots

Power riots in sport often involve political or ideological groups, who 'hijack' sports events to make serious protests about their causes. There have not been many examples of this type of riot in recent years, and those protests which have taken place around sports events have largely been peaceful, though some of the violent anti-hunt protests by animal rightists that have taken place at fox hunting meets in England in recent years might come into the category of power riots. There is also some anecdotal evidence that some of these protesters, unconcerned about the real cause, come from hooligan-type elements who latch on to fox hunting protests in the hope of provoking violence. If this is correct, these individuals would be taking part for the thrill rather than to further a cause.

Power riots were common at sports events in the late 1970s and early 1980s, when the anti-apartheid movement disrupted and forced cancellations in sports events between South Africa and other countries. For example, there were huge demonstrations at each match on the 1981 South African rugby union tour of New Zealand. At Hamilton, hundreds of protestors occupied the stadium and forced the cancellation of the match. The New Zealand public was shocked by scenes of fortress-like stadiums behind barbed wire and police beating and fighting with protestors (Nauright and Black, 1996).

Telic-mastery is the influential metamotivational state combination in the case of power riots. The rioters are very serious about their activities, often believing passionately in their cause. This, along with their determined efforts to disrupt or prevent an activity taking place, means that the mastery state must be operative and they will be experiencing high levels of felt significance and felt toughness. It is also likely that the alloic state will be added to the telic-mastery state combination, as the individuals concerned will have very strong feelings of felt identification with their cause and the other people rioting with them. These rioters will be convinced that they are 'in the right' and any means justifies the end.

Difficulties in categorising riotous behaviour

As with the different forms of violence, it is possible for a riot to change from one type to another as situational or environmental factors change. Play or thrill riots could easily become anger riots if the appropriate reversals take place. For example, measures taken by the police, like firing pepper or tear gas at groups of rioting fans, may induce reversals, angry reactions may occur and the police may become the targets of anger violence.

It should also be pointed out that, without actually having access to the thoughts of the rioting fans, it is impossible to know their real motivation for causing trouble. Consequently, the examples of actual sports riots that were placed under the sub-headings for anger, thrill and play riots are done so with caution. In addition, in any group of rioting fans, individual motivation may differ. For example, while the majority of individuals may be participating in what might generally be categorised as a play riot, some individuals may actually be experiencing anger. This is quite acceptable under reversal theory, which emphasises the importance of individual subjective experience, and should not detract from the general categorisation of crowd disturbances and sports riots in which large groups of people will have similar metamotivational profiles at the time of the riot.

It is interesting that the play riots by winning basketball and ice hockey fans, in Maryland and Minnesota respectively, mentioned earlier, were mirrored by riots by losing fans in Indiana and New Hampshire. In Indiana, basketball fans torched couches, toppled street signs and threw beer bottles at police officers. Police used tear gas to disperse a crowd in Bloomington, Indiana and arrested about 30 students on charges including public intoxication, criminal mischief and disorderly conduct ('Indiana fans', 2002). Losing New Hampshire hockey fans also became violent. New Hampshire police fired pepper gas into a bottle-throwing crowd of about 4,000 people in the downtown area of Durham, New Hampshire and arrested 90 people ('Fans riot', 2003).

These two examples, where both winning and losing fans rioted, illustrate the difficulty in categorising riotous behaviour. Although the behaviour of the fans might seem similar, the underlying motivation might well be different. The riots by the losing Indiana and New Hampshire fans could be examples of either anger or thrill violence. Categorisation depends on the motivation behind the riots and whether or not anger was involved. If the fans were rioting as an angry reaction to losing, then they are additional examples of an anger riot. If, however, they were rioting just for the hell of it, or for kicks, then both incidents could be placed in the thrill riot category.

Unlike sport in Europe, especially soccer, where often large numbers of fans travel to support their team at away games, it is less common for fans to travel in North America (Roadburg, 1980). Consequently, when losing Indiana and New Hampshire fans rioted, it was in their home towns, well away from winning fans. One can only speculate as to the extent and focus of the riots, if both sets of fans rioted at the same location. Indeed, it is possible that the riots could have involved European-type soccer hooligan confrontations between rival fans rather than, or as well as, the police. Such confrontations might well have resulted in different forms of violence and rioting as reversals to different metamotivational state combinations were induced.

Related research findings

In a well-planned and comprehensive series of some nine studies on sports rioters, Gordon Russell and his colleagues studied the personality of rioters from ice hockey and soccer in Canada, Finland and the Netherlands (see Russell, 1993; Wann *et al.*, 2001, for reviews). Though none of the scales used in their extensive battery of tests was a reversal theory measure, a number of their results provide support for reversal theory notions about the metamotivation involved in fan violence and riots. The researchers found that men who are angry and physically aggressive are more likely than others to become involved in a riot, supporting the idea that telic and/or mastery metamotivation underlies some forms of riots (anger and power). They also found that rioters show strong tendencies towards sensation-seeking activities and impulsive behaviour, supporting the idea that paratelic metamotivation lies behind some other forms of riots (play and thrill). There is considerable evidence from reversal theory sport studies that sensation or arousal seeking and impulsiveness are characteristics associated with partici-pation in risky, dangerous or 'paratelic' sports (e.g. Kerr, 1991; Svebak and Kerr, 1989). As Wann *et al.* (2001) pointed out:

> For example, given choices between exciting activities (e.g. surfing and sky diving) and less exciting pastimes (e.g. chess or reading a book), they choose the former. Sensation seekers express a 'need for varied, novel, and complex sensations and experiences and the willingness to take physical and social risks for the sake of such experience' (M. Zuckerman, 1979, p. 10). A crowd disturbance, containing as it does an element of risk, would understandably act like a magnet for these people.
>
> (Wann *et al.*, 2001, pp. 143–144)

Riotous behaviour was also found to be linked to psychopathology and anti-social behaviour, which tends to support the notion put forward by Kerr (1994) that some hard core soccer hooligans may well be psychopaths. Rioters were also males who had a history of fighting, and the time since their last fight was one of the two strongest predictors of violent behaviour. The second strong predictor was whether or not they liked attending ice hockey games because they liked to watch the fights on the ice.

It would be worthwhile for future research to test the validity of the conceptual ideas behind the motivation involved in the different types of riots within the reversal theory typology. There are some obvious practical difficulties. However, those convicted of riotous or hooligan offences might be willing to be interviewed and, if confidentiality could be maintained, it might be possible to interview others who escaped prosecution after a sports riot has occurred. The examples provided at the beginning of this chapter were short and designed to illustrate briefly the different categories of riot in the new reversal theory typology. In the following sections of the chapter, two examples are compared in more detail. The first of these focuses on riotous behaviour between groups of Dutch soccer hooligans, and the second on a hooligan non-event in Sapporo during the 2002 soccer World Cup.

Anatomy of a sport-related thrill riot: Soccer hooligan confrontation in the netherlands[1]

Although this thrill riot took place between two sets of hooligans claiming allegiance to soccer clubs, there was no actual sports event between the two soccer clubs on the day of the confrontation; one of the clubs was playing a different team. The riot was not connected to the outcome of a particular game, nor did the riot take place in either of the cities in which the soccer clubs were located. Although there have been numerous hooligan incidents in the Netherlands since the late 1970s, and few of the games between the top clubs can take place without the presence of a heavy contingent of riot police, at the time this incident was a new development in Dutch soccer hooliganism.

In March 1997, news of a prearranged and well-planned violent confrontation between 200–300 Feijenoord and about 150 rival Ajax hooligans shocked the Netherlands. In the confrontation, Carlo Picornie, one of the ex-leaders of the infamous Ajax F-side soccer hooligans, died from multiple injuries. Picornie, the owner of a hotel in Amsterdam, aged 35 years and married with two children, had been stabbed in a lung and received injuries to his scalp and brain. Several other hooligans were seriously injured, including another Ajax hooligan, 27-year-old Fred Joos, who received stab wounds and a battering similar to the one dealt out to Picornie. He survived, but only just. About 200 weapons, including steel poles, chains, bats, and hammers, found by police after the fight, were shown at a press conference. It is interesting to examine the details of the aggressive and violent behaviour which occurred at Beverwijk and to explain the motivation of the Dutch hooligans involved. Details of what actually occurred at the hooligan confrontation at Beverwijk, on Sunday 23 March 1997, have been reconstructed below from newspaper reports of eye-witness accounts and videotape evidence taken from a surveillance camera used by the Dutch transport authority to monitor traffic on a section of the A9 motorway between Haarlem and Alkmaar. The final minutes of the hooligan fight were recorded by this camera.

Reconstructing the hooligan riot

12 noon

Feijenoord was due to play a soccer match against AZ in Alkmaar. At about noon, 200–300 Feijenoord hooligans on their way to Alkmaar assembled at a restaurant on the motorway near Schiphol, Amsterdam's international airport. At about the same time, some 150 Ajax hooligans were beginning to gather in a large car park in the town of Beverwijk, close to the motorway route to Alkmaar that the Feijenoord group would take.

12:30 pm

Feijenoord supporters left the restaurant and continued on their way toward Alkmaar, accompanied by police. The police knew that a confrontation between the two groups was planned, but because the location was not known they could not prevent it. (The police had originally thought that it might take place at the motorway restaurant.) The real location was arranged by members of the two hooligan groups who were in contact with each other using mobile phones.

3:00 pm

The Feijenoord hooligans took the motorway through the Wijkertunnel, which runs alongside the town of Beverwijk but does not have an exit leading into the town. Taking the police by surprise, they stopped their cars on the motorway, climbed over the crash barrier, and ran toward the car park, where they were met in an adjoining field by the Ajax supporters. There, a massive fight began.

3:02 pm

Picornie and Joos, two Ajax hooligans, became isolated from the main Ajax group. In the melee, Picornie was brought down as Feijenoord hooligans continued to strike him. He got to his knees and tried to stand up. As he raised himself, a bald man, one of two men seen standing near Picornie at the end of the fight, made a stabbing motion toward Picornie's back and then threw a large object away.

3:07 pm

The fight only lasted a few minutes. Vehicles parked in a nearby car park were also vandalised. Police arrived quickly, but they could not prevent the hooligans escaping in their cars. Picornie died of serious wounding, and Joos, although alive, was also left seriously wounded.

Later the same afternoon

After the Feijenoord versus Alkmaar match, the police arrested 28 men on suspicion of causing public violence and causing grievous bodily harm (earlier at Beverwijk). A badly wounded man was also arrested.

The following Thursday afternoon

Carlo Picornie's funeral took place at the Nieuwe Oosterbegraafplaats in Amsterdam. Ajax 'supporters', most of whom were about 30 years old and some of whom were possibly former hooligans, attended in silence. Some were crying.

Five months later

The trials of the accused soccer hooligans began in Haarlem on 18 August. Despite some 48 arrests, not all those responsible for the death of Picornie and the severe injuries received by Joos were tracked down. The man who was seen stabbing Picornie in the back was never found. Two Feijenoord hooligans were found guilty of being jointly responsible for the death of Picornie and sentenced to four years in prison. Two other Feijenoord and three Ajax hooligans also received prison sentences.

Background to the riot

There has been an extended history of trouble involving hooligans claiming allegiance to Ajax and Feijenoord soccer clubs. It appears that this particular confrontation was sparked by insults issued by a Feijenoord hooligan (Daniel de Cavalho, one of those sentenced). In a television interview about a previous minor incident between Ajax and Feijenoord hooligans on the Amsterdam ring road a few weeks before the Beverwijk confrontation, he called the Ajax hooligans 'mietjes' (homosexual wimps) because, in this earlier incident, they ran away when faced by superior numbers of Feijenoord hooligans. This public insult was deliberately calculated to provoke a response from the Ajax hooligans, a challenge they would find difficult to ignore.

Measures taken by the Dutch authorities to combat soccer hooliganism have mirrored developments in England, with the result that the possibility for hooligan fighting to take place inside soccer grounds has become increasingly restricted. These measures include heavy police presence in and around the soccer grounds, police escorts for away-team supporters, perimeter fencing and segregated areas for groups of rival fans and, more recently, the use of police undercover agents to infiltrate hooligan groups. However, perhaps the most important development has been the use of video systems at the stadia that allow the police to monitor crowd behaviour and direct police action to hot spots where hooligan violence has been observed. In addition, the Dutch have developed the Centraal Informatiepunt Voetbalvandalisme, the equivalent of England's National Criminal Intelligence Service (NCIS), which keeps computer records of active soccer hooligans. Some hooligans have been identified through image enhancement of video recordings of hooligan aggression and fighting in and around the soccer grounds. Because of these control measures, the police have taken the initiative away from the hooligans. Hooligans are being forced to conduct their violent activities away from the soccer stadia, where they can regain the initiative from the police and experience the thrills and excitement that they desire.

Ajax and Feijenoord hooligans chose a date and a venue for their Beverwijk confrontation that would not attract a police presence. In this regard, their planning was extremely effective. First, there was no match between Ajax and Feijenoord soccer clubs on the day in question. Second, even though the police knew about a possible confrontation, they were caught off-guard by the choice of a location in an inconspicuous town far removed from the hooligans' home stadia in Amsterdam and Rotterdam and the Feijenoord match in Alkmaar. Third, communication on the day of the confrontation via mobile phones allowed the final details to be easily arranged.

As with English hooligans, outwitting the police provides extra challenge, excitement and fun for Dutch hooligans. In the case of the Ajax and Feijenoord hooligans, the planning and preparation, the secrecy in choosing the date and location, and the use of modern technology in the form of mobile phones for communication were all part of their response to the challenge of avoiding the police.

Some members of the hard core Ajax hooligan group, known as the F-side, interviewed anonymously by the press in the days before Picornie's funeral, indicated that the group barely existed anymore. The group had once consisted of a few hundred people based in De Meer, an area of Amsterdam. Many were now 30, and some even 40 years old, and most were family men holding down regular jobs. The older members of the F-side were very surprised that Carlo Picornie had gone to Beverwijk, as he too had recently settled into a quiet life with his wife and two children.

The aftermath

Considering that 200–300 Feijenoord and about 150 Ajax hooligans, armed with steel poles, chains, bats and hammers, met for conflict in an open field without the police present, it might seem unusual that many more people were not killed or seriously injured. Picornie's death sparked an enormous response from government ministers, the soccer authorities, the police, and the press and other media precisely because death as a direct result of soccer hooliganism is unusual, even though soccer hooligan violence has been occurring in the Netherlands for years.

As in the case of the disasters at the Heysel (1985) and Hillsborough (1989) stadia, there was a general expectancy that the terrible events would lead to a cessation of hooligan violence. This did not occur, and, similarly, there was no cessation in Feijenoord hooligan activity after the Beverwijk confrontation. It continued again at a match between Feijenoord and the English club Manchester United early in November 1997.

On 23 September 1997, a meeting in Apeldoorn was attended by representatives of the Dutch Football Association (KNVB), the Ministries of Public Affairs, Internal Affairs, Justice, and Sports, the mayors of major cities, and the police. A decision was made at this meeting to reschedule matches for which there was a high risk of hooligan trouble. If necessary, matches could be played in the afternoon rather than in the evening. This decision was made in an attempt to reduce hooligan violence and allow the police to escort fans to and from matches during daylight hours. In addition, at the end of September, 19 Ajax hooligans were taken into custody by an Amsterdam police special investigation team. Later, using prolonged observation and telephone taps, another 18 Ajax hooligans, thought to be part of the Ajax hard core, were arrested. The police thought that they had identified all the dangerous hooligans and that, with these arrests, the Ajax hard core had been neutralized.

Evidence from England suggests that adopting increasingly stringent punishments in the form of fines and longer periods of detention is not effective in terms of eliminating the problem. As was the case in England, it is highly likely that the effect of the arrests of hooligans in Amsterdam would be relatively short-lived, with new groups of hooligans moving in to replace the former hard core, and that when those arrested are eventually released, they are likely to return as hooligan heroes.

Soccer hooligans and World Cup 2002 in Japan

In contrast to the Netherlands, where soccer hooliganism has been a largely national affair and incidents of Dutch hooligans abroad have been few, English soccer hooligans frequently set aside club allegiances and inter-group rivalry for English international away matches. In England, where groups of hooligans align themselves with different club teams, like Chelsea and Arsenal, not because they necessarily care about the success of the team, but because it provides a convenient way of pursuing their violent activities, rival hooligan gangs frequently amalgamate to form a 'hooligan coalition' for the English national team's international matches overseas. The temporary coalition is disbanded when they return to England and old rivalries are renewed.

This 'coalition' violence was prevalent at both the 1998 World Cup in France and the Euro 2000 tournament where, at the England–Germany game in Charleroi, police arrested about 450 hooligans. When the draw was made for the 2002 World Soccer Cup, in Pusan, South Korea, it became apparent that England would play in Japan, rather than in South Korea. Given the background of English hooligan violence in recent international events, Japan took steps to deal with the expected soccer hooligan problem. To many people's surprise these preparations were apparently successful, as the 2002 World Cup passed without any major disruption by soccer hooligans. Why was it that no noteworthy incidents involving English hooligans occurred?

Anti-hooligan preparations

In Japanese professional soccer, which only began with the setting up of the J-League in 1993, incidents which could be classed as real soccer hooliganism have been scarce. Those few incidents that have been reported in the press or discussed on supporter group websites are relatively minor when compared with English soccer violence (Shimizu, 2002). Despite a lack of serious domestic incidents, the Japanese people were generally well aware of the violence that had occurred at previous tournaments, because hooliganism featured strongly in media coverage during the build-up to the World Cup. As a result, once it was decided that England would play in Japan, soccer officials, civic authorities, police and citizens in the host cities became increasingly nervous about the potential hooligan problem.

To counter these feelings of nervousness, the general secretary of the Fédération Internationale de Football Association (FIFA) and the security advisor of the English Football Association (FA) visited Japan and gave reassurances that hooliganism would not be a problem at the World Cup. They argued that new passport control laws in Britain and directives to magistrates to take tough action against football hooligans to prevent convicted troublemakers from travelling to the World Cup had been implemented. Much was made by British politicians about cooperation between the English and Japanese police and the fact that English police spotters would be on duty at airports to identify known hooligans as they arrived in Japan. Soccer officials also claimed that difficulties with the local language, Japan's distance from England and the high cost of living would mean that English hooligans would probably not travel to Japan. A new bill was approved in the Japanese parliament allowing immigration officials to refuse entry to soccer hooligans and to expel those convicted of offences.

In spite of all the assurances from soccer officials and diplomats, some Japanese citizen groups were not convinced and made their own preparations. For example, schools near World Cup stadia, or entertainment districts, were particularly concerned about the safety of their students. Head teachers sent letters to parents describing the emergency procedures which would take effect if rioting took place. Some schools asked parents to pick up their children (relatively unusual in Japan); others decided to send them home in groups; one school provided students with personal anti-crime alarms; and some schools closed altogether (Gordenker, 2002). Shop owners near Yokohama stadium, which was to host three first-stage World Cup soccer matches and the final, persuaded an insurance company to provide 'hooligan insurance' to cover fire or possible damage to their properties during the period of the World Cup. ('Nisshin', 2001). Also, in Sapporo, the district court put off criminal trials scheduled for early June, as prosecutors expected to be busy dealing with hundreds of hooligans arrested during the first round games between Germany–Saudi Arabia, Italy–Ecuador and England–Argentina ('Court puts', 2002).

The police also began to prepare for trouble with a number of anti-hooligan measures, following liaison with English police. For example, information from the NCIS 'hooligan profiling' database was made available to police in Japan. Although Japanese police were totally inexperienced in handling boisterous foreign soccer groups, they were taking no chances. For example, 7,000 police reinforcements from elsewhere in Japan were drafted in to support the local force in Sapporo ('Sapporo braces', 2002). Police measures also included large-scale terrorist and hooligan drills, as well as practice runs for medical staff who might have to deal with medical emergencies. One rather humorous development involved police plans to use a gun which could fire a 25 square metre net to trap hooligans, bringing to mind the gladiators in Roman times or Spiderman of comic book fame (Gilhooly, 2002).

Despite all claims and preparations, however, the potential for hooligan violence remained. In the past, hooligans have often found enough money to travel abroad, and a large number of those arrested in recent years for hooligan offences had jobs and reasonable salaries. In addition, due to financial problems in the airline industry at the time, cheaper airfares were available and, by taking indirect routes with non-major carriers, travel costs to Japan could be reduced. Furthermore, hooligans could take roundabout routes to Japan via other European countries, the US, or other Asian countries, rather than fly direct from London to Tokyo where the Japanese authorities, supported by English police, would be waiting for them. As for language difficulties, English hooligans have travelled all over Europe without difficulty and their inability to speak European languages has not been a hindrance. Why then would Japan pose a particular problem? From the point of view of the hooligans, the reasons put forward for hooligans not coming to Japan were precisely the things that could make Japan a new and interesting challenge. Hooligans, in the past, have shown creativity and resourcefulness in getting to games (Kerr, 1994).

One press story which seemed to confirm the view that hooligans were making plans to circumvent the authorities concerned Chris Henderson and Steve Hickmott, two ex-members of the infamous hooligan group known as the Chelsea Headhunters (see for example Kerr, 1994, pp. 91–93). Henderson and Hickmott, now aged 42 and 46, were reported to be running a bar in Pattaya, Thailand, called the Dog's Bollocks. The story in the British *Sunday Mirror* newspaper claimed that more than 100 soccer hooligans were secretly plotting to slip into Japan from Thailand and cause trouble at the England versus Argentina match in Sapporo. An undercover reporter found out that hooligans were planning to use local flights from Bangkok to Japan or to fly via co-host South Korea on the day of the England versus Argentina game. The article said that Henderson and Hickmott were arranging flights and getting tickets for the game, with the additional possibility that criminals in Thailand could prepare false identification papers for the hooligans ('Hooligans planning', 2002).

The lack of experience of the police in dealing with hooligan violence meant that, even if the rival Argentinian supporters or hooligans did not materialise, battles with the police could provide an ideal alternative for the English. Of England's first round games, the England versus Argentina game in Sapporo was targeted as the match where hooligan violence and rioting was most likely to occur.

Background to the England versus Argentina Sapporo game

There is a long history behind England–Argentina games, going back at least as far as the1966 World Cup, when England won an ill-spirited quarterfinal match in which the Argentinian captain, Rattin, was penalised and sent off for a series of violent tackles. However, he refused to leave the pitch for quite a time, causing a huge controversy. England eventually went on to win the 1966 World Cup. In the 1986 World Cup in Mexico, when Argentina played the ball into the England goal mouth, Maradona went up to head the ball, but instead, unnoticed by the referee, played the ball into the net with his hand. The goal was awarded and England was eliminated from the tournament. When questioned, Maradona would not admit to using his hand and claimed it was the 'Hand of God' which scored. Just prior to the Korea–Japan World Cup, while playing for Manchester United against Spanish team Deportivo La Coruna in the European Champions League, England's best player and captain, David Beckham, was badly injured by a wild two-footed tackle from Aldo Duscher, an Argentinian national team player. Beckham sustained a broken bone in his foot. At first it was thought that the injury would prevent him playing in the World Cup, but he recovered faster than expected and was able to play. In addition to these soccer incidents, the Falklands War remains a source of ill-feeling between the two countries.

Events in both England and Argentina prior to the start of the World Cup were also a cause for concern. A few months before the tournament, the English authorities were unable to prevent violence at a Cardiff versus Leeds match, and over 600 Millwall hooligans from rioting after a match with Manchester City ('A night', 2001; 'Violence mars', 2002). Also, in the four months prior to the tournament, several deaths occurred in violent clashes between supporters and the police in Argentina ('Fan shot', 2002; 'Teenage fan', 2002; 'Violence returns', 2002).

In Sapporo, the 8.30 p.m. kick-off for the England versus Argentina game meant that fans and hooligans had the chance to spend most of the day drinking in Odori Park in the city centre. Trouble also seemed possible in and around the Sapporo Dome, but would more likely occur after the match, in the Susukino entertainment district. What seemed most likely was the type of incident which occurred both at the 1998 World Cup and Euro 2000 where trouble arose when large groups of supporters, including hooligans, congregated in city centre and entertainment districts, drinking in pubs and bars. Finally, the results of the opening games, where England could only manage a draw with Sweden (1–1) while Argentina won against Nigeria (1–0), could also act as a spur to the hooligans. All the necessary conditions appeared to be in place for hooligan riots and fighting in Sapporo.

What actually took place?

By May 2002, over 1,000 hard core football hooligans had been banned from travelling to Japan and were required to surrender their passports to the police for the duration of the tournament (Cobain, 2002). Some hooligans who did manage to leave England and took roundabout routes to Japan were arrested and had their visas revoked. One of those hooligans denied entry to Japan was found to be carrying 175 tickets for the World Cup, about half of which were for the England versus Argentina game, even though a complex system designed to prevent tickets ending up in the hands of ticket touts or hooligans had been implemented ('British hooligan', 2002).

Several convicted hooligans who had flown in from Singapore via Bangkok on a Singapore Airlines flight were denied entry at Kansai airport. Andrew Cooper, a 37-year-old who flew to Japan from Seoul, and two other 34-year-old men, who flew to Narita airport from Istanbul, were among the 22 individuals denied entry. Cooper had a previous conviction for possessing tear gas, and the names of the two others were on a NCIS hooligan list with some 324 names of people to be denied entry ('Brits on', 2002; 'English fan', 2002; 'Security tightens', 2002; 'Sixteen Brits', 2002).

The game passed off without any real hooligan incidents occurring at the Sapporo Dome or in Odori Park and the Susukino entertainment district before, during or after the game. Politicians, the police and the soccer authorities were mightily relieved. In the game, England captain David Beckham scored a penalty and Argentina was defeated 1–0.

While there were no real hooligan incidents in Sapporo during the 2002 World Cup, it is interesting that thousands of miles away in Moscow an anger riot took place. On 9 June Russia were playing joint hosts Japan and were favourites to win. In Moscow, thousands of fans, many of them drinking, had congregated to watch an outdoor broadcast of the game on a giant screen on the side of the Moskva Hotel, next to Red Square. When Russia eventually lost 0–1, thousands of soccer fans turned into hooligans and went on the rampage, setting cars ablaze, smashing store windows in up-market Tverskaya Street, beating up people and fighting the poorly prepared police. Two people were killed, about 50 people hospitalised and 60 hooligan rioters arrested. Russian fans, whose team 'on paper' were a much superior team to the Japanese, feeling angry and humiliated, reacted with serious violence in an anger riot when their team lost to Japan in the important World Cup tournament (Lagnado, 2002; 'Russia soccer', 2002).

Comparing the Beverwijk and Sapporo hooligan scenarios: Reversal theory explanations

As Kerr (1994) has described in detail, a complex interaction of factors produces the positive psychological experience associated with soccer hooligan activities. To summarise briefly, being involved in aggressive and violent acts supplies hooligans with the immediate sensation associated with taking risks and being negativistic 'just for the hell of it'. For them, these activities are perceived as fun and exciting, and they provide a satisfying and rewarding experience which works well in counteracting boredom. Using these basic ideas and the framework of reversal theory, a comparison of the Beverwijk hooligan confrontation and events around the England versus Argentina World Cup match in Sapporo will be undertaken in the following sections of the chapter.

Trying to outwit the police and authorities adds to the excitement and thrills experienced by hooligans in a paratelic-negativistic state combination as arousal levels are increased and experienced in a positive way. Hooligans often respond to what they perceive as new challenges by adopting different and more creative strategies (Kerr, 1994). In fact, it was in response to police tactics that the Beverwijk confrontation took place, and it is probable that the hooligans involved used mobile phones to avoid police surveillance techniques. In terms of the ongoing struggle between police and hooligans, the use of undercover observation and telephone taps only adds to the mastery game by making it more interesting. These days hooligan groups have their own websites and frequently communicate with other groups using the internet ('Football violence', 2001).

In the case of Beverwijk, the Ajax and Feijenoord hooligans were totally successful in outwitting the police. Although much of the initial planning activity may well have been carried out in a serious telic manner, both during and after the riot, when plans came to fruition and the police had been outwitted the planners would have felt satisfaction and even pride as they thought back and considered the successful outcomes, thus adding to their psychological rewards in terms of improved positive affect and hedonic tone. In a sense, telic-oriented planning was necessary in the preparation stages for reversals and paratelic-oriented pleasure later.

Attempts by English hooligans to outflank the British and Japanese police and authorities and travel to World Cup 2002 in Japan were much less successful. A few hooligans may have managed to get to Sapporo, but not in sufficient numbers to be effective. In addition, policing in Sapporo was extremely heavy and there was always the possibility that inexperienced police might misinterpret fans' boisterous behaviour as violent and retaliate with serious violence. Also, for anyone arrested and subsequently prosecuted there was the prospect of languishing in a Japanese jail under a tough regime with an uncertain prospect of an early release. On this occasion the hooligan game became unbalanced in favour of the police.

The opportunities for hooligans to engage in thrill riots and paratelic-negativistic 'fun' violence were minimised to such an extent that the hooligan game was not worth playing. The risks involved outweighed the possible rewards and paratelic protective frames did not come into effect. The outcome was that the psychological 'payoff' in terms of positive affect and pleasant hedonic tone provided by both the thrills and excitement of participating in rioting and fighting, and the emotional rewards of taking part in effective and accomplished planning was denied to English hooligans. The pleasant experience for many of the Dutch hooligans at Beverwijk was only possible because their safety-zone and confidence protective frames were operative and the risks associated with rioting and fighting could be taken with the perception that there was no danger.

The truth is that soccer-related hooligan fighting generally appears to be much worse than it actually is. There is a play-fight element in much of it that Marsh

(1978) has called 'the illusion of violence'. According to reversal theory notions about protective frames, in order for hooligans to continue to perceive the aggression and violence associated with soccer hooliganism as thrilling and exciting, it has to retain an element of physical risk. Put bluntly, stabbings, beatings, and occasional deaths are necessary. Without the element of danger, excitement would be much reduced and the hooligan game would be spoilt. However, there must be a kind of balance, with enough danger to maintain the perception of risk but not so much that the risk becomes too great, because then any protective frame will be 'broken' and many of the combatants will drop out. Soccer hooligans have their own rules of engagement, which permit their aggressive and violent activities to be experienced within protective frames. This allows feelings of excitement to be maximised, but also allows usually unpleasant telic-oriented emotions such as fear, anxiety and anger, when they occur, to be experienced as pleasant parapathic emotions (Apter, 1992; Kerr, 1994).

Many of the Feijenoord hooligans who attended the confrontation at Beverwijk would likely have been buoyed up by the media attention and their success against Ajax hooligans. For most, Picornie's death and Joos' injuries would not have been sufficient to break the paratelic protective frame that encompasses their hooligan activity. Quite the opposite: knowledge of the death and injuries would have been likely to enhance the challenge, danger, and excitement associated with hooligan fighting. Consequently, further hooligan aggression and violence by Feijenoord hooligans was almost inevitable.

The discussion above comparing Beverwijk and Sapporo has emphasised paratelic-negativitism as a central feature of the motivation of those involved in hooligan activities and thrill riots. As mentioned earlier, however, it is entirely possible that some of the rioters with a telic-negativistic or a paratelic-mastery state combination operative could easily have been engaging in anger or power violence and rioting. This may well have been true for those involved in killing Picornie and seriously injuring the other Ajax hooligans.

Closing comments

A reversal theory typology was used in this chapter to classify riots into general categories. These general categories involve large groups of people predominantly in the same state of mind (i.e. with the same metamotivational state combination operative). This common state of mind can change in a group of rioters as a riot unfolds (e.g. thrill riots could change to anger riots). It must also be remembered that the experience of the individuals participating in the riot may well be diverse and that riots are dynamic. Reversals are likely to occur and states of mind change.

In chapter 2, the idea was put forward that players involved in competition, or more specifically team contact sports, enter into a kind of contract in the pursuit of aggression and violence between consenting adults. Spectators and fans who buy tickets to watch games can also be thought of as entering into a contract, but a different kind of contract. For them, the contract involves behaving in a way which is in accordance with the law while watching a sports event. Should they break the contract then they are subject to a different set of rules and conditions than the players. As Russell stated:

> It is worth pointing out that the conduct of the spectators and athletes is governed by different legal systems during a contest. Physical violence among spectators is summarily dealt with by the police and thereafter by the courts, whereas a few feet away the same violence by players is adjudicated by referees or umpires under the de facto authority of the 'rules of play'. Thus, players in most combatant sports risk considerably weaker punishments for illegal aggression than do their fans.
>
> (Russell, 1993, pp. 181–182)

This is an important difference and grounds for separating athletes' sanctioned aggression and violence and violent behaviour by fans. Where there may be a similarity is between athletes' unsanctioned aggression and violence and similar behaviour by fans, where both are subject to the law. However, to go further at this point takes the discussion into legal territory and that topic will be dealt with in more detail in the final chapter. Before that, however, the penultimate chapter is concerned with the observation of aggression and violence in sport and the possible role of the media in escalating violence.

Note

1   This part of the chapter is based on Kerr, J. H. and de Kock, H. (2002). Aggression, violence and the death of a Dutch soccer hooligan: A reversal theory explanation. *Aggressive Behavior*, 28, 1–10. Sections have been reproduced by permission John Wiley and Sons, Inc. (© 2001).

References

A night of shame in lion's den. (2001, 31 December). *The Japan Times*, p. 17.

Apter, M. J. (1992). *The dangerous edge*. New York: The Free Press.

Apter, M. J. (1997, July). *The experience of being violent*. Paper presented at the Eighth International Conference on Reversal Theory, University of East London.

British hooligan, loaded with Cup tickets, gets the boot. (2002, May 30). *The Japan Times*, p. 3.

Brits on 'hooligan list' detained, await deportation from Japan. (2002, 28 May). *The Japan Times*, p. 1.

Brownout in Cleveland. (2001, 18 December). *The Japan Times*, p. 24.

Cobain, I. (2002, 18 May). 1,000 soccer thugs told to surrender their passports. *The Times*, p. 9.

Court puts priority on hooligans. (2002, 9 April). *The Japan Times*, p. 2.

English fan becomes first to be denied entry. (2002, 21 May). *The Japan Times*, p. 21.

Fan shot to death. (2002, 19 February). *The Japan Times*, p. 22.

Fans riot following NCAA game. (2003, 15 April). *The Japan Times*, p. 21.

Football thugs slip through FA's net. (2001, 31 August). *The Times*, p. 9.

Football violence on the rise. (2001, 15 August). *BBC News* 16.35 GMT (17.35 UK time).

Gilhooly, R. (2002, 22 January). Sapporo soccer hooligans face police-fired dragnet. *The Japan Times*, p. 3.

Gordenker, A. (2002, 14 June). Football fallout: Fūrigan [hooligan] fears prompt school safety drills. *The Japan Times*, p. 15).

Hooligans planning Thailand sneak. (2002, 6 April). *The Japan Times*, p. 2.

Indiana fans riot after loss in final. (2002, 4 April). *The Japan Times*, p. 23.

Kerr, J. H. (1991). Arousal-seeking in risk sport participants. *Personality and Individual Differences*, *12*, 613–616.

Kerr, J. H. (1994). *Understanding soccer hooliganism*. Buckingham: Open University Press.

Kerr, J. H. and de Kock, H. (2002). Aggression, violence, and the death of a Dutch soccer hooligan: A reversal theory explanation. *Aggressive Behavior*, *28*, 1–10.

Lagnado, A. (2002, 10 June). Russian rage: World Cup defeat triggers riots. *The Times*, p. 1.

Mann, L. (1979). Sports crowds viewed from the perspective of collective behaviour. In J. H. Goldstein (Ed.), *Sports, games and play: Social and psychological viewpoints* (1st Edition, pp. 337–369). Hillsdale, NJ: Erlbaum.

Marsh, P. (1978). *Aggro: The illusion of violence*. London: Dent.

Nauright, J. and Black, D. (1996). 'Hitting them where it hurts': Springbok–All Black rugby, masculine national identity and counter-hegemonic struggle, 1959–1992. In J. Nauright and T. J. L. Chandler (Eds), *Making men: Rugby and masculine identity* (pp. 205–226). London: Frank Cass.

Nisshin to sell hooligan insurance. (2001, 10 June). *The Japan Times*, p. 2.

Roadburg. A. (1980) Factors precipitating fan violence: A comparison of professional soccer in Britain and North America. *British Journal of Sociology*, *31*, 265–276.

Russell, G. W. (1993). *The social psychology of sport*. New York: Springer-Verlag.

Russia soccer riot leaves two dead; one Japanese hurt. (2002, 11 June). *The Japan Times*, p. 3.

Sapporo braces itself. (2002, 5 May). *The Japan Times*, p. 12.

Security tightens for the big kick-off. (2002, 31 May). *The Japan Times*, p. 1.

Shimizu, S. (2002). Japanese soccer fans: Following the local and national team. In J. Horne and W. Manzenreiter (Eds), *Japan, Korea and the 2002 World Cup* (pp. 133–46). London: Routledge.

Sixteen Brits denied entry in lead up to World Cup. (2002, 1 June). *The Japan Times*, p. 2.

Smith, M. D. (1983). *Violence in sport*. Toronto: Butterworth.

Spectators turn violent after game. (2001, 11 April). *The Japan Times*, p. 21.

Svebak, S. and Kerr, J. H. (1989). The role of impulsivity in preference for sports. *Personality and Individual Differences*, *10*, 51–58.

Teenage fan shot, in serious condition. (2002, 2 April). *The Japan Times*, p. 23.

Violence mars game. (2002, 21 January). *The Japan Times*, p. 22.

Violence returns to haunt Argentine soccer. (2002, 5 March). *The Japan Times*, p. 22.

Wann, D. L., Melnick, M. J., Russell, G. W. and Pease, D. G. (2001). *Sport fans: The psychology and social impact of spectators*. London: Routledge.

Zuckerman, M. (1979). *Sensation seeking: Beyond the optimal level of arousal*. Hillsdale, NJ: Erlbaum.

8   Blood and guts

Observing violence in sport

This chapter begins with an examination of why people watch aggression and violence in sport and find it enjoyable and entertaining. This examination will compare four very different kinds of violent 'sports'. These have been chosen because they represent 'sport' in the broadest sense of the term, they involve either real or fake violence, and they have or have had a high profile in terms of providing entertainment for very large numbers of spectators. In trying to explain why people enjoy these sports, concepts from reversal theory, including cognitive synergies, protective frames and parapathic emotions, will be included in the discussion. The chapter will go on to discuss broader aspects of a current academic debate on the possible effects of viewing media violence in general, and will then focus more specifically on the possible effects of viewing violence in sports. The sports chosen for discussion in the early part of this chapter are K-1, or ultimate fighting as it is sometimes known, professional wrestling, the manufactured-for-television 'sport' *The American Gladiators*, and violent sports depicted in science fiction sports films such as *Rollerball* and *The Running Man*.

K-1, or ultimate fighting, involves a mix of boxing, kickboxing, karate, wrestling and 'kakutogi', or martial arts. With the very minimum of rules, fights are kept short so that fighters are encouraged to go all-out for victory rather than conserve their energy for later rounds. This has produced an 'anything goes', action-filled and fear-inducing violent spectacle in which many fights end before the final bell. At a recent K-1 fighting Grand Prix, in March 2002 in Tokyo, the highlight of the night was a mixed fight between Royce Gracie from Brazil and Hidehiko Yoshida from Japan. Gracie is a member of the famous Gracie family, who have been proponents of a form of freestyle jujitsu in Brazil (Gracie jujitsu), and Yoshida is a former Japanese Judo World Champion and Olympic gold medalist. The fight ended in controversy; the referee stopped the fight after 7 minutes 24 seconds in the first round and declared Yoshida the winner when the Brazilian apparently lost consciousness. Gracie and his corner were extremely unhappy with the decision, claiming that the fighter had not lost consciousness and should have been allowed to continue fighting (Maylam, 2001; Nishiyama, 2001; 'Yoshida is', 2002).

The contrast between K-1 and professional wrestling could hardly be greater. Indeed, although marketed as a sport, pro-wrestling has been more appropriately described as 'an explicitly dramatic form of entertainment' (Mondak, 1989), and Pallo has explained in detail how the wrestlers work together to make the moves look real:

> In the pro game everything has to be greatly exaggerated, much larger than life – just like pantomime. And to achieve this it is necessary to supplement the genuine amateur moves and holds – known as 'shoot moves' – with spectacular gimmick moves and holds, which are bugger all to do with the true sport, but are purely to entertain the punter. . . . Many of these working moves rely considerably on the cooperation of a wrestler's opponent. He has to let you put on the hold (often seeming to be dazed at the time) or he has actively to help you to put it on.
>
> (Pallo, 1985, pp. 22–23)

Since the 1960s when Pallo was in the ring, pro-wrestling has changed dramatically. The World Wrestling Entertainment company (WWE; formerly known as World Wrestling Federation, WWF) utilises all the techniques of modern television, stereo sound and special effects to ensure that spectators are constantly faced with new and stimulating match-ups and wrestling scenarios. Each major event or series of fights between wrestlers has become more like a mini soap opera than a simple wrestling match. The audience is never allowed to become bored, and the scheduling of matches between different wrestlers is very important in ensuring that this does not happen. Yet, take away the glitzy modern television presentation and the story lines have been much the same in US pro-wrestling since the 1930s:

> The message of wrestling is embodied in the heroes and villains of wrestling's ethical system. That message is relayed to the audience via numerous routes. The nature of each competition between hero and villain is verbalized during pre-match interviews with the combatants, while non-verbal signals including wrestlers' dress, mannerisms, tactics and ethnic identification further clarify the wrestling drama.
>
> (Mondak, 1989, p.140)

The American Gladiators was a television show which has since developed into a business enterprise involving American Gladiators-sanctioned events and sport and fitness promotion and merchandising, in addition to computer games. The original show, produced by the American Broadcasting Company, which ran for four seasons in the early to mid 1990s, has been variously described as being an example of 'junk', 'trash', 'pseudo' or 'marginal' sport (Rinehart, 1994). Contestants competed for prize money in a sporting contest contrived especially for television. The contests tended to mimic aspects of well-established sports, carried to extremes, and contestants competed for cash and prizes with the specially chosen Gladiators who were regulars in the show and specialised in certain events. For example, as described by Rinehart:

> In 'Break Through and Conquer,' contestants attempt to rush a football twenty yards past a tackling Gladiator, then get into a small ring with another Gladiator and, in imitation of sumo wrestling, attempt to displace the Gladiator from the ring. In 'The Wall', contestants get a ten-second head start, begin climbing a nearly vertical wall (à la mountain climbing), but then are pursued by Gladiators attempting to pull them off the wall.
>
> (Rinehart, 1994, p. 30)

The American Gladiators' shelf life as a pseudo or marginal sport was relatively short-lived, although fan websites do exist and repeat showings can be seen on some television networks.

'Manufactured sports', in films such as *Rollerball* and *The Running Man*, have also featured in the cinema. Both films, which are brutally violent science fiction thrillers, involve futuristic games. The original *Rollerball* film, based on a short story by William Harrison (*The Roller Ball Murders*), was released in 1975 and a remake came out in 2002. In the remake, a few changes to the story were made, but the two films have the same common theme. *Rollerball* is set in a future where the world is at peace, controlled by large corporations. In this world, there is no dissent or crime and the major sport is a violent, brutal game known as 'Roller-ball'. The game is a combination of American football, motor cross, ice hockey and roller derby, played by gladiator-types, protected by helmets and padding, who skate inside a bowl-shaped arena . Motor cycles tow and release players to build up and maintain speed. Players have weapons (e.g. spiked gloves) which they use to fight off opponents, and score by dropping a metallic ball into a lit up goal. The central character in the original film, Jonathan E, is played by James Caan and the plot concerns his refusal to retire and his survival, even after the game's evil corporate executives make the game's rules progressively more extreme, in each subsequent game. The stage is finally reached where there are no rules and teams play until one or the other is destroyed, but Jonathan E prevails against his evil adversaries.

The movie *The Running Man*, based on a book written by Stephen King (writing as Richard Bachman) came out in 1987. The film is about a violent television game show in which criminals can participate in an attempt to prove their innocence. Arnold Schwarzenegger plays Ben Richards, a contestant in the game who has been framed for a crime he did not commit. In the game, Richards must survive against a series of 'stalkers' whom he meets in a series of violent confrontations in the 'gaming grid'. The stalkers are armed with, for example, deadly swords, electric guns and buzz saws. One is garrotted by Richards using a length of barbed wire, while another dies by being mutilated by a chainsaw. Needless to say, Richards, the hero, eventually kills all the stalkers, survives the game and is proven innocent.

K-1 fighting, pro-wrestling, *The American Gladiators*, and the films *Rollerball* and *The Running Man* provide an interesting comparison of different types of real and unreal extreme violence. In K-1, the violence is real, very real, whereas in pro-wrestling the violence is not at all real. Although not close to K-1 in terms of violence, *The American Gladiators* does have 'real' physical contact between contestants and Gladiators, but the context is one of an unreal manufactured sport. *Rollerball* and *The Running Man* are science fiction and the violence is, of course, not real. In spite of differences in the real/unreal nature of the fighting and violence, all four types of 'sport' have been, or continue to be, immensely popular with audiences. For example, in the 2002 K-I fighting Grand Prix, over 90,000 people came to the national stadium in Tokyo to watch, while thousands, perhaps millions, around the world watched the event on television. The first Grand Prix was held in 1993 and in a decade it has become the most popular fighting sport after boxing (Maylam, 2001). About the time that K-1 fighting was starting up, huge numbers of people were already watching pro-wrestling events. For example, in addition to those watching the events live, *Wrestlemania V* reached 915,000, and *Wrestlemania VI* 825,000 homes on a pay-per-view basis (Rinehart, 1994). What is it about these 'sports' that make them attractive and enjoyable to watch for so many spectators and viewers?

Why do people enjoy extreme sport violence?

Some of the answers can be found in *Why we watch: The attractions of violent entertainment* (Goldstein, 1998). Among other important contributions that are interesting and relevant here are the chapters by Guttmann, on the appeal of violent sports, and Zillmann, on the psychology of watching violence in general. Guttmann (1986,1998), taking a historical perspective, argues that spectators have always been interested in violent sports through the ages. He sees little difference between those who watched chariot racing and gladiatorial contests in ancient Greece and Rome, those who attended jousting tournaments in medieval Europe, and those who attend modern day soccer matches. In addition, he is also able to identify incidents of crowd trouble and riots at events like these throughout history, pointing out that the spectator riots in Roman times make modern day soccer hooliganism seem relatively innocuous (Guttmann, 1998, p. 14).

Zillmann (e.g. 1998) has been investigating aspects of aggression for over thirty years and is probably best known for his theory of excitation-transfer (Zillmann, e.g. 1971, 1983). Briefly, excitation transfer is thought to occur because of a time discrepancy between cognitive processes (immediate) and excitatory components of the emotions (slower and persistent as a result of relatively slow physiological changes) in responding to changing environmental stimuli. Therefore, residues of previous excitation may be transferred and intensify any emotional response to new stimulation. In one experiment, physical exercise was used to increase arousal in one group of participants, but not in another group. Both groups were then provoked by researchers and the participants who had exercised were found to respond more aggressively than the non-exercise participants (Zillmann and Bryant, 1974). In other words, the arousal left over from the exercise produced increased levels of aggression in those who had exercised (Zillmann, 1998, p. 209). How might the results of Zillmann and Bryant's (1974) study and the excitation transfer model be applied to those watching violent sports? Simply put, as the drama of an event unfolds, spectators may experience high arousal negative emotions (e.g. anxiety, anger) if, for example, their favourite performer's opponent takes a clear lead in the scoring. However, if their favourite athlete stages a comeback and triumphs over the opponent, the spectators' enjoyment of victory will be enhanced by residual arousal from the previously experienced unpleasant emotions.

Both Guttmann (1998) and Zillmann (1998) emphasise the important role that sensation-seeking or arousal-seeking plays in the attractiveness of violence for those watching. In this connection, they refer to the work of Elias (1969/1982) and Elias and Dunning (1970) who argued that modern society had become too protected in comparison with the risky existence that humans faced in earlier times. Contemporary life is therefore not very exciting and people have to actively seek out thrills and vicarious risk-taking through, for example, watching sports. As Guttmann stated:

> . . . a propensity to commit acts of interpersonal expressive violence is precisely what modern society most strongly inhibits and what sports spectatorship most gratifyingly permits – either directly, in the case of fans who run amok, or vicariously, in the case of fans who merely empathize with and take pleasure in the violence they witness. . . . It is doubtful that the vicarious sensations experienced by the sports spectator can be as thrilling or as satisfying as those experienced by the athletes, but the importance of these sensations should not be underestimated.
>
> (Guttmann, 1998, p. 21)

The fact that watching violent sports produces increases in levels of arousal, and that people deliberately watch to achieve elevated arousal, has been recognised by other scholars and researchers, and fits neatly with the reversal theory approach.

Reversal theory explanations

The need for people, at certain times, to seek heightened levels of arousal is a basic concept in reversal theory and has been a constant theme throughout this book, whether referring to the motivation of competitive adult athletes, young performers, or that of rioting fans or hooligans. Therefore, it should come as no surprise that this is also true for spectators who enjoy aggressive and violent sports events (live or in the media), especially where those spectators may have relatively risk-free and, perhaps, rather boring lifestyles. Other concepts from reversal theory can further explain spectators' enjoyment of violent entertainment. These are the experience of parapathic emotions when spectators' protective frames are in operation, and the concept of cognitive synergies.

Parapathic emotions

Describing *Rollerball* and *The Running Man*, or violent films in general, as being attractive forms of entertainment is not to say that they are attractive to all people, or that, for those people who do find such films attractive, all the emotions they experience will be pleasant ones. Clearly, much of their attraction lies in the experience of unpleasant or negative emotions like fear, disgust or hatred (e.g. through scenes of raping, maiming and violent death). McCauley (1998, pp. 159–160) argues that there would appear to be two ways of explaining how people are capable of being frightened, disgusted or saddened and changing this experience into a positive experience. The first is to assume that unpleasant emotional reactions are necessary and tolerated for the benefits of a subsequent pleasant emotional experience (e.g. as evil villains are defeated and killed by 'good' heroes at the end of the fiction or drama). This assumption fits with the excitation transfer model (Zillmann, e.g. 1983) mentioned earlier, in which enjoyment is boosted by prior distress and the residual excitation from negative hedonic tone. This model is generally not at odds with reversal theory concepts and actually provides support for reversal theory arguments that a certain level of arousal can be interpreted in different ways and that changes from pleasant to unpleasant experience (or vice versa) are possible at any given level of arousal (Apter, 1982). This is one way in which people might derive enjoyment in these situations, and it makes sense in reversal theory terms.

McCauley's (1998) second option is to assume that the emotions induced by fiction and drama are fundamentally different from real world emotions experienced outside fiction and drama. According to McCauley (1998), dramatic emotions are a parallel but different reality best understood through reversal theory's notion of protective frames and parapathic emotions. It is the safe, secure, and detached experience of danger and risks in a paratelic protective frame that allows unpleasant emotions like anxiety or fear, anger, hatred and disgust to be experienced as pleasant parapathic emotions by observers (see chapter 2). Indeed, it is often the parapathic emotion-inducing moments of greatest violence and horror that are likely to be the most memorable scenes and the ones viewers talk about after watching a violent drama or film. As Apter emphasised:

> A horror film would be nothing without the vampires, the corpses coming to life, the ghouls, and the ghosts. (You would feel cheated if a horror film left you not horrified.) And the most memorable moments, the ones we go over with pleasure afterwards and look forward to with pleasure on seeing the film again, are the moments of greatest horror – like the shower scene in Hitchcock's original *Psycho* – which provide the sought after *frisson*.
> (Apter, 1992, p. 67)

Those people who have their safety-zone and detachment frames intact will look out for violent films and watch them with great parapathic emotion-oriented pleasure, but other individuals are likely to avoid violent films completely. These are viewers who do not have protective frames in place when watching violent films and their experience will be decidedly unpleasant. These viewers do not experience unpleasant emotions as pleasant parapathic ones, but rather as real anxiety, disgust or hatred, for example. To continue Apter's quote above:

> . . . of course a piece of fiction may go all the way and actually produce the real form of the emotion; but if it does so it has failed in its task of producing emotions of all kinds within a protective framework which allows them to be enjoyed.
>
> (Apter, 1992, p. 67)

Cognitive synergies

To fully understand the attraction of the violence in K-1 fighting, pro-wrestling, *The American Gladiators*, and films like *Rollerball* and *The Running Man*, the reversal theory concept of cognitive synergy needs to be brought into the discussion. An individual can experience cognitive synergy when a given 'identity' (e.g. an object, event, situation, another person) is perceived by the individual to have opposite, mutually exclusive, or incompatible characteristics (Apter, 1982; Coulson, 2001). This synergy, or bringing together of contradictory properties, which can occur either simultaneously (*identity synergy* where mutually exclusive characteristics in a person or object are observed, for example a man in women's clothing or a talking cartoon animal) or successively (*reversal synergy* where mutually exclusive characteristics are perceived in such quick succession that the feeling of identity 'carries over' momentarily, for example the Necker cube or other ambiguous figures involving perceptual changes), produces a phenomenological effect that neither property could have produced by itself (Apter, 2001). These opposite qualities are only synergistic if they relate to the same thing or person, thus causing a paradox in a person's perception. Cognitive synergies[1] play a role in humour, art and music, and the enjoyment of sports, including those under discussion. Synergies are closely related to the telic and paratelic states and, as they have the effect of increasing felt arousal and enhancing the intensity of experience, they tend to be sought after and enjoyed in the paratelic state.

In thinking about cognitive synergies in televised entertainment, Coulson (1991, p. 78) grouped game shows, quiz shows and sport together and argued that there were at least six common synergistic elements in these forms of competition. The first two, safe/risky and win/loss synergies, are related to the nature of competitions, the second two, human/machine and natural/preternatural synergies, are concerned with athletes' bodies and performances, and the last two, reality/fantasy and adult/child synergies, are a means of enhancing the fun and fantasy elements in, for example, pro-wrestling.

As mentioned in chapter 2, the secure context of sporting contests was stressed in relation to the establishment of protective frames. It is interesting that a secure context is also necessary for safe/risky cognitive synergies in violent sports to work and be enjoyable as part of the paratelic experience. In K-1 fighting, pro-wrestling and *The American Gladiators*, there is a recognised and established arena, referees, judges and some kind of framework of rules and regulations, which provide a safe and secure context. Yet at the same time, there is the uncertainty and risk of injury to the protagonists. In K-1 fighting and, to a much lesser extent, *The American Gladiators*, the risk is real, while in pro-wrestling the injuries are faked, but there is still the possibility that the wrestlers will make mistakes and real injuries will occur. (In 1999, for example, pro-wrestler Owen Hart died as the result of a fall during a wrestling stunt.)

In win/loss synergies, the surprise and uncertainty of ongoing incidents and the unpredictable nature of the contest contribute to this type of synergy. Spectators are more likely to experience a synergy when competitions are close than when competitions are boring one-sided affairs where one of the combatants loses easily. A sudden reversal of fortunes could cause a win/loss synergy. For example, when a team's seemingly impenetrable defence cracks and the team's fans are suddenly confronted with the possibility of loss just when the game seemed secure; the certainty of winning has been suddenly disrupted and, for a short time, the observer's experience is coloured by some of the idea of winning being carried over to his or her perception of losing.

Although not linking it to reversal theory, Guttmann (1998, p. 21) also appreciated the importance of the secure structural framework of a sport's rules and regulations. He recognised that, although particular contests may be unpredictable, because there are always more contests and new seasons, they are also reassuringly repeatable. The repetition of the unexpected outcome within the familiar format is a crucial factor in both safe/risky and win/loss synergies. In a similar way to sports arenas, a film theatre (or watching a video at home) also provides a secure context for watching aggression and violence in films. The warm rooms, comfortable seats, availability of snacks and drinks, dimmed lighting, and likely presence of friends or family all contribute to feelings of security.

When watching athletes performing, especially where their build or uniform enhances their appearance, both the human/machine and natural/preternatural synergies may come into effect. Consider, for example, the enormous size of sumo wrestlers in Japan and pro-wrestlers in the US, the exaggerated height of basketball players, and the padding and depersonalising helmets worn by American football players (as well as Gladiators in *The American Gladiators*). One might almost imagine that the athletes involved have been specially developed for their sports, and they might be perceived as non-human or even machine-like. This is especially true for Sumo wrestlers who, aside from their size, have a distinctive, unusually stiff, walk, with their arms held slightly out, that suggests the mechanical motion of a robot.

Competitive athletes, when compared to the average person, often appear to have almost superhuman abilities and have the capacity to perform skills beyond those normally endowed by nature. For example, it is obvious that high-level K-1 fighters' training, fitness, flexibility, muscularity and skill in punching, kicking and other ring manoeuvres, in addition to their ability to absorb violent blows, go far beyond the average person's capabilities.

Although not usually present to the same extent in real sporting competition, the adult/child and reality/fantasy synergies can come into play in some types of violent sport like pro-wrestling. Apter called pro-wrestling 'a celebration of synergy' in which audiences experience the pro-wrestlers in two ways at the same time:

> This institution bristles with obvious synergies. The wrestlers are very large men behaving like small children, taunting each other, having temper tantrums, and generally showing off. They are highly 'macho', but at the same time feminine in their vanity and fondness of self-decoration and dressing up. They are both strong (physically) and weak (intellectually). And they are abstract symbols (e.g. of the Wild West, Cossack Russia, the Marines, comic super-heroes) while remaining particular individuals with their own personalities. And the wrestling contest as a whole is theatre masquerading as sport.
>
> (Apter, 1989, pp. 135–136)

The 'sports' films *Rollerball* and *The Running Man* also provide good examples of synergies. Both films involve competitive 'games' and that means that the safe/risky and win/loss synergies can come into play. Elements of the human/machine and natural/preternatural synergies are also invoked; in the case of *Rollerball*, for example, champion Jonathan E outlives all his adversaries, emphasising his superhuman and machine-like characteristics (added to by his protective helmet and padding).

Having explored the reasons why people watch violent sports, further questions arise about the possible effects of watching aggressive and violent sports on those who watch them. In the following part of the chapter, providing answers to those questions brings the discussion firmly into the controversial area of the 'media effects' debate. This part will begin with an examination of the coverage of aggression and violence in the media in general, and then proceed to consider the media and the portrayal of sports violence.

Aggression and violence in the media

It is opportune that a number of recent reviews reflecting current thinking about instances of media violence and their potential influence on audiences are available (e.g. Barker and Petley, 2001a; Carter and Weaver, 2003; Geen, 2001; Goldstein, 1998; McCauley, 1998; Zillmann, 1998). However, it becomes clear from these reviews that, stated simply, academic opinion is split roughly into two camps (Barker and Petley, 2001a; Carter and Weaver 2003). One camp, the positivistic empiricist or behavioural effects camp, emanating mostly from the US, analysed the alleged ill effects of media violence using psychology-based laboratory-type research methods, the results of which gave rise to a behavioural model of media effects. A second, the cultural and critical studies camp, developed largely in Europe, provides an alternative view, using qualitative research methods to investigate the meaning of activities like watching television (and televised violence) in the context of people's everyday lives (Gunter, 2001). A historical perspective and the criticisms each side has directed at the other have been neatly summed up by Gunter:

> The criticisms of the simplistic behavioural model of media effects that was ascendant in the 1960s was already being questioned in the late 1970s and early 1980s by the cognitive perspective, which recognised the need for more sophisticated theoretical models and methodologies to analyse how people engaged with the media.
>
> The problem with media studies grounded in a cultural and critical studies framework is that it has tended to be largely theoretical with, until fairly recently, an almost complete lack of data to back up its conclusions about the way people respond to media content.
>
> (Gunter, 2001, p. 656)

The tension between these approaches has become known in the literature as the media effects debate (e.g. Barker and Petley, 2001a; Carter and Weaver, 2003). Although opinion generally tends to be polarised into rather black and white views of the topic, consideration of some of the arguments put forward by each theoretical stance will help to establish the difficulty of forming definite conclusions about the effects that portrayals of violence in the media have on viewers and whether or not those effects are harmful.

The positivistic empiricist or behavioural effects approach

Beginning with the positivistic empiricist camp (which would include some of the work of Bandura and Berkowitz summarised in chapter 1), Geen (2001) has produced an extensive review of research and theory development. He summarised the findings from laboratory and field experiments, as well as longitudinal studies, which generally support a link between viewing aggression and violence and increases in aggression in the viewers. This was found to be especially true when the violence portrayed was realistic rather than fictional with, for example, real violence producing more excitement and arousal than fictional violence. Given the discussion earlier in this chapter, another interesting finding was that media violence elicits greater violence in observers when it is considered morally justified. For example, Geen (1981) had participants in an experiment observe a scene from *Rollerball*, involving a violent attack by several members of one team against an individual opponent. Participants were told either that the attack was retaliation for earlier dirty play or that it was unjustified. Later, when insulted by another participant, participants' verbal aggression was greater in those who had been told that the violence in the *Rollerball* scene was justified violence, than in those told it was unjustified. This finding is in accord with Zillmann's (1998) arguments about what he terms *moral monitoring*. He claims that viewers constantly monitor the behaviour of both fictional and real characters and events in moral terms as 'good or evil', 'right or wrong', 'virtuous or selfish', and, as a result of this, develop a positive disposition towards 'good' and a negative disposition toward 'evil' characters. In this connection, experiments where violence by an aggressor was perceived as being motivated by revenge brought out more aggression in observers than the same violence attributed to different motives. However, laboratory experiments carried out to investigate the possible cathartic effects of viewing screen violence produced little evidence in support of the notion (Geen, 2001).

Finally, according to Geen (2001), in the 1970s laboratory experiments began to lose ground to field experiments, where the natural settings were considered superior in terms of ecological validity, and to longitudinal studies which varied in length between one and 22 years. The results from both types of research were considered to provide additional evidence, supporting laboratory-based work, that observation of media aggression and violence had the effect of inducing aggressive behaviour in viewers which was maintained over time.

In attempting to explain the processes involved in media-elicited aggression, Geen (2001), adding a cognitive perspective, argued that televised violence was a source of material for the construction of complex 'aggressive behavioural scripts'. He drew attention to extensions of social learning theory by Huesman (1986) and research results (Huesmann *et al.*, 1983) which supported the idea that, in simple terms, when people find themselves in a violent scenario, they will respond following a script based on similar violent scenarios they have previously seen on television:

> How the violent stimulus is represented conceptually depends on a number of factors, such as the perceived justification of the observed action, the motivation of the aggressor and the realism of the aggression (Geen and Thomas, 1986). The consequences for the perpetrator of violence seen in media presentations also affect the information that is assimilated to cognitive scripts. Portrayals of rewarded (i.e. successful) aggression have been found to elicit aggressiveness in viewers whereas scenes showing punished aggression bring about an inhibition of aggression.
>
> (Geen, 2001, p. 109)

In addition, Geen (2001, p. 109) referred to the concept of 'cognitive priming' in relation to the processes underlying media violence effects (Berkowitz, 1984). Cognitive priming refers to the idea that observing violent media presentations may induce aggressive thoughts in the observer, especially where that observation might facilitate access to previously formulated cognitions, linked to violence and associated affective states, in a person's memory.

The cultural and critical studies approach

Those academics who advocate the cultural and critical studies approach in the media effects debate do not accept the arguments of the behavioural effects approach, arguing that it is too simplistic to provide a true understanding of the psychological processes involved. For example, the main thrust of Barker and Petley's (2001b) arguments also follow the line that the research questions asked by the behavioural effects researchers are too narrowly cast to provide meaningful answers. They contend that the 'assumption that violence is an abstractable unit whose presence can be counted and whose influence can be studied' is erroneous (Barker and Petley, 2001b, p. 3). They underline the benefits of qualitative research and go on to reason that, in relation to the media effects debate:

> . . . this tradition of research begins by acknowledging that people who watch TV, or go to the cinema, or play video games, or whatever, do so because these activities *mean* something to them. 'Violent' media produce different kinds of pleasure. They are used and, yes, sometimes even abused, but always within the contexts of people's lives. If we don't notice and study these media and their uses with respect for their patterned complexities, it is a dead cert that we will end up understanding nothing.
>
> (Barker and Petley, 2001b, p.3)

Among a selection of the most important quantitative work which gives credence to this approach are studies by Gerbner and his associates on the content of programmes on US prime-time television (e.g. Gerbner and Gross, 1976; Gerbner *et al.*, 1995), by Schlesinger *et al.* (1992) and Schlesinger *et al.* (1998) on women and men viewing violence, and Buckingham's (1993,1996, 2000) work on the perceptions and understanding of children and young people when watching television. Space here does not allow a detailed summary of these wide-ranging studies; only brief accounts of the main findings and conclusions will be included.

Gerbner and his associates investigated the amount of violent content in US prime-time television programmes and the people or characters who were portrayed in programmes as the victims or perpetrators of this violence. The idea behind the research was that repeated portrayals of certain groups as perpetrators or victims makes an impact on the audience's cultivation of social conceptions about victims (mostly women) and perpetrators of violence. These social conceptions were thought to be learned over time, depending on the amount of television a person watched. In this way, media violence was seen to act as a form of social control.

Schlesinger and his colleagues carried out two separate studies, using questionnaires and interviews, with women and men to explore the detailed patterns of their responses to viewing violence in four different forms of media violence. The findings showed that perception and judgements of media violence varied considerably within the samples of women and men participants, and although these were very different for women and men, they were related to their specific community rules and norms. In particular, women and men (more strongly) were found to differentiate between 'realistic' and 'unrealistic' violence. For example, one middle-class white male from Glasgow said:

You see the guy getting pierced all over the place and blood spurting out, it doesn't really bother me, but having to watch a documentary or something like that, and there was an operation getting carried out, you just saw a simple incision and stuff like that, you'd be cringing, turning away from the telly. Although they try to get it as realistic as possible you sort of still know deep down what is happening and what is not happening.

(Schlesinger *et al.*, 1998, p. 41)

Incidentally, one of the forms of media violence in the Schlesinger *et al.* (1998) study was televised violence involving boxing and soccer. The researchers asked men to view material from a boxing video, *Lords of the Ring* and then used focus groups to elicit their reactions. The men's responses revealed some disagreement about the effects of viewing boxing. For example:

In this focus group there was one man, who while hating boxing, told how his father had been a keen fan and took him to fights as a youngster. Boxing, however, had not made his father physically aggressive: 'I agree with all that is being said, its [*sic*] brutal . . . but I think to say that affects everyone in that way is a bit sweeping. It didn't affect my father. He got enjoyment out of it.'

(Schlesinger *et al.*, 1998, p. 53)

Buckingham (1993, 1996, 2000), in a series of quantitative studies of children's attitudes to media violence, also found that children's perceptions of violence were extremely diverse and that they too learned to distinguish between realistic and unrealistic violence. Also, even if children became desensitised to unrealistic or fictional violence, this did not desensitise them to real-life violence. In addition, Buckingham, examining responses to a wide range of television programmes (some quite innocuous), found that they could induce positive and negative responses in children. While some of these programmes contained unpleasant material (e.g. news bulletin items), they were found to be important in terms of children's learning about the real world, a point made by some of the children themselves. Children were also found to have developed means or strategies of coping with material that they found upsetting and this suggests that they are active interpreters of meaning and can be, within certain limits, sophisticated or even critical (Buckingham, 2001).

Confirming Buckingham's (2001) findings, a more recent report by Millwood-Hargrave (2003) has shown that children are well able to recognise the difference between real and fictional violence. Fictional violence was found to have no lasting effect, but children were found to be disturbed by even mild depictions of real violence when it was shown, for example, as part of news bulletins. What this means in reversal theory terms is that televised violence has different effects depending on whether or not the protective frame provided by fiction is present. Indeed, in all the examples covered in this chapter, whether it be K-1 fighting, pro-wrestling or Rollerball, the enjoyment of those watching involves the detachment frame. Not only is there the detachment of being an observer or spectator, but what is being observed also has a kind of fictional and theatrical quality which increases feelings of detachment.

Making definite conclusions about the possible effects of media violence and trying to establish whether those effects are harmful or helpful is not an easy task. Certainly research findings, like those by Buckingham (1993, 1996, 2000), challenge popular wisdom about children (and adults) being passive and impressionable recipients of media messages. Part of the problem is that the media effects debate has become politicised, with the conservative arguments of the so-called 'moral majority' being ranged against those of the 'liberal left'. There may be an element of over-reaction in terms of the emphasis on the negative effects of violence in the media, as moral panics have been associated with media effects for well over a hundred years (Murdock, 2001). According to Murdock (2001), the demands for increased regulation and control of the media (often put forward by the media themselves) after the release of the latest violent horror movie or a particularly heinous crime being blamed on screen violence, are not new.

Sports violence and the media

In addition to the screening of controversial incidents of violence in regular sports television coverage, some sportsmen have featured in commercially available videos which have shown, some might say glorified, unsanctioned violent incidents from their sports. For example, former England and British Lions rugby union hooker, Brian Moore, provides commentary to violent fights in *Pitbull's punch ups*; former captain of Wales, FA Cup winner and Wimbledon soccer hardman Vinnie Jones features in *Soccer's hardmen*. Dermott Brereton, the former Australian Rules centre half forward, who had an outstanding career with Hawthorn and later with the Sydney and Collingwood clubs, brought out a video entitled *Hits and Memories*, which covered on-field violence in Australian Rules football. The involvement of these ex-athletes in these videos and the fact that the videos were on sale to the general public has been highly controversial.

The sale of sport 'video nasties' raises a number of other questions. For example, do portrayals of aggression and violence on television and in commercial videos encourage adult players to start engaging in unsanctioned violent play? Would watching these videos have an adverse effect on young athletes? Also, would these violent video images influence spectators? In attempting to answer these questions there are lessons to be learned from the general media effects debate.

Smith (1983, pp. 112–118) argued that young players do learn aggressive and violent acts through modelling the behaviour of their sports heroes or models. Much of the evidence for his conclusion at that time was based on the results of laboratory-type research undertaken by researchers who advocated a behavioural effects approach to film violence. The cultural and critical studies approach cautions against there being a simple cause and effect relationship between media violence and increased levels of violence in those who observe the violence. Perhaps Smith's (1983) conclusions need to be modified in the light of more recent research and thinking.

Wann *et al.* (2001, p. 115) have argued that the media tend to 'talk up or hype up' the antagonism between two opponents or two teams before competitive events to increase viewer interest, but that this may activate increased levels of hostility in spectators. Yet they also point out (p. 104) that the media have been quick to condemn violence in sports and in a similar, but opposite manner, the presumption is that this condemnation might act to reduce violence in sports. Which is it to be? On the one hand, the media are accused of increasing hostility and, on the other, praised for condemning violence in sports. This possible duality in the effects of media coverage of violent sports is rather similar to what occurs in general with the media and violent material. For example, a violent film or video is released by the media, then the media condemn it and demand increased regulation and control of the media (Buckingham, 2001; Murdock, 2001). A second point concerns the perceptions of those who watch or read about sanctioned and unsanctioned violence in sport. Are they passive and impressionable, accepting everything offered at face value, or do they perceive and make judgements on media sports violence in a critical fashion, as the advocates of the cultural and critical studies approach would have people believe?

Evidence from Australian rugby league suggests that fans and viewers are critical and, in this case, were self-regulating with regard to watching unsanctioned violence in sport (Hutchins and Phillips, 1997). Australian rugby league, in the 1970s and early 1980s, was dominated by excessive levels of unsanctioned violence. Sanctions and regulation were relatively weak and there was a general approval of unsanctioned violence by large sections of the rugby league community (Heads, 1992). As a result, the general public, especially women and families, became disillusioned. Attendances by fans at matches and the numbers of viewers watching on television declined, and junior players changed to other sports. Fans, viewers and junior players were critical of what was happening in Australian rugby league at the time and 'voted with their feet'. Faced with reduced income and a poor public image, commercially-driven Australian rugby league administrators were forced to make changes which would de-brutalize the game by eliminating unsanctioned violence.

Consider another example, the popular notion that watching violent sports has a beneficial cathartic effect, providing a chance for spectators to 'let off steam', thus reducing their general levels of aggression and hostility and making society safer. This proposition sounds reasonable, especially to those who have participated as spectators at sports events or other rowdy recreational activities like rock concerts and festivals. However, Wann *et al.* (2001, pp. 197–198) state directly that: 'Simply put, there is virtually no empirical evidence validating the existence of catharsis in sport'. This is a position shared by Guttmann (1998) and Zillmann (1998), based on the results of early behavioural effects experiments which failed to find any link:

Given the persuasive evidence that sports spectatorship *increases* rather than decreases aggressiveness, we can turn the catharsis theory on its head and conjecture that spectators *desire*, consciously or unconsciously, to experience an intensification of aggressiveness.

(Guttmann, 1998, p. 20)

However, might it not be better to think of catharsis in a wider sense, not limited to just aggression and hostility, but as a form of emotional or psychological purging, which might include a more complete palette of emotions within the whole experience of being a spectator or fan? This is an idea to which Wann *et al.* later gave some credence:

The point is although frustration and anger may not be eliminated at the ball-park, other emotions can and do get a vigorous workout. To the extent sport fans choose to express their emotions, freely and openly, they and society are the better for it.

(Wann *et al.*, 2001, p. 198)

Indeed, individuals who attend sports events on a regular basis may use them as opportunities for the modulation of emotions and arousal (e.g. Kerr, 1994; Thayer, 1989, 1996).

In trying to establish the truth about the effects of watching media sports violence, qualitative research, one of the methodologies advocated by cultural and critical studies researchers, might help to clarify some of the issues involved. For example, a research project by Barker and Brooks (1998) investigated how fans of the film *Judge Dredd* reacted to the violence, and got them to talk about their involvement and pleasure. From their interviews, the researchers were able to identify a number of sources of involvement and pleasure, which included physical satisfaction, being part of a crowd, creating imaginative worlds, game playing and role playing, taking risks, defying convention, confirming membership of communities of response, and critical appreciation. A contemporary series of qualitative studies with fans of violent and aggressive sports might prove equally revealing. After all, Colburn's (1985, 1989) qualitative research about ice hockey players and violence in Canadian ice hockey, described in chapter 4, certainly provided some useful insights about athletes. This is not to say that the experiments of the behavioural effects researchers are without value. Taken together with research findings from other approaches, the combined findings could provide an enhanced understanding of the involvement, pleasure and possible effects of observing both sanctioned and unsanctioned violent action in the media coverage of sports. In other words, a melding of the two research traditions might produce much more powerful results than either can produce independently.

A recurring theme throughout this book has been that sanctioned aggression and violence in sport is an inherent, enjoyable aspect of play in, for example, team contact sports. It should, therefore, not be objectionable and neither should reading about or viewing sanctioned aggression and violence in the media be problematic. If there is a problem concerned with media portrayal of sports violence, in terms of the effect it may have on those observing, then it is likely to be with unsanctioned aggression and violence. However, it is just as difficult to come to definite conclusions about the effects of portrayals of unsanctioned sports violence in the media on viewers as it is about media violence in general. As Kerr cautioned:

> Popular wisdom supported by some academic opinion and research evidence has it that violence on television and violent films and videos cause increased violence and aggression in viewers. However, the issues involved are complex and caution is required before jumping to definite conclusions about the influence of the media and their portrayal of violent acts in sport.
>
> (Kerr, 1999, p. 85)

Closing comments

Large numbers of people enjoy watching or reading material which includes portrayals of violence and, equally, large numbers of people enjoy watching live or televised sports events which include both real and fake violence. The main theme in this chapter has been to probe and explore the reasons why people enjoy the violence in these activities, and whether or not watching them has any effect on the viewers. The principal conclusion from the chapter is that popular wisdom which suggests media violence and media sports violence has harmful effects on people, especially where those viewers are young children, may not be correct. Sweeping statements, suggesting simple cause and effect, including even some based on early academic research, do not always stand up to detailed scrutiny. A good deal more research, involving a range of methodologies, is necessary before more definite conclusions can be drawn.

In examining the sources of pleasure identified by Barker and Brooks' (1998) research with *Judge Dredd* fans, it can be seen that many, if not all, can be neatly explained by reversal theory concepts. These include activities requiring the establishment of paratelic protective frames to allow the enjoyment of parapathic emotions and others which might allow the enhancement of emotional experience through cognitive synergies. It is therefore perhaps surprising that Zillmann (1998), in his condemnation of psychologists' lack of attention to portrayals of violence as entertainment, has not mentioned reversal theory as an exception to this neglect:

> Given that our attraction to portrayals of violence and its aftermath is obtrusive in filling movie and television screens and books and papers, in both fiction and non-fiction, it is astounding how little attention psychologists have paid to this phenomenon. Both the construction of the theories that might explain the extraordinary appeal of the portrayals in question and the empirical exploration of this appeal have been neglected. In untiring

fashion, social psychologists and others have investigated the antisocial consequences of exposure to fictional violence. . . . But they have essentially bypassed the issue of the appeal of fictional and non-fictional violence as a salient element of entertainment.

(Zillmann, 1998, pp. 181–182)

Clearly, reversal theory has addressed itself to the task of explaining why both fictional and non-fictional violence are appealing forms of entertainment in the past (e.g. Apter, 1982, 1992), and will do so in the future.

To date in this book a number of topics concerned with aggression and violence in sport have been covered. Numerous examples were examined in detail and scholarly work in the area was explored and critically analysed. Notions of sanctioned and unsanctioned aggression and violence, as they apply to both adult and young athletes, have been debated. In addition, a new typology of sports riots, including soccer hooliganism, has been proposed. Also, the motivation behind the popularity of watching sports involving real and fake violence was explored, and arguments about the possible effects of watching media portrayals of violence in sports have been discussed. In the next, and final, chapter much of the discussion is devoted to a critical analysis of the control of aggression and violence in sport.

Note

1   More detailed information on the characteristics, mechanism and structure of cognitive synergies can be found in Coulson (2001).

References

Apter, M. J. (1982). *The experience of motivation: The theory of psychological reversals.* London: Academic Press.

Apter, M. J. (1989). *Reversal theory: Motivation, emotion and personality.* London: Routledge.

Apter, M. J. (1992). *The dangerous edge.* New York: The Free Press.

Apter, M. J. (Ed.) (2001). *Motivational styles in everyday life: A guide to reversal theory.* Washington DC: American Psychological Association.

Barker, M. and Brooks, K. (1998). *Knowing audiences: Judge Dredd, its friends, fans and foes.* Luton: University of Luton Press.

Barker, M. and Petley, J. (Eds) (2001a) (2nd Edition). *Ill effects: The media/violence debate.* London: Routledge.

Barker, M. and Petley, J. (2001b). Introduction: From bad research to good – a guide for the perplexed. In M. Barker and J. Petley (Eds), *Ill effects: The media/violence debate* (2nd Edition, pp.1–26). London: Routledge.

Berkowitz, L. (1984). Some effects of thought on anti- and prosocial influences of media events: A cognitive neo-associationist analysis. *Psychological Bulletin, 95,* 410–427.

Buckingham, D. (1993). *Children talking television: The making of television literacy.* London: Falmer Press.

Buckingham, D. (1996). *Moving images: Understanding children's emotional responses to television*. Manchester: Manchester University Press.

Buckingham, D. (2000).*The making of citizens: Young people, news and politics*. London: Routledge.

Buckingham, D. (2001). Electronic child abuse: Rethinking the media's effects on children. In M. Barker and J. Petley (Eds), *Ill effects: The media/violence debate* (2nd Edition, pp. 63–77). London: Routledge.

Carter, C. and Weaver, C. K. (Eds) (2003). *Violence and the media*. Buckingham: Open University Press.

Colburn, K. (1985). Honor, ritual and violence in ice hockey. *Canadian Journal of Sociology, 10*, 153–170.

Colburn, K. (1989). Deviance and legitimacy in ice hockey: A microstructural theory of violence. In D. H. Kelly (Ed.), *Deviant behaviour*. New York: St. Martins Press

Coulson, A. S. (1991). Cognitive synergy in televised entertainment. In J. H. Kerr and M. J. Apter (Eds), *Adult play: A reversal theory approach* (pp. 71–85). Amsterdam: Swets and Zeitlinger.

Coulson, A. S. (2001). Cognitive synergy. In M. J. Apter (Ed.), *Motivational styles in everyday life: A guide to reversal theory* (pp. 229–248). Washington DC: American Psychological Association.

Elias, N. (1969/1982). *The civilising process*. New York: Pantheon.

Elias, N. and Dunning, E. (1970). The quest for excitement in unexciting societies. In G. Luschen (Ed.), *Cross-cultural analysis of sport and games* (pp. 31–51). Champaign, IL: Stipes.

Geen, R. G. (1981). Behavioral and physiological reactions to observed violence. Effects of prior exposure to aggressive stimuli. *Journal of Personality and Social Psychology, 40*, 868–875.

Geen, R. G. (2001). *Human aggression*. Buckingham: Open University Press.

Geen, R. G. and Thomas, S. L. (1986). The immediate effects of media violence on behavior. *Journal of Social Issues, 42*, 7–27.

Gerbner, G. and Gross, L. (1976). Living with television: The violence profile. *Journal of Communication, 26*, 173–199.

Gerbner, G., Gross, L., Morgan, M. and Signorielli, N. (1995). Violence on television: The Cultural Indicators Project. *Journal of Broadcasting and Electronic Media, 39*, 278–283.

Goldstein, J. (Ed.) (1998). *Why we watch: The attractions of violent entertainment*. New York: Oxford University Press.

Gunter, B. (2001). Ammunition in the violence debate. *The Psychologist, 14*, 656–657.

Guttmann, A. (1986). *Sports spectators*. New York: Columbia University Press.

Guttmann, A. (1998). The appeal of violent sports. In J. Goldstein (Ed.), *Why we watch: The attractions of violent entertainment* (pp. 7–26). New York: Oxford University Press.

Heads, I. (1992). *True blue: The story of NSW rugby league*. Randwick, NSW: Ironbark Press.

Huesmann, L. R. (1986). Psychological processes promoting the relation between exposure to media violence and aggressive behavior by the viewer. *Journal of Social Issues, 42*, 125–139.

Huesmann, L. R. , Eron, L. D., Klein, R., Brice, P. and Fischer, P. (1983). Mitigating the imitation of aggressive behaviours by changing children's attitudes to media violence. *Journal of Personality and Social Psychology, 44*, 899–910.

Hutchins, B. and Phillips, M. G. (1997). Selling permissible violence: The commodification of Australian rugby league 1970–1995. *International Review for the Sociology of Sport, 32,* 161–176.

Kerr, J. H. (1994). *Understanding soccer hooliganism.* Buckingham: Open University Press.

Kerr, J. H. (1999). The role of aggression and violence in sport: A rejoinder to the ISSP position stand. *The Sport Psychologist, 13,* 83–88.

Maylam, J. (2001, 21 October). K-1 hits the spot. *The Japan Times,* p. 9.

McCauley, C. (1998). When screen violence is not attractive. In J. Goldstein (Ed.), *Why we watch: The attractions of violent entertainment* (pp. 144–162). New York: Oxford University Press.

Millwood-Hargrave, A. (2003). *How children interpret screen violence.* London: British Broadcasting Corporation.

Mondak, J. J. (1989). The politics of professional wrestling. *Journal of Popular Culture, 23,* 139–149.

Murdock, M. (2001). Reservoirs of dogma: An archaeology of popular anxieties. In M. Barker and J. Petley (Eds), *Ill effects: The media/violence debate* (2nd Edition, pp.150–169). London: Routledge.

Nishiyama, G. (2001, 31 January). K-1's 'anything goes' fighting captivates Japan. *The Japan Times,* p. 3.

Pallo, 'Mr. TV', J. (1985). *You grunt and I'll groan: The inside story of wrestling.* London: McDonald Queen Anne Press.

Rinehart, R. (1994). Sport as kitsch: A case study of *The American Gladiators. Journal of Popular Culture, 28,* 25–35.

Schlesinger, P., Dobash, R. E., Dobash, R. P. and Weaver, C. K. (1992). *Women viewing violence.* London: British Film Institute.

Schlesinger, P., Haynes, R., Boyle, R., McNair, B., Dobash, R. E. and Dobash, R. P. (1998). *Men viewing violence.* London: Broadcasting Standards Council.

Smith, M. D. (1983). *Violence and sport.* Toronto: Butterworths.

Thayer, R. E. (1989). *The biopsychology of mood and arousal.* New York: Oxford University Press.

Thayer, R. E. (1996). *The origin of everyday moods.* New York: Oxford University Press.

Wann, D. L., Melnick, M. J., Russell, G. W. and Pease, D. G. (2001). *Sport fans: The psychology and social impact of spectators.* London: Routledge.

Yoshida is a knockout in mixed martial arts (2002, 30 August). *The Japan Times,* p. 23.

Zillmann, D. (1971). Excitation transfer in communication mediated aggressive behavior. *Journal of Experimental Social Psychology, 7,* 419–434.

Zillmann, D. (1983). Transfer of excitation in emotional behavior. In J. T. Cacioppo and R. E. Petty (Eds), *Social psychophysiology: A sourcebook.* New York: Guilford.

Zillmann, D. (1998). The psychology and the appeal of portrayals of violence. In J. Goldstein (Ed.), *Why we watch: The attractions of violent entertainment* (pp. 179–211). New York: Oxford University Press.

Zillmann, D. and Bryant, J. (1974). Effect of residual excitation on the emotional response to provocation and delayed aggressive behavior. *Journal of Personality and Social Psychology, 30,* 782–791.

9 The final whistle

Rounding off

The theme for this final chapter is the control of aggression and violence in sport. It will take a critical look at how the law deals with violent acts in sport, and at the arguments and recommendations for 'reducing the incidence of aggression and violence in the athletic domain' contained in the International Society of Sport Psychology's (ISSP) position stand. Following on from this critical review, measures are proposed for (a) reducing unsanctioned violent acts in sport, based on successful strategies implemented by the Australian Rugby League (ARL) and (b) dealing with soccer hooliganism and other types of sports riots. Finally, the usefulness of reversal theory in providing a new and integrated framework for understanding aggressive and violent behaviour in sport and the implications of this approach for research are discussed.

Violence in sport and the law

Until recent years, there has been a kind of unwritten code of silence amongst players and some officials in team contact sports. This ensured that 'what happened on the playing area during a game stayed there' and the possibility of taking an opponent to court was rarely, if ever, realised. Even in cases where players had been injured, they were generally reluctant to testify against any aggressor. Part of the background to this code was the fact that there was always the chance for 'evening the score' the next time the two players or teams met. However, recently some violent incidents in sport have resulted in criminal assault court cases, as well as claims for compensation. Anecdotal evidence suggests that, since the early 1990s, legal cases may also have been increasing (e.g. Henderson, 1996; James and Gardiner, 1997; Young, 1993), but it is not known if it is the actual number of violent incidents, or just the number of court cases, that have been increasing. The police and courts have generally been reluctant to get involved in incidents of unsanctioned violence on the playing area during games. In England, for example, although the police are entitled to intervene at their own discretion, they only do so as a last resort (Henderson, 1996). One example where police did decide to intervene was at the 1996 British ice hockey championship playoff between Durham Wasps and Humberside Hawks. A fight broke out during the pre-game warm up, and police arrested two players.

It has been argued in this book that, when unsanctioned violent actions occur, they should be exempt from the special status given to sanctioned violent acts in sport. It is the unique status given to sanctioned violent and aggressive acts which characterises the special nature of, for example, team contact sports. As such, those unsanctioned acts which fall outside the rules of the sport and player norms should then be considered as unacceptable by players, coaches and officials, but are they considered illegal in the eyes of the law?

Consider an example of unsanctioned violence from English rugby union. In 1995, Hendon rugby union player William Hardy was charged with manslaughter following the death of an opposing Centaurs player, Seamus Lavelle, in a Middlesex and Hertfordshire Division One match. Hardy went to the aid of some of his teammates who were embroiled in a fracas with opposing players, involving punching and kicking. Apparently, Hardy tried to cool things down verbally, but was attacked with two punches from behind by Lavelle. Hardy turned around and lashed out with an uppercut punch which caused Lavelle, a much bigger man, to fall backwards and hit the back of his skull on the ground. He suffered severe swelling of the brain and, after being put on a life-support machine in hospital, later died from his injuries. Hardy claimed in court that he hit out in self-defence because he was being hit, and did not actually know beforehand which player he had punched. He also stated that he 'did not mean to hurt the man. I did not mean to kill him'. Hardy was later acquitted of the manslaughter charge by the judge and jury (Cleary, 1995; Conagh, 1994).

There are some important similarities and differences between this case and the McSorley–Brashear ice hockey incident mentioned in chapter 1 (McGregor, 2000; 'McSorley found guilty', 2000). For example, Brashear, like Lavelle, struck his head after being hit, and McSorley, like Hardy, also stated that he had not intended to hurt Brashear. There are also some differences. For example, Hardy apparently acted in self-defence, whereas McSorley's attack was an act of revenge, not self-defence. Brashear was seriously injured in a top-level National Hockey League (NHL) ice hockey game, while Lavelle died in a relatively lower-level English rugby union match. Hardy was found not guilty, and even though McSorley was found guilty and was suspended from playing for a year by the NHL, his sentence from the court was eighteen months' probation. Were the courts' decisions in either case correct? Had Hardy's uppercut been part of a street fight or pub brawl would he have been acquitted? Had McSorley's deliberate slash with his stick to Brasher's head not taken place on the ice during a game, would he have been fined or given a prison sentence, like any other member of the public found guilty of assault?

In an attempt to shed more light on the thinking behind these types of decisions and the law's interpretation of unsanctioned violent acts carried out in a sporting context, some examples of court decisions in Canadian and Scottish law will be examined in the following sections. The notion of consent in Canadian court decisions and apparent inconsistencies in recent Scottish court decisions will be addressed.

The Latin legal term *violenti non fit injuria* (to one who consents no injury is done) is often quoted in relation to cases involving athletes injured in violent sports. However, a crucial question with regard to this term is, exactly what do participants consent to in terms of level of risk? At one extreme, consent might be considered to apply to all risks, at the other only to limited risks. Also, can the notion of consent be interpreted to the extent that it might include consent to a degree of unsanctioned violence? The Centre for Sport and Law at Brock University in Canada published two articles ('Dealing with violence', 2003; 'Violence in sport', 2002) which summarised some of the legal decisions made in Canadian courts that are relevant to the discussion here. With regard to the notion of consent, in one negligence case concerning an intercollegiate Canadian football[1] game (Dunn versus University of Ottawa), the court accepted that Dunn had consented to a degree of violence, but it only covered what might be 'reasonably expected under the circumstances':

> The court found that while a punt returner consents to being hit hard by a tackler, he does not consent (and in this instance the player did not consent) to 'being head butted or speared in the face by an onrushing 225-pound linebacker while in that vulnerable position [that is, looking up, tracking the ball within the five yard no-tackle zone.]' The court found that the actions of the defendant fell far below the standard that might reasonably be expected of, or accepted by, a university football player.
>
> ('Dealing with violence', 2003, p. 2)

It would appear that the court's decision was based on the fact that Dunn gave his consent to sanctioned acts of violence (being hit hard by the tackler), but not to a particularly vicious unsanctioned act (deliberately using the helmet in a tackle to 'spear' an opponent) in the no tackle zone that not only contravened the rules of Canadian football, but was highly dangerous. The judge wrote:

> Not every breach of the rules, by any stretch of the imagination, will result in a finding of negligence within the context of a game such as football. Such non-compliance is but one factor in any judicial determination. Only when there is a deliberate intention to cause injury or a reckless disregard for the consequences of one's actions in an uncontrolled and undisciplined manner will a finding of negligence result.
>
> ('Dealing with violence', 2003, p. 2)

The Dunn versus University of Ottawa case was a negligence case, but the issue of consent arises again in assault cases where intention to inflict force, and lack of consent by the victim to that force, must be established. Following three cases involving ice hockey incidents, Canadian 'courts have recognized that even where a particular level of violence is expected, and indeed may have been consented to, it may be so inherently dangerous as to preclude such consent' ('Violence in sport', 2002). Indeed, a set of points to be considered in these kind of cases has been developed by the courts:

- *Nature of the game* Was it an amateur or professional league? Competitive? Contact or non-contact?
- *Nature of the act(s) and surrounding circumstances* Was the act common or uncommon? Did it occur away from the play or after the whistle? What degree of force was applied?
- *Degree of risk* Was serious injury possible or probable?
- *State of mind* Was the act done in retaliation or to intimidate?

('Violence in sport', 2002)

Although these points represent a step forward in terms of objectivity, they are still rather unspecific, and the importance of the answers to the questions that have been posed still has to be decided on subjectively by judge and/or jury. In coming up with a decision, judge and/or jury may have considerable difficulty in interpreting these points. The list of points was developed some time after the McSorley–Brashear case but, for example with regard to point 1, the nature of the game, if NHL ice hockey player McSorley had been playing in a competitive amateur contact ice hockey league would that mean that his stick attack on Brashear should be interpreted differently? While it is true that the same action in a non-contact league might be considered differently because, presumably, players in a non-contact league have not given their consent to physical contact and/or a degree of violence, this would not apply to amateurs playing competitive ice hockey with full contact. Also, it is difficult to decide about point 3, the degree of risk. For example, in the McSorley–Brashear and Hardy–Lavelle cases, after the initial blow was struck, the serious injuries occurred as a result of heads striking the ice or the ground. Could a judge and/or jury decide whether, in the particular circumstances of each case, the injuries had been possible or probable? Difficulties in interpretation of these points do not assist the legal profession in their attempts to be consistent in court decisions.

James and Gardiner (1997) compared three different cases of sportsfield violence in Scottish soccer to illustrate the inconsistent nature of legal intervention. In the first, an 'off the ball' headbutt, which caused little injury to the recipient, resulted in a three month prison sentence (the offending player was also on probation for a previous violent offence); in the second, an 'on the ball' elbow in the face, requiring five stitches, resulted in no legal action; and in the third, a player was fined for kicking the ball into the crowd with more force than necessary and concussing a spectator (the player kicked the ball out so that an injured teammate could receive medical attention).

In 1996, the Lord Advocate (chief justice) in Scotland issued 'Instructions' (a statement of guidelines) to chief constables of police to cover potentially volatile situations, which stated that the priority at sports fixtures is crowd control. In addition, the instructions also made it clear that those involved with the playing and administration of the game are primarily responsible for conduct on the field, but players cannot be regarded as exempt from the criminal law (James and Gardiner, 1997). In particular, James and Gardiner (1997) pointed out that the police are given little guidance in the Lord Advocate's statement and must use their discretion in the same way as they would when dealing with any other violent incident outside of sport. A relevant part of the statement is included here:

> ... the Lord Advocate wishes the police to investigate and, where appropriate, report to the Procurator Fiscal [public prosecutor] incidents where the violence used by the participant goes *well beyond* that which would be expected to occur during the normal run of play and that which the rules of the sport concerned are designed to regulate. In deciding which incidents to investigate the police should pay particular regard to incidents where the violence or disorderly behaviour has occurred after the whistle has blown and whilst the ball is dead and to incidents where the violence or disorderly behaviour has occurred in circumstances designed or liable to provoke a disorderly or violent response from spectators.
>
> (James and Gardiner, 1997, pp. 42–43)

The statement is rather vague; no specific explanation of terms like 'well beyond' and 'normal run of play' is provided. Vague terms like these leave considerable doubt as to what is actually intended and who should decide whether or not an athlete's behaviour is illegal: match officials, administrators, the police, public prosecutor, or the courts? James and Gardiner (1997, p. 44) also note that the Lord Advocate's Instructions give the impression that all 'normal play' is lawful, but query, for example, whether high tackles in rugby (which, despite being against the rules of the game, happen quite often during play) should be immune from prosecution as part of normal play, or subject to criminal prosecution as being well beyond what is considered normal play?

More attention needs to be given to legal aspects of violent incidents in sport. As demonstrated by the cases and decisions in Canadian and Scottish law, the point made by James and Gardiner in 1997 of the need for more detailed definitions, either by prosecution policy or on a case by case basis in the courts (backed up by a rigorous system of internal measures developed by the sports governing bodies), is relevant.

In the same way that there is a lack of clarity on legal aspects of aggression and violence in sport, there is also a general lack of understanding of the nature and role of aggression and violence in sport. The International Society of Sport Psychology's position stand (Tenenbaum, *et al.*, 1997; Tenenbaum, *et al.*, 2000) is a case in point. Although prepared on behalf of ISSP members, it is also typical of the misguided views held by many people. In particular, the position stand contains a number of recommendations for reducing the incidence of aggression and violence in sport and it is important, therefore, to examine the position stand and Kerr's (1999, 2002) criticisms of the document in more detail.

The ISSP position stand and misconceptions of aggression and violence in sport

In his rejoinder to the ISSP position stand, Kerr concluded:

> It has been argued here that the ISSP position stand is unacceptable and would need to be radically altered if it is ever to be taken on board by sport psychologists and the wider sport community. This is especially true for the concluding Recommendations. In a nutshell, the majority of these recommendations are unrealistic and/or unworkable and need to be radically revised and redrafted.
>
> (Kerr, 1999, p. 87)

What was it about the ISSP position stand that warranted such strong criticism? It is impossible to reproduce all the details of the four published papers (Kerr, 1999, 2002; Tenenbaum, *et al.*, 1997; Tenenbaum, *et al.*, 2000) debating the issues of aggression and violence in sport raised by the ISSP position stand, so discussion here will be limited to some of the main points. Kerr (1999) criticised the ISSP position stand on five major points: (1) a lack of rationale and background information on how and why it was developed; (2) a failure to provide a real understanding of the motivation behind aggression and violence in sport; (3) a failure to distinguish between on-field violence and spectator or fan violence; (4) the overly concrete conclusions about the influence of media; (5) the blame placed on officials for making errors which result in player or spectator violence. Each of these points will be expanded on below.

First, the position stand lacked clear statements about how and why it was developed, who it was aimed at, and how it might be used. While it did include a review of some of the general sport aggression literature, the review was neither current nor comprehensive.

Second, Kerr (1999) argued that the ISSP position stand failed to provide a real understanding of the motivation behind aggression and violence in sport, especially in team contact sports. For example, the position stand did not provide a specific definition of aggression and violence in sport. Rather, it relied on some of the definitions prevalent in the sport psychology literature (see chapter 1, page 7) which are too general and not flexible enough to distinguish between sanctioned and unsanctioned aggression and violence in, for example, team contact sports. In particular, LeUnes and Nation's (1989; see page 7 of this volume) definition containing the phrase *intent to injure* was emphasised by the position stand and Tenenbaum *et al.* (2000, p. 317). However, as is apparent from the discussion in chapter 1, deciding on whether an athlete had an intent to injure when carrying out an act of sanctioned or unsanctioned violence is especially problematic, a fact that has been recognised by other academics studying sports violence (Isberg, 2000; Russell, 1993: Smith, 1983). Any satisfactory definition, has to recognise that sanctioned acts of aggression and violence in sport are willingly sought by athletes as a primary source of pleasure and that these acts are fundamentally different in nature from unsanctioned violent acts, both inside and outside the sports context (e.g. page 8 this volume; Kerr, 1997; Russell, 1993). Also lacking credibility were claims in the position stand that sanctioned aggressive acts were *assertive* rather than aggressive (pages 11–12 this volume, Kerr, 2002)

Third, the position stand failed to differentiate between on-field violence and spectator or fan violence and, apart from one brief reference, ignored soccer hooliganism and the substantial literature on the topic that has accumulated since the 1960s. Later it was claimed that: 'the definitions of aggression given in the PS can be applied to the behaviors of both participants and spectators, though they have different triggers' (Tenenbaum, *et al.*, 2000, p. 318), but this argument is unconvincing. The motivation behind athletes' and fans' aggressive and violent behaviour can take a variety of forms and result in a number of different outcomes. However, direct links between the two are not always apparent and, for example, violent acts by fans are only occasionally sparked by particular events on the playing arena. In addition, it has been established that many acts of soccer hooliganism take place because of motives that have little to do with actual play during soccer matches (Chapter 7 this volume; Kerr, 1994; Kerr and de Kock, 2002). Therefore, it would be prudent to consider violent athlete and fan behaviour separately.

Fourth, the position stand made very definite conclusions about the effects of portrayals of aggressive and violent behaviour in sport and the influence of the media (especially television). It cited Bandura's research work on the supposed learning of aggressive acts through imitation (Bandura *et al.*, 1963a, 1963b). However, as Kerr (page 14 this volume; 2002) pointed out, the experimental conditions in Bandura and his colleagues' studies have been criticised by other psychologists as merely reflecting vigorous play rather than aggression. The position stand also cited other studies (e.g. Comisky *et al.*, 1977; Bryant *et al.*, 1981; Bryant *et al.*, 1982) which, it was argued, suggested that 'fans like violence in their sports'. These studies were carried out on the effects of watching televised rough play in American football and ice hockey, and hostility between tennis players. Kerr (2002) drew attention to comments later made by some of the researchers in reviewing these studies which questioned the effects of observing violence in televised sports. They stated:

> In spite of the pervasiveness of the claim that violence in sports has considerable entertainment value, and regardless of the coherent and contrived rationales that have been proposed to account for it, pertinent empirical evidence is scarce. Only three investigations have directly assessed the appeal of sports violence for spectators.
>
> (Bryant and Zillman, 1983, p. 200)

And later:

> Notwithstanding speculations, research fails us at this point. The effect of

injurious play in sports on spectators' enjoyment is simply not known at present.

(Bryant and Zillmann, 1983, p. 203)

The relationship between television viewing of violence and the amplification of violence or antisocial behaviour in observers is more complicated than the rather simplistic view presented by the position stand. Kerr (1999) urged caution because the issues involved are complex and there is no simple cause and effect relationship. It was argued on page 125 that evidence from the behavioural effects approach (which would include most of the research studies cited in the position stand and Tenenbaum *et al.*, 2000) is somewhat limited, and the use of more sophisticated theoretical models and methodologies to analyse how people interact with media portrayals of violence are necessary (e.g. Gunter, 2001).

Fifth, game officials were incorrectly blamed in the position stand for making errors which act as a catalyst for arousing emotions which may then result in player or spectator violence. The position stand went on to suggest that improving officials' mental skills, including 'improving their ability to concentrate, control unnecessary arousal, and cope with pressure' (Tenenbaum *et al.*, 1997, p. 4), would minimise violent behaviour amongst athletes and spectators. Kerr (1999) considered that such a statement was inappropriate because, while officials may make an occasional erroneous decision and these may result in a violent response from players or spectators, incidents are relatively few in number. Kerr stated:

> The number of violent acts amongst spectators sparked by an official's wrong decision, in relation to the number of games played week in week out, must be very small indeed. With respect to players, aggressive and violent acts between players or perpetrated against officials by players in most sports are minimal.

(Kerr, 1999, pp. 85–86)

This view was contrary to that put forward in the position stand and Tenenbaum *et al.* (2000) that 'aggressive and violent behavior toward officials by athletes, coaches and spectators are not rare occurrences'. The authors attempted to support their arguments by the citation of studies by Rainey (1994) and Rainey and Hardy (1999), which investigated assaults on baseball umpires and rugby referees. However, examining the results of these studies closely, Kerr (2002) was, for example, (a) able to quote Rainey and Hardy (1999) who said: 'Only a small minority (5.6%) of the rugby referees reported that they had been assaulted', and (b) able to point out that neither study reported the reasons why the assaults took place and therefore the results could not be used to substantiate the standpoint that officials make errors that inflame aggressive acts in athletes and spectators.

The arguments in the position stand regarding these five major points were inaccurate at best and misguided at worst. Unfortunately, this was also true for the majority of the nine ISSP recommendations for 'dramatically reducing the incidence of aggression and violence in the athletic domain', made towards the end of the position stand (Tenenbaum *et al.*, 1997, p. 5). In spite of an appeal for these to be 'radically revised and redrafted' (Kerr, 1999, p. 83) these remained unchanged (Tenenbaum *et al.*, 2000). The recommendations were:

Recommendation 1 Management should make fundamental penalty revisions so that rule-violating behavior results in punishments that have greater punitive value than potential reinforcement.

Recommendation 2 Management must ensure proper coaching of teams, particularly at junior levels, which emphasises a fair code-of-conduct among all participants.

Recommendation 3 Management should ban the use of alcoholic beverages at sporting events.

Recommendation 4 Management must make sure facilities are adequate regarding catering and spacing needs and the provision of modern amenities.

Recommendation 5 The media must place in the proper perspective the isolated incidents of aggression that occur in sport rather than making them 'highlights.'

Recommendation 6 The media should promote a campaign to decrease violence and hostile aggression in sport which will also involve the participation and commitment of athletes, coaches, management, officials and spectators.

Recommendation 7 Coaches, managers, athletes, media, officials, and authority figures (i.e. the police) should take part in workshops on aggression and violence to ensure that they understand the topic of aggression, why it occurs, the cost of aggressive acts, and how aggressive behavior can be controlled.

Recommendation 8 Coaches, managers, officials and the media should encourage athletes to engage in prosocial behavior and punish those who perform acts of hostility.

Recommendation 9 Athletes should take part in programs aimed at helping them reduce behavioral tendencies toward aggression. The tightening of rules, imposing of harsher penalties and changing of reinforcement patterns are only part of the answer to inhibiting aggression in sport. Ultimately, the athlete must assume responsibility for his or her behavior.

(Tenenbaum *et al.*, 1997, p. 5)

Even a quick glance through these recommendations should reveal to the reader that, with the exception of recommendation 1 and the last two sentences of recommendation 9, the majority were unrealistic and/or unworkable and some patronising and/or insulting (Kerr, 1999). Take recommendation 7, for example; rather than demand that coaches and others take part in aggression and violence workshops, it might have been preferable to recommend that professional psychologists offer educational programmes on aggression and violence for anyone interested. With regard to the police, who often deal with extreme violence on a regular basis in their daily work, the suggestion that they need to attend workshops was both patronising and insulting. Similarly, recommending that athletes take part in programmes aimed at helping them reduce behavioural tendencies toward aggression (recommendation 9) is to misunderstand athletes' motivation for participation in aggressive and violent sports and the real nature of aggression and violence in sport. This recommendation is certainly not helpful for those athletes involved in sports where aggression and/or violence is a necessary and sanctioned characteristic. If reinforcement patterns have to be changed then it should be to inhibit unsanctioned violence in sport, not sanctioned aggression and violence.

The stance adopted in the position stand is one which appears to be arguing for a world of politically correct, sanitised sports. While it may be necessary for sport psychologists to draw up a position stand on unsanctioned aggression and violence in sport, a general attack on all aggressive and violent acts (including sanctioned acts) was unwarranted. As Kerr stated:

> The kind of 'sanitized' sports that the PS and Tenenbaum *et al.* (2000) seem to be arguing for actually already exist. They are known as touch rugby, touch or tag American football, and no-contact ice hockey. Without the element of sanctioned aggressive and violent physical contact, they bear scant resemblance to the real games of rugby, American football and ice hockey.
>
> (Kerr, 2002, p. 76)

Caution should be exercised by sport administrators and officials, and the courts, before interfering with sanctioned aggression and violence in sport. There is a danger that, for example, team contact sports would become too benign and therefore much less interesting for both players and spectators. Unsanctioned violence in sport needs to be reduced, but what measures can be taken to control such acts? The next section examines how they might be controlled, making reference to the successful strategies adopted by the Australian Rugby League, which radically changed rugby league into a sport where unsanctioned violence is now the exception rather than the rule.

How to reduce unsanctioned aggressive and violent acts in sport

Sport governing bodies are already taking action against blatant acts of unsanctioned violence and, in some cases, have been doing so for some time. The example of Australian rugby league and its domination by a subculture of excessive unsanctioned violence during the 1970s and early 1980s (Heads, 1992; Hutchins and Phillips, 1997) was used in the previous chapter to illustrate the fact that sports fans and viewers are self-regulating when it comes to watching unsanctioned violence in sport. Beyond showing that fans could be critical in their viewing and attendance, the Australian rugby league example could almost be held up as a reference model for other team contact sports, for how to dramatically reduce unsanctioned violence in sport. Driven by technological, cultural, social, and economic factors, a number of radical changes were introduced, over a period of years in the 1980s, that dramatically transformed the game (Hutchins and Phillips, 1997). Rules were changed (e.g. the use of 'sin bins', where offending players had to leave the field for 10 minutes without being replaced) and the interpretation and enforcement of the rules became much stricter, as referees and other match officials stamped down on acts of unsanctioned violence. A solicitor was made chairman of a post-match adjudication panel which examined incidents of violence using television and video replays. If found guilty of an impermissible violent act by the panel, players were given much more severe penalties than in the past. The outcome was a substantial improvement in player conduct and a marked decrease in unsanctioned violent incidents. More than this, however, well aware of their poor public image, the ARL also began a television advertising campaign as part of its marketing strategy and commercial restructuring. All of these changes contributed to what Hutchins and Phillips (1997) called the commodification of rugby league in Australia. The game became faster, the players became fitter and more skilful, the play became much more spectacular and there was a great reduction in incidents of punching and fighting. The measures pioneered in Australia have been adopted by other countries and, in contemporary rugby league, there is little tolerance for acts of unsanctioned violence.

It is interesting that rugby union, which lagged behind rugby league for some years, has now adopted most of the measures implemented in that sport. In the 2003 Rugby World Cup, for example, video replay assessments by a so-called 'independent citing official' and judiciary panels were used to examine incidents of unsanctioned violent play, and some players were suspended as a result. In addition, game officials tightened up their interpretation and enforcement of the laws of the game, and used red and yellow cards for 'sending off' and 'sin bin' offences. Game officials' effectiveness was greatly assisted by technology. The referee and his two assistants, as well as the video referee in the grandstand, were connected by interactive radio communication links that allowed them to communicate easily. This changed the role of touch judges to that of 'referee assistants', who could advise the referee during play of any infraction of the laws (including unsanctioned violent play) that the referee might have missed. These changes made it very difficult for any rugby union player at the 2003 Rugby World Cup to escape detection for an act of unsanctioned violence.

These days most, if not all, team contact sports use video replays to examine aspects of play, including incidents of violence. However, the use of technology to aid officials has not been adopted to the same extent by all team contact sports. Some, like soccer, limit its use to investigating incidents after matches. Others, like rugby union, allow limited use during a game to adjudicate when the on-field officials were unsighted during the scoring of a try, as well as for post-match analysis. Similarly, in American football:

> Each week the league's supervisors of officials review every play of every game, sometimes from as many as five angles, and red-flag anything they think might be a finable offense. Washington [the NFL director of football development] then views each play and renders a decision, often fining players for transgressions that didn't draw a penalty during the game. Though the system has its flaws . . . it has undoubtedly helped clean up the game.
>
> (Silver, 1998, p. 52)

More recently, in American football, video apparatus is also placed at the side of the field, which allows the referee to review plays during games when necessary. Individual sports have their particular reasons for the degree to which they have adopted technology, but it might be beneficial for each sport to check on the way technology is used in other team contact sports. For example, soccer could well benefit from having its referee and touch judges linked by communication systems in the way, for example, that the technology is now used in rugby union. This might in turn expand the role of touch judges in soccer to provide greater assistance to referees, while at the same time reducing the possibility of 'off the ball' incidents.

While most team contact sports have engaged to a greater or lesser extent in trying to eliminate unsanctioned violence, one team contact sport, ice hockey, stands out as the one sport which continues to allow unsanctioned violent acts in the form of fighting. The authorities have resisted making any changes to hockey rules, arguing that fighting is a part of hockey and claiming that it acts as a means of preventing other, more vicious types of unsanctioned violent acts coming to the fore. In countries such as Canada, fighting and other violent acts in hockey are extremely controversial and, like rugby league in Australia in the 1970s and 1980s, its public image is not good among large sections of the population. One can only speculate that, if contemporary ice hockey, especially the National Hockey League, adopted an approach similar to that adopted in rugby league and, increasingly, rugby union, the game of hockey might be transformed, in a way similar to these two other sports.

Trying to deal with sports riots and soccer hooliganism

Sports riots can occur for various reasons, and it may be necessary to vary the methods adopted to contain or prevent them. Play and thrill riots often occur for no obvious reason, just for the hell of it. In trying to deal with or prevent thrill and play riots, the choices are similar to those outlined below for dealing with soccer hooliganism. On the one hand, the authorities and police can try to anticipate when and where trouble is likely to take place, prepare carefully and respond with overwhelming force as the police in Sapporo did during the soccer World Cup in 2002. On the other hand, innovative ways could be found, especially around large sport events like the US student basketball and ice hockey finals described in chapter 7 (pages 97–8), to allow young people to take risks and have fun without rioting. This would require finding activities which would appeal to highly aroused, excited people in the paratelic state. For example, in the case of the US students, if the universities had organised post-game rock concert-type festivals or parties for both winning and losing fans in their respective locations, well away from downtown or shopping areas in relatively controlled situations, perhaps the rioting, injuries and arrests could have been avoided.

Anger and power riots are more difficult to deal with. When power riots occur, the people concerned are very serious about their 'cause'. For them the end justifies the means and this type of sports riot is likely to continue until, for example, the 'problem' (e.g. fox hunting or apartheid) has been solved. This usually means that there is often no obvious way of reducing or eliminating power riots until major decisions are made by governments. The police are often left to try and contain the protestors and prevent them from disrupting sports events. The often spontaneous nature of anger riots makes it very difficult to anticipate when they might take place. One might argue that large numbers of police should be available, for example in and around sports stadia and/or downtown areas, just in case an anger riot should occur. However, this strategy may not only be financially unfeasible, but could be counter-productive in terms of maintaining public order, as over-zealous responses by police might escalate low-level rioting to more serious levels of fighting and destruction. Herein lies a dilemma for the police; if they respond to rioting with too little force they may add to the fun for rioters, but if they respond with too much force they may on some occasions provoke an escalation in rioting and violence.

Soccer hooliganism

Given the motivation behind this form of antisocial behaviour, what possible options are there for dealing with hooliganism? One possible option, often advocated by sports authorities, police forces and the law courts, is to 'get tough' with or 'crack down hard' on offenders. Even though this strategy has been pursued in Europe over the last 40 years without lasting success, some would argue that it was successful in preventing hooligan behaviour in Japan during the Soccer World Cup in 2002. The important implication from events in Japan is that, if the authorities and the police do decide to take action to prevent outbreaks of soccer hooliganism, they need to do so with a great deal of preparation and overwhelming force. Anything less than this and they may simply add to the fun of the hooligan game. Also, the optimistic conclusion that the authorities and the police may be tempted to make after events in Japan in 2002 is that it is possible to prevent soccer hooliganism. While the very heavy police presence and other measures worked in a one-off soccer tournament in Japan, over the longer term waging a successful war against soccer hooliganism may just displace hooligan behaviour to some other destructive activity in other locations.

Other options for preventing or reducing soccer hooliganism involve finding alternative forms of rewarding activities to replace hooligan behaviour (i.e. hooligan rehabilitation). These activities would need to be able to provide the same levels of excitement, pleasure and intensity of experience and be useful for weaning hooligans away from their reliance on the negativistic state. Kerr proposed three possibilities:

> Firstly, hooligan fighting might be relocated to a context which was not anti-social, such as that associated with combat sports; boxing, judo or the Eastern martial arts. This strategy, however, would require the ex-hooligan to move away from negativistic activity, as most of these sports require a high degree of conformity to rules or etiquette. Secondly, activities which the hooligan engaged in before starting on a hooligan career might be regenerated. However, keep in mind that these activities were rejected before as inadequate in producing the desired levels of hedonic tone, and so may not prove as effective as adopting the third strategy. The third possibility is to find a new set of self-satisfying experiences. This approach offers perhaps the best option for successful treatment as it would have added appeal, in terms of novelty, for producing paratelic-oriented experience.
>
> (Kerr, 1994, p. 114)

Although these three options might appear to be geared to the level of the individual, in principle there is nothing, apart from logistics, to prevent them being applied to larger groups. For example, if hooligans in sufficient numbers could be encouraged to take part in dangerous risk-sports, like sky diving, mountaineering, skiing or car or motor cycle racing, it might allow them to get their 'kicks' in a more socially acceptable, non-destructive way. Such strategies may at first glance appear to be unworkable. However, if one considers the very large sums of money that, for example, soccer hooliganism costs the British government, these strategies might well be successful if even part of those sums could be invested at a local societal level to provide alternative risk-taking activities for established and apprentice hooligans and other disaffected youth. The British government shows no sign of trying out innovative solutions to the hooligan problem, possibly not wanting to reward hooligan behaviour in this way. Unfortunately, without new initiatives, local patterns and traditions in leisure or individual patterns of lifestyle and finance may govern the choice of alternative activities (Kerr, 1994; Plant and Plant,1992) and these will already probably have been rejected by hooligans.

An integrated approach to understanding aggression and violence in sport

There has been something of a campaign in this book to get across the message that not all aggression and violence in sport should be viewed in a negative light. On the contrary, there are situations where certain types of aggressive and violent acts are central to people's enjoyment of activities. These activities range from athletic contests to viewing violent sports as a spectator, or watching violent sports movies. Being a part of these activities does no psychological harm to the vast majority of those who participate and may actually benefit their psychological health (Kerr, 1997). It is unusual to find a psychological theory that takes a positive view of certain kinds of violent acts in the context of sport and, moreover, one that can explain the psychological dynamics involved across the wide range of topics associated with aggression and violence.

Tthe reversal theory approach (Apter, 1982, 2001), and the importance of metamotivational state combinations, the salience of particular states in those combinations, and reversals between individual pairs of states has been emphasised throughout this text. In addition, the role played by metamotivational variables, like felt arousal or felt toughness, and cognitive synergies has also been stressed. However, the key concept from reversal theory which permeates all the various examples of aggression and violence described in this book is that of paratelic protective frames. For example, it is only through the notion of safety-zone and confidence frames that it is possible to understand how people, both adults and youth, would voluntarily subject themselves to possible physical damage for the pleasures of taking part in violent sports. Safety-zone and detachment frames also add to an understanding of why people feel secure and enjoy spectating and being a fan at sports events. In addition, detachment frames and the enjoyment of parapathic emotions are crucial in explaining the motivation behind watching such diametrically opposed sports as K-1 fighting and pro-wrestling, as well as violent sports films like *Rollerball* and *The Running Man*. Furthermore, the concepts of confidence, safety-zone frames and parapathic emotions greatly assist with explanations of why people engage in antisocial sport-related rioting and soccer hooligan behaviour. The lack of hooliganism in Sapporo at the 2002 Soccer World Cup, for example, may well have been an example of a situation where the hooligans 'chickened out' because no protective frames were in operation and they perceived the risks involved as being too high. As demonstrated in this book, reversal theory is in the unique position of being able to provide an integrated approach to understanding virtually all aspects of aggression and violence in sport.

This integrated approach has a number of implications for future research on the topic. For example, it should immediately be obvious that taking a general scale of hostility or aggression (e.g. Buss and Durkee, 1957; Buss and Perry, 1992) and administering it to athletes to measure aggression and violence in sport is liable to produce invalid results. Any measure of aggression and violence in sport needs to allow not only for possible differences between, for example, an athlete's attitude to aggression and violence in the sports context and his or her attitude to aggression and violence in everyday life, but also to possible differences in their attitude to sanctioned and unsanctioned aggression and violence in sport. Such measures would benefit from being tailored to individual sports, where the idiosyncrasies of each sport and the contexts where different types of violence might be acceptable could be explored. Before meaningful progress can be made, new measures incorporating the concepts of sanctioned and unsanctioned aggression and violence need to be developed.

In attempting to identify sport-specific attitudes to aggression and violence, qualitative methods may have considerable advantages over quantitative methods. The comparatively more flexible approach of various types of interviews (e.g. structured or semi-structured interviews, interviews and later metamotivational coding, post-competition interviews with video recall) may provide richer results than self-report scales. For example, interviews conducted as part of research by Colburn (1985, 1989) on male, and Theberge (1999) on female ice hockey players' attitudes to aggression and violence were particularly revealing in providing the subjective views of individual athletes.

Closing comments

It is time for sport psychologists, and other interested groups, to take a long, hard look at popular wisdom and the sports literature and re-think some contemporary notions of aggression and violence in sport. This book has examined aggression and violence in sport in the broadest sense of the term, and is intended to challenge and test contemporary notions, while at the same time offering alternative interpretations and explanations. Most important of all in this process is to come up with explanations which mean something to those people 'at the coalface' who, in some way or other, are involved in aggression and violence in the name of sport: primarily athletes, coaches, officials and administrators, but also spectators, fans and television commentators as well as law enforcement agencies. To be considered at all adequate by members of these groups, any theoretical explanations must have a sound basis in reality. As this book draws to a close, it is hoped that it has provided just such a realistic understanding of aggression and violence in sport.

Note

1   Canadian football is similar to American football, but there are some differences in the rules of the two games.

References

Apter, M. J. (1982). *The experience of motivation: The theory of psychological reversals.* London: Academic Press.

Apter, M. J. (Ed.) (2001). *Motivational styles in everyday life: A guide to reversal theory.* Washington: American Psychological Association.

Bandura, A., Ross, D. and Ross, S. A. (1963a). Imitation of film-mediated aggressive models. *Journal of Abnormal and Social Psychology, 66,* 3–11.

Bandura, A., Ross, D. and Ross, S. A. (1963b). Vicarious reinforcement and imitative learning. *Journal of Abnormal Psychology, 67,* 601–603.

Bryant, J., Comisky, D. W. and Zillmann, D. (1981). The appeal of rough and tumble play in televised professional football. *Communication Quarterly, 29,* 256–262.

Bryant, J., Brown, D., Comisky, D. W. and Zillmann, D. (1982). Sports and spectators. *Journal of Communication, 32,* 109–119.

Bryant, J. and Zillmann, D. (1983). Sports violence and the media. In J. H. Goldstein (Ed.), *Sport violence* (pp. 195–211). New York: Springer-Verlag.

Buss, A. H. and Durkee, A. (1957). An inventory for assessing different kinds of hostility. *Journal of Consulting Psychology, 21,* 296–349.

Buss, A. H. and Perry, M. (1992). The Aggression Questionnaire. *Journal of Personality and Social Psychology, 63,* 452–459.

Cleary, M. (1995, January). The killing fields? *Rugby World,* pp. 59–61.

Colburn, K. (1985). Honor, ritual and violence in ice hockey. *Canadian Journal of Sociology, 10,* 153–170.

Colburn, K. (1989). Deviance and legitimacy in ice hockey: A microstructural theory of violence. In D. H. Kelly (Ed.), *Deviant Behaviour.* New York: St. Martins Press.

Comisky, D. W., Bryant, J. and Zillmann, D. (1977). Commentary as a substitute for action. *Journal of Communication, 27,* 150–153.

Conagh, D. (1994, 24 July). Judge clears rugby player who killed man on pitch. *The Times,* p. 5.

Dealing with violence as a legal issue (2003). *Coaches' Report, 9* (3). (Centre for Sport and Law Inc., Brock University, website: www.sportlaw.ca).

Gunter, B. (2001). Ammunition in the violence debate. *The Psychologist, 14,* 656–657.

Heads, I. (1992). *True blue: The story of the NSW Rugby League.* Randwick, NSW: Ironbark Press.

Henderson, J. (1996, 17 March). Why sport gets its collar felt. *Observer,* p. 2.

Hutchins, B. and Phillips, M. G. (1997). Selling permissible violence: The commodification of Australian Rugby League 1970–1995. *International Review for the Sociology of Sport, 32,* 161–176.

Isberg, L. (2000). Anger, aggressive behavior, and athletic performance. In Y. L. Hanin (Ed.), *Emotions in sport.* Champaign, IL: Human Kinetics.

James, M. and Gardiner, S. (1997). Touchlines and guidelines: The Lord Advocate's response to sportsfield violence. *Criminal Law Review, 1,* 41–45.

Kerr, J. H. (1994). *Understanding soccer hooliganism.* Buckingham: Open University Press.

Kerr, J. H. (1997). *Motivation and emotion in sport.* Hove: Psychology Press.

Kerr, J. H. (1999). The role of aggression and violence in sport: A rejoinder to the ISSP position stand. *The Sport Psychologist, 13,* 83–88.

Kerr, J. H. (2002). Issues in aggression and violence in sport: The ISSP position stand revisited. *The Sport Psychologist, 16,* 68–78.

Kerr, J. H. and de Kock, H. (2002). Aggression, violence, and the death of a Dutch soccer hooligan: A reversal theory explanation. *Aggressive Behavior, 28,* 1–10.

LeUnes, A. D. and Nation, J. R. (1989). *Sport psychology: An introduction.* Chicago: Nelson-Hall Inc.

McGregor, R. (2000, 9 March). McSorley puts hockey on trial with him. *The National Post,* p. B8.

McSorley found guilty but escapes jail sentence (2000, 8 October). *The Japan Times*, p. 22.

Plant, M. and Plant, M. (1992). *Risk-takers: Alcohol, drugs, sex and youth*. London: Routledge.

Rainey, D. W. (1994). Assaults on umpires: A statewide survey. *Journal of Sport Behavior*, *17*, 148–155.

Rainey, D. W. and Hardy, L. (1994). Assaults on rugby union referees: A three union survey. *Journal of Sport Behavior*, *22*, 105–113.

Rainey, D. W. and Hardy, L. (1999). Assaults on rugby referees: A three union survey. *Journal of Sport Behaviour*, *22*, 105–113.

Russell, G. W. (1993). *The social psychology of sport*. New York: Springer-Verlag.

Silver, M. (1998, 26 October). Dirty dogs. *Sports Illustrated*, 45–57.

Smith, M. D. (1983). *Violence and sport*. Toronto: Butterworths.

Tenenbaum, G., Stewart, E., Singer, R. N. and Duda, J. (1997). Aggression and violence in sport: An ISSP position stand. *The Sport Psychologist*, *11*, 1–7.

Tenenbaum, G., Sacks, D. N., Miller, J. W., Golden, A. S. and Doolin, N. (2000). Aggression and violence in sport: A reply to Kerr's rejoinder. *The Sport Psychologist*, *14*, 315–326.

Theberge, N. (1999). Being physical: Sources of pleasure and satisfaction in women's ice hockey. In J. Cloakley and P. Donnelly (Eds), *Inside sports* (pp. 146–155). London: Routledge.

Violence in sport – it's your responsibility too (2002). *Coaches' Report*, 9 (2). (Centre for Sport and Law Inc., Brock University website: www.sportlaw.ca).

Young, K. (1993). Violence, risk and liability in male sports culture. *Sociology of Sport Journal*, *10*, 373–396.

Author index

Subject index